That's the Ticket!

A Century of American Political Ballots

That's the Ticket!

A Century of American Political Ballots

Selections from the Charles H. McSorley Collection

Donald L. Ackerman
Jonathan H. Mann

The Rail Splitter Press
New York

The Rail Splitter Press
Post Office Box 275, New York, NY 10044
www.railsplitter.com

Layout & Design: Peter J. Klarnet
Photography & Imaging: Christopher Day
Contributing Editors: Timothy H. Bakken and Dr. Dean W. Rudoy

Manufactured in the United States of America

ISBN 978-0-615-64070-9
LCCN: 2001012345

Chapter illustration credits on page 146.

Contents

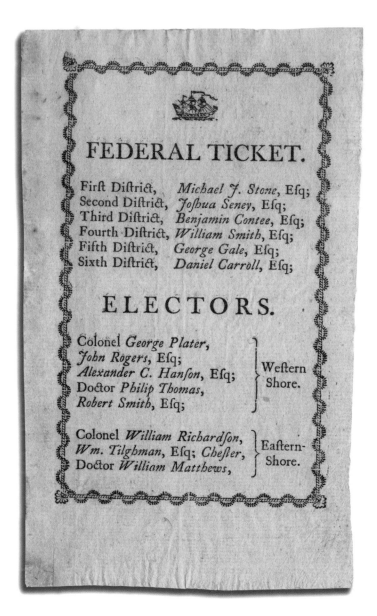

A rare ballot from the first presidential election in U. S. history. There were five states in which eligible voters selected Presidential Electors: New Hampshire, Virginia, Delaware, Maryland and Pennsylvania. This ballot was cast by a Maryland voter on January 7, 1789. It lists Congressional candidates as well as eight Presidential Electors, five from the Western Shore and three from the Eastern Shore. When the Electoral College met on April 6th, only six of the eight Presidential Electors actually cast votes. (We are unaware of the existence of any other ballots from this first election.)

[Courtesy of the Division of Political History, National Museum of American History, Smithsonian Institution.]

Introduction

"…Ballots are the rightful and peaceful successors of bullets; and…when ballots have fairly and constitutionally decided, there can be no successful appeal back to bullets… Such will be a great lesson of peace: teaching men that what they cannot take by election, neither can they take it by war; teaching all the folly of being the beginners of a war."

–Abraham Lincoln, Address to Congress, July 4, 1861.

"…Among freemen there can be no successful appeal from the ballot to the bullet, and that they who take such appeal are sure to lose their case and pay the cost."

–Abraham Lincoln, letter to J.C. Conkling, August 26, 1863.

Americans have always held a keen interest in politics and electioneering, but despite such passion, few actually participate in the process. The percentage of qualified voters who actually exercise their franchise is traditionally low in comparison to newer democracies. There also seems to be little interest in American political history. Qualification for elective office does not include a thorough knowledge of American history; periodic misstatements and gaffes by candidates reflect that reality. Regardless, the electoral process in America has always been popular sport.

Abraham Lincoln fully understood that the promise of America – its ideals as delineated in our founding documents – was something that we as a people *continually* strive to attain. Although we may fall short and engage in counterproductive actions, we yet remain "… the last best hope of earth." Lincoln knew that America had failed to live up to its full promise, but he had faith in its eventual fulfillment.

The gap between reality and the ideals embodied in the Declaration of Independence and the Constitution was wide indeed in 1789 when George Washington became our first president. Only 5% of the population was eligible to vote. Typically one needed to be a Caucasian male, over 21 years of age, a landowner, and with few exceptions a Protestant ("religious tests" were on the books in a majority of states). Among those excluded were women, Native Americans and African Americans, whether slave or free. Fortunately the history of our country is the tale of tearing down barriers to participatory democracy and expanding the elective franchise.

Clearly the "establishment" in our formative years had a strong idea of who "counted" in society, of who had the wisdom and judgment to make weighty decisions affecting the nation. This was largely driven by a desire to preserve personal property and privilege; a class system was thus hidden within a democratic republic. This elitism was increasingly challenged as the country grew. Changed demographics coincided with an evolution in public opinion and new political pressures. But there were setbacks along the way. Early on, reactionary forces led some states to overturn laws that had granted the vote to free blacks and some propertied women. Later, Mexicans living in the territory acquired during the war with Mexico were denied the right to vote, as were large numbers of Asian immigrants. Most of these exclusionary restrictions remained in force well into the first half of the 20th century.

Even Presidents Collected Ballots!

This diminutive Jackson ballot from Ohio dates from the election of 1828. It once belonged to future President William McKinley, an Ohio native. He apparently acquired this relic of a past election while serving as a prosecuting attorney of Stark County, Ohio (1869–71).

That our system of government remains imperfect is abundantly clear. There is ongoing debate over the Electoral College, particularly in those rare instances when a candidate for President receives the most popular votes yet loses the election. Disagreement remains over voter registration and identification requirements and as to which method for casting votes is secure and accurate. Much of this figured in the disputed election of 2000, the closest in our history. Al Gore's loss to George Bush ignited a "perfect storm" of contention: Gore lost the election despite a 500,000+ majority in popular votes. Use of butterfly ballots in Florida (a state with a critical electoral vote) gave "hanging chads" to the lexicon and the victory to George Bush. Despite widespread criticism many of these problems remain three elections later.

Few people fully understand the somewhat convoluted procedure for electing our nation's leaders. Presidents and Vice Presidents are chosen by members of the Electoral College. These individuals, known as Presidential Electors, are *pledged* to vote for *specific* candidates. Opposing slates of electors are voted upon in the general election. The slate receiving the largest number of votes within a given state meets the following month in their state capital to cast sealed ballots known as Electoral Tickets. These are forwarded to Washington, opened and tabulated in front of Congress by the Vice President, and the results announced and made official. To be elected, a presidential candidate must have 50% of the total number of electoral votes plus at least one additional vote, constituting a majority of the total.

Laws related to the selection of Presidential Electors and qualifications to vote vary widely and are, generally speaking, the domain of each individual state. Until 1832 Presidential Electors were usually chosen by state legislatures and until 1914 U.S. Senators were elected by their respective state legislatures, *not* by popular vote. For our first presidential election under the Constitution, held January 7, 1789, only five states allowed selection of Presidential Electors by popular vote. (Delaware reverted to election by the state legislature for the 1792 contest.) By 1820 most property requirements had been abolished, but religious tests continued until 1828 when Maryland ended the exclusion of Jewish voters. With the advent of Jacksonian Democracy in the 1820's, selecting Presidential Electors finally became the prerogative of white, male citizens over the age of 21 (South Carolina being the sole exception). The popular vote nationwide was first recorded in 1824. By 1828 it had risen dramatically to over one million. Unfortunately this trend toward democratization was offset by the enactment of poll taxes, literacy tests, onerous naturalization requirements and other exclusionary laws.

The concept of voting – and the dignity of Democracy – is credited to the ancient Greeks. Its origins date back to the 5th century B.C. Votes were taken on important issues that impacted a majority of citizens, including the punishment of ostracism. The word "ballot" has its origin in the Italian *ballotta*, or "little ball." White balls indicate the affirmative, while black balls indicate the negative. The term "blackballed," denoting an exclusion or denial of privileges, has its origin in the Renaissance. It is uncertain when paper ballots first came into service. There is no reference to them in Colonial America prior to the 1690's.

Ballots as historical records furnish a great deal of information. Beyond the individual candidates for office, they often reveal issues, both recurring and temporal. They chronicle ongoing adjustments and improvements in the electoral process. Printed on paper for temporary use, they are fascinating ephemeral artifacts, and in many instances none are thought to remain extant from a given election. Some examples printed on silk and linen from the mid-19th century were ornamental and never meant to be actually cast. There was never a central source for ballots such as the U. S. Government Printing Office or Bureau of Engraving & Printing. They were printed by regional printers, often in newspapers, and sometimes written out by hand. Another interesting aspect is ballots that include names of Presidential Electors who went on to greater things. Jefferson Davis was a Polk elector in 1844; Lincoln was a Presidential Elector in 1840, 1844 and 1856, his archrival Stephen A. Douglas was an opposition Presidential Elector in 1840. (In fact, while most know of the Lincoln-Douglas debates held during the 1858 Illinois Senate campaign, the two first debated in the election of 1840 "on the stump" as proponents respectively of William Henry Harrison and Martin Van Buren.)

Finding presidential ballots that predate 1820 can be challenging. Less than half the states admitted to the Union up until then allowed selection of Presidential Electors by popular vote. In states where the legislatures selected Presidential Electors, there was little need to print ballots. It should also be noted that statewide elections often took place earlier in the fall, with the traditional November date ("first Tuesday after the first Monday") reserved for the general or presidential election. Because of this peculiar scheduling it was often possible to predict a state's presidential preference in advance, regardless of its method for selecting Presidential Electors.

Small localities typically set up a polling place at some convenient location, often the general store, school, wayside inn or post office. Judges and clerks were hired to supervise the process and record votes in a poll book. This practice was widespread prior to the Civil War. After a voter identified himself, he voted verbally or submitted a ballot. His name and the slate of electors for whom he voted were then recorded in the poll book. Abraham Lincoln served as polling clerk at New Salem, Illinois in 1832, a task for which he received $2.50. It is known he cast a vote verbally for the losing slate of electors pledged to Whig candidate Henry Clay. In larger cities voters lined up at the polling place on election day and placed ballots in ballot boxes or glass globes. Under these methods the preference of a voter was readily apparent, negating any semblance of a *secret* ballot.

Casting secret ballots did not become commonplace until the adoption of the "Australian ballot" following the presidential election of 1884. Standard practice in Australia beginning in 1857, the (*American*) secret ballot had four requirements: official ballots had to be printed at public expense; the ballot had to list names of nominated candidates of all parties as well as all legislative proposals; they had to be distributed *only* at the polling place; and then they had to be marked in secret. The first president elected under widespread use of the Australian ballot was in 1888. At about the same time, technology to enable casting of secret ballots was facilitated by the introduction of the Myers Automatic Booth, the first automated polling system to be mass-marketed.

As seen in the following pages, there is little uniformity in the size, style or format of political ballots. Some list only the slate of Presidential Electors, while others include the name of the presidential candidate. Some picture the candidate, some don't. Some have overprinting or designs printed on the back. Some are very small, others gargantuan in comparison. Some states, like Virginia, had voters sign their name on the back of each ballot to document their legitimate use. Often they were "spindle cast" to avoid fraud: when presented to a poll-worker the ballot was immediately stabbed onto a metal spindle. Voters would often customize their ballot, writing in names of alternative candidates for statewide office or voting contrary to pre-printed ballot initiatives and amendments.

More than 220 years following our first national election, officials still struggle with the best means to accurately record votes and discourage voting fraud. Scanned punch cards or electronic voting machines; "reliable" paper records; computerized data entry – changing technology will always attempt to improve what will surely remain an imperfect system. But, as imperfect as it remains, our votes still count!

Every ballot pictured in this study, unless otherwise noted, was collected over many decades by Charles H. McSorley, a man who delighted in American history and always strove to improve his knowledge. His tireless research contributed to the scholarly database we all draw upon. By saving these ephemeral scraps of paper, Charlie helped preserve and enlighten American history; we hope to preserve his efforts and legacy herein, and in the process, perhaps ignite some of the same passion and curiosity that characterized his life. ✂

Preface

REMEMBERING THE COLLECTOR—HISTORIAN

Charles McSorley was born in Philadelphia in 1926. He came from a working class family and was raised in an Irish-German neighborhood where his German grandfather owned a fruit and produce market. Charlie worked many an hour in this market. In the early 1940's it was not uncommon for people to spend Indian-head cents, Liberty-head nickels and even an occasional large cent. For Charlie this was the real fruit that came from his grandfather's produce market – he became a coin collector.

Charlie made many trolley trips to the Philadelphia Library to read numismatic publications. He began to frequent the coin shops in Philadelphia, first buying coins from Ira Reed and later from his successor, David Bullowa. It was from Bullowa that Charlie once purchased 10 pounds of foreign coins. Mixed in were some small brass campaign tokens for William Henry Harrison and Henry Clay. These rekindled an interest in such artifacts, which had been born when his Irish grandfather gave him a Garfield "Canal Boy" token. Charlie was hooked – he became a political collector.

After serving in the U.S. Navy, Charlie went to work for a graphite firm owned by the Skakels, Ethel Kennedy's family. He hated it. "The dullest job in the world!" he recalled. He decided to try something he knew he would like. Charlie became a professional numismatist and a dealer in political memorabilia. He followed the adage that, "If you want to get lucky in this hobby, get smart!" Early on, he spent more hours in the New York Historical Society and like repositories of learning than most dealers or collectors spend in a lifetime.

Although Charlie was known in political circles primarily for his 19th century tokens, he also had an abiding love for political ephemera. This has been a much-neglected area with little scholarship and study. Perhaps this is because there is little in this area that lends itself to both systematic collecting and display. One salient exception to this is the ballot. The depth of his passion for these little-appreciated election relics is revealed in the following pages. Charlie collected them up until the end, on July 8, 2011. The auction catalog of his token collection and this work breathe life into the body of his beloved ballots and will be his legacy to collectors for years to come. For those of us who knew him on a personal basis, however, the love for our friend will be everlasting.

—*Joe Levine*
Presidential Coin & Antique Company

One

The Rise and Fall of Federalism:
Origins of the Two-Party System

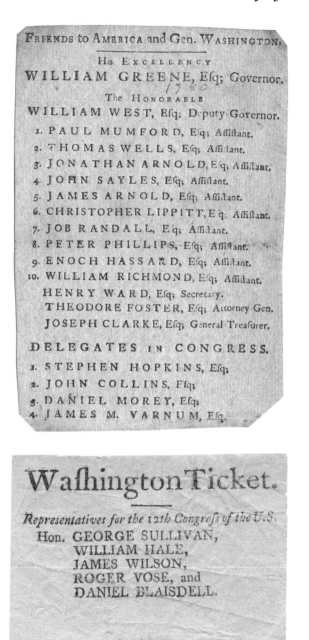

"Always vote for principle, though you may vote alone, and you may cherish the sweetest reflection that your vote is never lost."

—John Quincy Adams

"I never vote for anyone. I always vote *against*."

—William Claude Dukenfield
(W. C. Fields)

Even before the adoption of the Constitution and the establishment of a central government in 1789, candidates for office associated themselves with George Washington. In 1780 a group of Rhode Islanders, headed by gubernatorial candidate William Greene, described themselves as "Friends to America and Gen. Washington." This election took place near the tail end of the American Revolution, when the goal of independence seemed within reach. Even after Washington's death Federalist candidates invoked his name as seen in this "Washington Ticket" dating from an 1811 congressional election held in New Hampshire. Although Washington's fame only grew with time, the Federalist Party faded fast, fielding their last presidential slate in 1816.

The terms "Democrat" and "Republican" so define our deeply entrenched two-party system that it is hard to believe there was a time when their battles did not represent "politics as usual." Their respective partisans have been slugging it out since 1856. Before these well-defined adversaries there were prior stakeholders who took each other on: the Democrats versus the Whigs, and before that Republicans versus Democratic-Republicans, and even earlier Federalists who disputed with the anti-Federalists. But in the beginning there were only the Federalists. The system we now take for granted did not exist in our earliest days: opposing slates of candidates, two major parties, occasional third parties, universal suffrage and the secret ballot. How things have changed! When America took her first steps toward self-government, the very concept of *competing* political parties actually seemed offensive.

In 1789 the Presidential Electors of the Electoral College unanimously cast votes for George Washington (he proved to be the only president so honored). Since each Presidential Elector had two votes to cast, a handful of other candidates also received votes; the person receiving the second highest number – John Adams – thus was chosen Vice President. (Balloting was not separated into a vote for President and a vote for Vice

Election of 1789

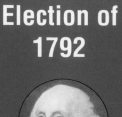

George Washington
Electoral Vote   69

John Adams
Electoral Vote   34

Balance distributed among ten individuals.

Election of 1792

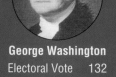

George Washington
Electoral Vote   132

John Adams
Electoral Vote   77

Thomas Jefferson
Electoral Vote   4

George Clinton
Electoral Vote   50

Aaron Burr
Electoral Vote   1

List of Republican Candidates, as Electors from the State of South-Carolina, on the approaching Election of President and Vice-President of the United States of America. Anno Domini, 1800.

E L E C T O R S.

Robert Anderson,
John Hunter,
Arthur Simkins,
Wade Hampton,
Andrew Love,
Theodore Gaillard,
Paul Hamilton,
Joseph Blythe.

In 1800 the Federalists chose John Adams and Charles Pinckney as their candidates, while the Democratic-Republicans chose Thomas Jefferson and Aaron Burr. This ballot records the votes received by the Democratic-Republican electors of South Carolina. With each elector permitted two votes, the general election resulted in a tie, with Jefferson and Burr each receiving 73 votes. The final decision was made by the House of Representatives in February 1801 with each state voting as a bloc. Neither candidate took an active part on his own behalf, in contrast to some rather heated wheeling and dealing among Capitol partisans. In the end Jefferson prevailed and was chosen President with Burr as his Vice President. In 1803 the 12th Amendment was ratified, requiring separate voting for President and Vice President. The possibility of candidates from opposing parties being elected President and Vice President, as had happened in 1796, continued through 1824, after which time Presidential and Vice Presidential candidates ran as a team. Popular voting for presidential electors was not permitted in South Carolina until after the Civil War; it was the last state to hold out against this defining feature of modern democracy.

Election of 1796

John Adams
Electoral Vote   71

Thomas Jefferson
Electoral Vote   68

Election of 1800

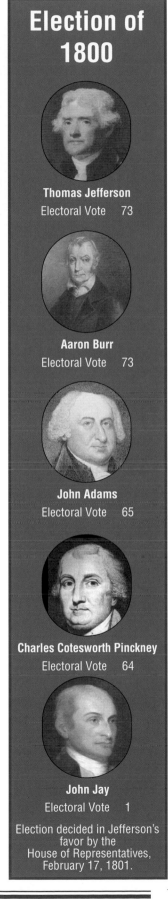

Thomas Jefferson
Electoral Vote   73

Aaron Burr
Electoral Vote   73

John Adams
Electoral Vote   65

Charles Cotesworth Pinckney
Electoral Vote   64

John Jay
Electoral Vote   1

Election decided in Jefferson's favor by the House of Representatives, February 17, 1801.

President.) Given that Washington was on everyone's "short list", the outcome was no surprise.

Three of the original colonies did not participate in the election of 1789. Of the remaining ten, only half selected Presidential Electors by popular vote, including Maryland. A ballot from that state marked "Federal Ticket" is known to exist. It was used in the election held in January of that year to choose the Electors who would vote George Washington into office the following month. These gentlemen ran unopposed, since at that time the Federal Party was the *only* party. The election was a procedural exercise, a formality, in the pre-determined process. But just two years later Thomas Jefferson and James Madison organized the country's first political opposition group: the anti-Federalists, also known as the Democratic-Republicans. Indeed most regard Jefferson as the founder of the modern Democratic Party.

Washington served two terms as President thus establishing a precedent for term-limits, breached only by four-term President Franklin Delano Roosevelt. Washington's successor, John Adams, proved not nearly as popular and failed to gain a second term. Washington and Adams were our only Federalist presidents; the party ceased to exist after 1816.

As Adams left office Jefferson attempted to reunite the country in non-partisanship. On March 4, 1801, he patriotically declared during his first Inaugural Address: "We are all Republicans, we are all Federalists." Yet his Democratic-Republicans (and their successors the Democratic Party) all but dominated the electoral landscape from 1800 to 1860. Their counterparts, the National Republicans (and Whigs), managed to elect just three presidents in that sixty-year span.

Few pre-1828 presidential ballots can be found. Jefferson, Madison and Monroe each served two terms. (Monroe, presiding during the

Election of 1804

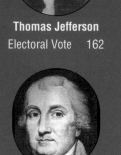

Thomas Jefferson
Electoral Vote   162

Charles Cotesworth Pinckney
Electoral Vote   14

Election of 1808

James Madison
Electoral Vote   122

Charles Cotesworth Pinckney
Electoral Vote   47

George Clinton
Electoral Vote   6

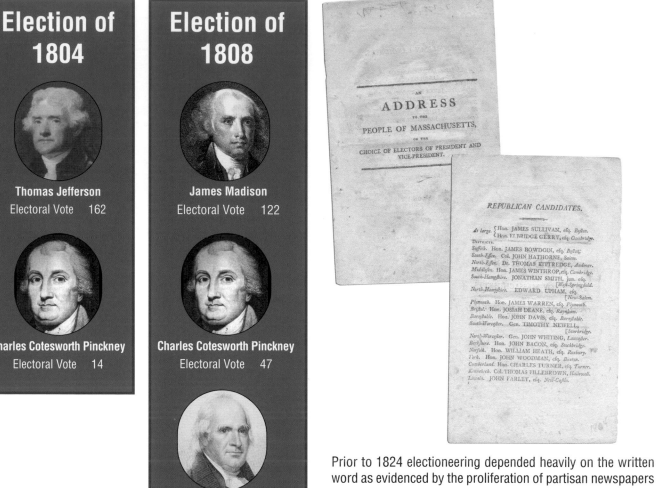

Prior to 1824 electioneering depended heavily on the written word as evidenced by the proliferation of partisan newspapers and pamphlets. This 16-page "Address to the People of Massachusetts, on the Choice of Electors of President and Vice-President" was published in 1804. Nineteen electors are listed on the inside cover pledging support for the re-election of Thomas Jefferson. The year before, the Louisiana Purchase had been finalized and the following year exploration of the territory by the Lewis & Clark Expedition went under way. Things were going well for Jefferson, but were destined to deteriorate towards the end of his second, and final, term.

DeWitt Clinton is celebrated as one of the greatest politicians of the era which succeeded the Founding Father period. He promoted and built the Erie Canal, his lasting legacy. In 1812 he was the candidate of the Federalist Party, which opposed Jefferson's Embargo Act of 1808 because of its devastating effect on domestic commerce, especially in New England. The embargo greatly contributed to the declaration of war with England in early 1812, which was even more vehemently opposed by the Federalists. This "Electoral Peace Ticket" from Massachusetts was issued in 1812 in support of Clinton. A similar Rhode Island ticket exists inscribed "Clinton, Peace and Commerce." The war lasted 2-1/2 years and witnessed the burning of Washington and the White House by the British.

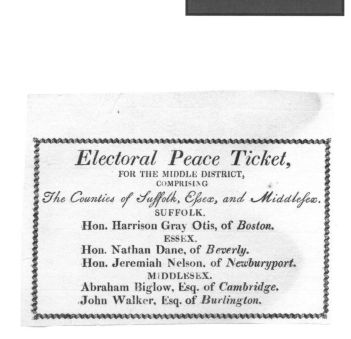

Election of 1812

James Madison
Electoral Vote   128

DeWitt Clinton
Electoral Vote   89

Election of 1816

James Monroe
Electoral Vote   183

Rufus King
Electoral Vote   34

Election of 1820

James Monroe
Electoral Vote   231

John Q. Adams
Electoral Vote   1

period known as the "Era of Good Feelings," fell just one vote shy of unanimous election in 1820.) The lack of ephemera from those early years is understandable, since party legislative caucuses chose presidential nominees, and nominating conventions had yet to be created. The right to vote was highly restricted and most states chose their Presidential Electors through their state legislatures. Hence there was little need for campaign material and printed ephemera.

Increasingly frustrated Federalists – who complained of an imperious "Virginia dynasty" (since every President except John Adams hailed from the Old Dominion State) – suggested rotating the nominating process to enable other states such as New York and those in New England to feel represented. Campaigns, as we know them today, were on the horizon. They would soon alter the political landscape. ∽

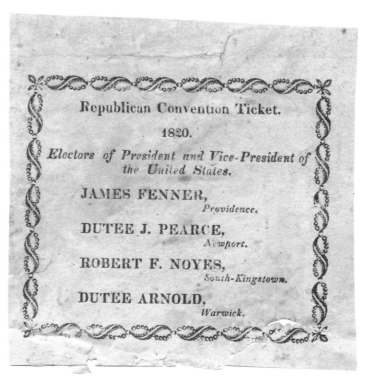

Rhode Island ballot from 1820, when all electors save one voted for the popular incumbent James Monroe.

Two

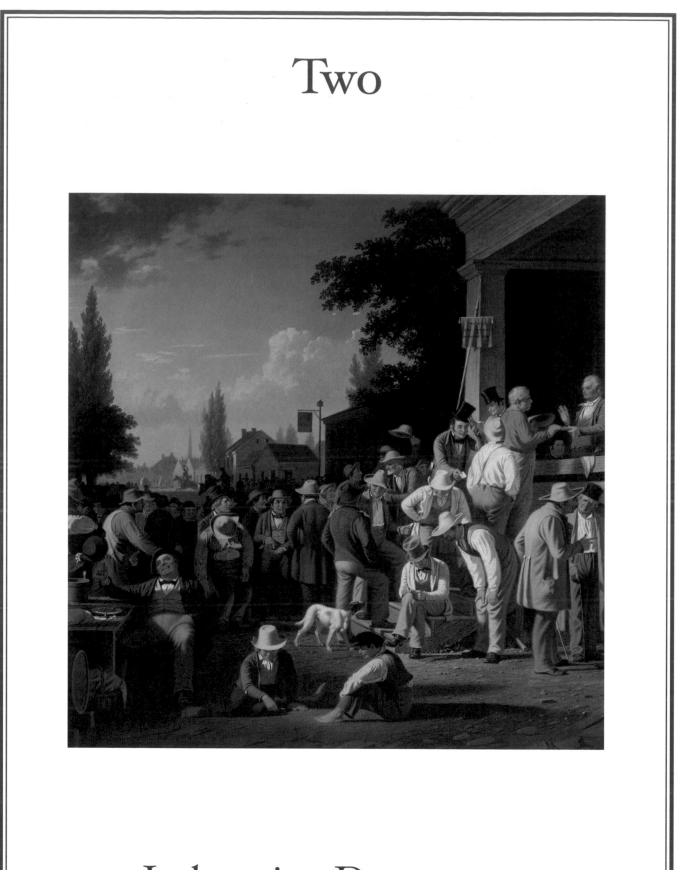

Jacksonian Democracy

Election of 1824

John Q. Adams
Popular Vote   108,740
Electoral Vote   84

Henry Clay
Popular Vote   47,136
Electoral Vote   37

Andrew Jackson
Popular Vote   153,544
Electoral Vote   99

William Crawford
Popular Vote   46,618
Electoral Vote   41

No candidate receiving a majority, the election was decided in Adams' favor by the House of Representatives.

Election of 1828

Democratic

Andrew Jackson
Popular Vote   647,286
Electoral Vote   178

National Republican

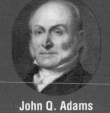

John Q. Adams
Popular Vote   508,064
Electoral Vote   83

"A share in the sovereignty of the state, which is exercised by the citizens at large, in voting at elections is one of the most important rights of the subject, and in a republic ought to stand foremost in the estimation of the law."

—Alexander Hamilton

Abolition of property restrictions allowed more and more citizens to participate in the political process. The popular vote, first recorded in 1824, grew dramatically by 1828 when it carried the military hero General Andrew Jackson into office. A native of the Carolinas and resident of Tennessee, he famously opened his inaugural celebration to any and all comers: the resulting crush along with fights in the Executive Mansion all but destroyed the place; much of the furniture was lost or damaged by roughnecks and hooligans.

Jackson's political allies held dear the sentiment that "to the victor belong the spoils". They blocked every bid for appointments from opposition party members. Only loyal Jacksonians found places in his administration. This came easy since "Old Hickory" was widely perceived as a man of the people championing their interests against the Eastern, moneyed establishment. Jackson was our first and only populist President. His 1828 campaign saw the advent of elections as we now know them, replete with rallies, barbeques, campaign songs, mudslinging and widespread dissemination of political paraphernalia. Ballots issued for his campaigns clearly reflected his political views and were targeted to his western, agrarian base. During his term in office another innovation was instituted: the national nominating convention. Inspired by an Anti-Masonic convention held at Harris-

ELECTORAL TICKET FOR **1824**

John Q. Adams, President.

ANDREW JACKSON, Vice-Pres't.

	Trumbull county.
Calvin Pease,	
Alexander Campbell,	Brown do
Elisha Hotchkiss,	Hamilton do
Francis Dunlavy,	Warren do
Asa Coleman,	Miami do
John Wallace,	Champaign do
Abraham Shepard,	Brown do
John Woodbridge,	Ross do
S. R. Holcombe,	Gallia do
Nathaniel M'Lean,	Franklin do
Michael Garrahty,	Fairfield do
Henry Howard,	Belmont do
John M'Laughlin,	Jefferson do
Thomas M'Millan,	Wayne do
Ephraim Quinby,	Trumbull do
Almon Ruggles,	Huron do

In pre-Civil War America various factions proposed "dream tickets" that rarely amounted to anything. The combination of John Quincy Adams and Andrew Jackson was not as outlandish as it first seems. Federalist Adams had supported Jefferson's Embargo Act of 1808 and was forced from his Senate seat by outraged colleagues. He then switched party allegiance. In the balloting that took place in the election of 1824, Jackson not only received the most votes for President, but also received a modest number as a Vice Presidential candidate. The person receiving the most votes for the second spot was John C. Calhoun. He served as Vice President under Adams and again under Jackson, the only person to hold that position under two Presidents. He and Jackson were at odds on more than one occasion, most notably during the Nullification Crisis of 1832, when Calhoun was obliged to back away from threats of secession. Few people ever got the best of "Old Hickory". Clay was one of the few exceptions. Upon his retirement, Jackson exclaimed that his only regret in life was that he "didn't shoot Henry Clay and hang John C. Calhoun."

William Crawford was the favorite in the campaign of 1824 but due to a debilitating stroke prior to the election, faded from contention. This Virginia ballot lists the election day as Monday the first, rather than the official date of Tuesday, November 2nd. When none of the candidates received a majority the contest was decided by the House of Representatives, which chose John Quincy Adams over Andrew Jackson even though the "Hero of New Orleans" had garnered both the most popular votes and the most electoral votes. Fourth place finisher Henry Clay was appointed Secretary of State in Adams' Cabinet, prompting charges of collusion and a "corrupt bargain".

The Crawford Ticket.

FOR PRESIDENT.
WILLIAM H. CRAWFORD.

FOR VICE PRESIDENT,
ALBERT GALLATIN.

William C. Holt, Norfolk.
Dr. Charles H. Graves, Surry.
John Cargill, Sussex.
Gen. Wm H. Brodnax, Greenville.
Gen. John Purnall, Prince Edward.
Dr. James Jones, Nottoway.
Maj. Charles Yancey, Buckingham.
Col. Joseph Martin, Henry.
Col. Tho's M. Randolph, Albemarle
Judge Wm Brockenbro', Richmond
John T. Lomax, Fredericksburg.
Col. Wm. Jones, Gloucester.
Robert Shields, Sen. York.
Col. Ellison Currie, Lancaster,
Robert Taylor, Orange.
Isaac Foster, Fauquier.
Daniel Morgan, Jefferson.
Wm. Armstrong, Hampshire.
Archibald Rutherford, Rockingham.
John Bowyer, Rockbridge.
James Hoge, Montgomery.
Andrew Russell, Washington.
Joseph H. Samuels, Wood.
William Marteny, Randolph.
Election on the first Monday in November.

OHIO ELECTORAL TICKET,
FOR
HENRY CLAY, President,
and NATHAN SANFORD, *Vice-President.*
"America will be *independent*, when she a-
dopts an *American Policy*."—*Clay's Speech.*

For Electors.
William H. Harrison, *of Hamilton Co.*
William M'Farland, *of Ross*   do.
Thomas Kirker, *of Adams*   do.
James Heaton, *of Butler*   do.
Henry Brown, *of Franklin*   do.
Ebenezer Buckingham, Jr. *of*
     Muskingum   do.
William Kendall, *of Scioto*   do.
William Skinner, *of Washington,*   do.
James Caldwell, *of Belmont*   do.
David Sloane, *of Jefferson*   do.
Samuel Coulter, *of Stark*   do.
Solomon Kingsbury, *of Geauga*   do.
Ebenezer Merry, *of Huron*   do.
James Cooley, *of Champaign*   do.
James Steele, *of Montgomery*   do.
John Bigger, *of Warren*   do.

Future President William Henry Harrison is listed as a Presidential Elector on this 1824 Ohio ballot. It may be the only ballot known from the first of Clay's three attempts at winning the Presidency. Except for some brass tokens issued on behalf on Andrew Jackson, political artifacts from this election are highly elusive.

burg, Pennsylvania in December 1831, the Democrats and Whigs followed suit, despite die-hards who yearned for the old party caucus system (Abraham Lincoln among them!). National politics polarized around the man lampooned as "King Andrew I" and two parties emerged to do battle: the Democratic-Republicans, or Democrats, who adhered to Jackson, and the National Republicans, or Whigs, who opposed his autocratic style.

For ill or good Jackson established himself as a role model for the strong executive, albeit one with little regard for other branches of government. In hindsight his public disdain for the Supreme Court and hostility toward the rights of Native Americans were despicable. But his firm authority in upholding the Union during the Nullification Crisis remains admirable. (South Carolina triggered the "Nullification Crisis" claiming a state had the right to *nullify* any federal law they didn't approve of – in this case, a tariff statute.) Many presidents who followed set far less confrontational courses, deferring to Congress and acting only within perceived, prescribed authority. Yet during times of crisis – such as the Civil War – Jackson's image has been used as an exemplar of leadership and dedication to the principles of the Founding Fathers. It is little wonder that his likeness appeared on both Republican and Democratic ballots for decades following his death in 1845. ෬

In 1824 voters in Maryland selected Presidential Electors by district, rather than in a statewide winner-take-all contest. The Fourth Electoral District was located in the western part of the state, with Pennsylvania bordering on the north. There were many German immigrants in the district. The results in Maryland gave Jackson 7 votes, Adams 3 and Crawford 1.

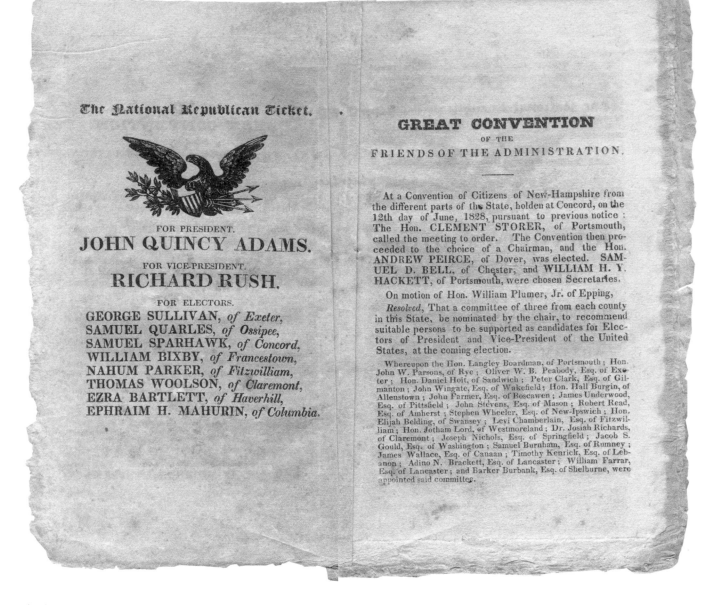

The National Republican Ticket.

FOR PRESIDENT.
JOHN QUINCY ADAMS.
FOR VICE-PRESIDENT.
RICHARD RUSH.
FOR ELECTORS.

GEORGE SULLIVAN, *of Exeter,*
SAMUEL QUARLES, *of Ossipee,*
SAMUEL SPARHAWK, *of Concord,*
WILLIAM BIXBY, *of Francestown,*
NAHUM PARKER, *of Fitzwilliam,*
THOMAS WOOLSON, *of Claremont,*
EZRA BARTLETT, *of Haverhill,*
EPHRAIM H. MAHURIN, *of Columbia.*

GREAT CONVENTION
OF THE
FRIENDS OF THE ADMINISTRATION.

At a Convention of Citizens of New-Hampshire from the different parts of the State, holden at Concord, on the 12th day of June, 1828, pursuant to previous notice: The Hon. CLEMENT STORER, of Portsmouth, called the meeting to order. The Convention then proceeded to the choice of a Chairman, and the Hon. ANDREW PEIRCE, of Dover, was elected. SAMUEL D. BELL, of Chester, and WILLIAM H. Y. HACKETT, of Portsmouth, were chosen Secretaries.

On motion of Hon. William Plumer, Jr. of Epping,

Resolved, That a committee of three from each county in this State, be nominated by the chair, to recommend suitable persons to be supported as candidates for Electors of President and Vice-President of the United States, at the coming election.

Whereupon the Hon. Langley Boardman, of Portsmouth; Hon. John W. Parsons, of Rye; Oliver W. B. Peabody, Esq. of Exeter; Hon. Daniel Hoit, of Sandwich; Peter Clark, Esq. of Gilmanton; John Wingate, Esq. of Wakefield; Hon. Hall Burgin, of Allenstown; John Farmer, Esq. of Boscawen; James Underwood, Esq. of Pittsfield; John Stevens, Esq. of Mason; Robert Read, Esq. of Amherst; Stephen Wheeler, Esq. of New-Ipswich; Hon. Elijah Belding, of Swansey; Levi Chamberlain, Esq. of Fitzwilliam; Hon. Jotham Lord, of Westmoreland; Dr. Josiah Richards, of Claremont; Joseph Nichols, Esq. of Springfield; Jacob S. Gould, Esq. of Washington; Samuel Burnham, Esq. of Rumney; James Wallace, Esq. of Canaan; Timothy Kenrick, Esq. of Lebanon; Adino N. Brackett, Esq. of Lancaster; William Farrar, Esq. of Lancaster; and Barker Burbank, Esq. of Shelburne, were appointed said committee.

In the days before television ads, whenever someone delivered a derogatory speech against a candidate, someone else would write a reply that might appear in pamphlet form or be published in newspapers. This 24-page booklet from 1828 consists of such a rebuttal to an anti-Adams speech, together with a ballot on the inside of the front cover.

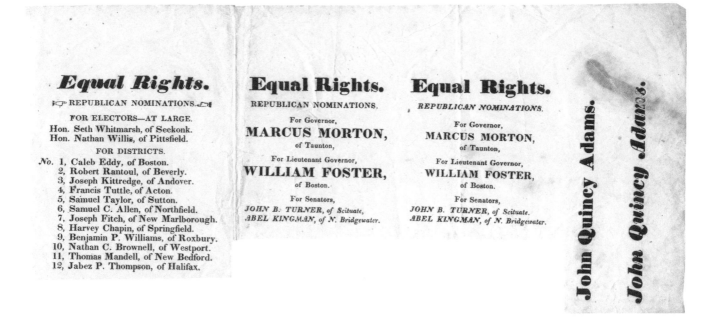

Marcus Morton was a perennial gubernatorial candidate in Massachusetts. Apparently, his slogan was "Equal Rights". This circa 1828 ticket(s) could be used in the statewide or national election which were traditionally held in different months. The name of the Presidential candidate, John Quincy Adams, appears separately and could be cut out and applied as a paste-down.

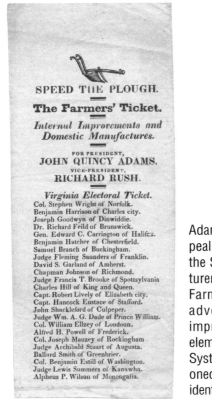

Adams here tries to appeal to both farmers in the South and manufacturers in the North. "The Farmer's Ticket" also advocates "internal improvements", a key element of the "American System" later championed and most closely identified with Henry Clay.

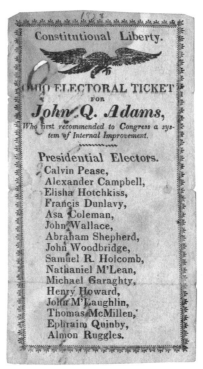

Ohio voters are reminded that John Q. Adams "first recommended to Congress a system of Internal Improvement." This policy encouraged Federal funding of roads, canals, bridges and other aspects of transportation related to commerce. Both Henry Clay and Abraham Lincoln were staunch supporters of the improvement system.

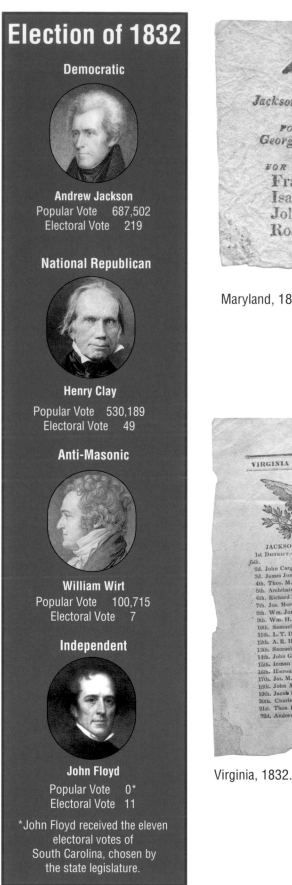

Election of 1832

Democratic

Andrew Jackson
Popular Vote 687,502
Electoral Vote 219

National Republican

Henry Clay
Popular Vote 530,189
Electoral Vote 49

Anti-Masonic

William Wirt
Popular Vote 100,715
Electoral Vote 7

Independent

John Floyd
Popular Vote 0*
Electoral Vote 11

*John Floyd received the eleven electoral votes of South Carolina, chosen by the state legislature.

Jackson Republican Ticket

FOR CONGRESS
George C. Washington

FOR THE ASSEMBLY
Francis Thomas
Isaac Shriver
John Kinzer
Roderick Dorsey

Maryland, 1828.

Jackson Democratic Ticket
President
Andrew Jackson
Vice President
John C. Calhoun
ELECTORS
Ethan A. Brown, Hamilton co.
Robert Harper, Ashtabula
1 William Piatt, Hamilton
2 James Shields, Butler
3 Henry Barrington, Miami
4 Thomas Gillespie, Green
5 Thomas L. Hamer, Brown
6 Valentine Keffer, Pickaway
7 Robert Lucas, Pike
8 John M'Elvain, Franklin
9 Samuel Herrick, Muskingum
10 George Sharp, Belmont
11 Walter M. Blake Tuscarawas
12 Benjamin Jones, Wayne
13 William Rayen, Trumbull
14 Hugh M'Fall, Richland

Ohio, 1828.

VIRGINIA ELECTORAL TICKET.

JACKSON ELECTORAL TICKET.
1st District—Geo. Loyall, of the Borough of Norfolk.
2d. John Cargill, of Sussex.
3d. James Jones, of Nottoway.
4th. Thos. M. Nelson, of Mecklenburg.
5th. Archibald Austin, of Buckingham.
6th. Richard Logan, of Halifax.
7th. Jos. Martin, of Henry.
8th. Wm. Jones, of Gloucester.
9th. Wm. H. Roane, of Hanover.
10th. Samuel Carr, of Albemarle.
11th. L. T. Dade, of Orange.
12th. A. R. Harwood, of King & Queen.
13th. Samuel Blackwell, of Northumberland.
14th. John Gibson, of Prince William.
15th. Inman Horner, of Fauquier.
16th. Hierome L. Opie, of Jefferson.
17th. Jas. M. Mason, of Frederick.
18th. John McMillan, of Brooke.
19th. Jacob D. Williamson, of Rockingham.
20th. Charles Beale, of Botetourt.
21st. Thos. Bland, of Lewis.
22d. Andrew Russell, of Washington.

Virginia, 1832.

ANTI-JACKSON TICKETS.

For Governor of the State of New-York—
FRANCIS GRANGER.
Lieutenant-Governor—
SAMUEL STEVENS.

Presidential Electors.

JAMES KENT	JOHN C. SPENCER
Silas Wood	George Huntington
Eleazer Lord	Nicholas Shoemaker
Henry Cotheal	Gerrit Smith
Joseph Tucker	Chauncey Baker
Ellis Potter	Orrin Wilbur
James Turk	James Hawks
Coert Dubois	Edmund G. Per Lee
George A. Gay	John Miller
Nathaniel Dubois	Calvin Burr
Charles Hathaway	Josiah Dunlap
Gideon Hawley	Hiram F. Mather
Martin De Freest	Robert Cook
Justus M'Kinstry	Robert S. Rose
William Turtle	Nathaniel W. Howell
John Gebhard	Asa B. Smith
Duncan M'Martin, jr.	Shubael Dunham
Gilbert Waring	Samuel Lacey
Joseph Boies	Hollam Hutchinson
John L. Curtenius	George H. Boughton
Robert Livingston	Nathan Mixer.

For Senator—ANTHONY LAMB.
For Assembly—JOHN MORSS,
SAMUEL G. RAYMOND,
JAMES MONROE,
MARTIN E. THOMPSON,
THOMAS J. DOYLE,
CHARLES STARR,
WILLIAM DUER,
JAMES VAN BENSCHOTEN,
JOHN REDFIELD,
JOHN I. LABAGH,
GABRIEL P DISOSWAY.
For Congress—JONATHAN THOMPSON,
DAVID B. OGDEN,
GEORGE F. TALMAN,
HUBERT VAN WAGENEN.

New York, 1832. "Anti-Jackson" newspaper ballot issued in support of Henry Clay. James Kent was Chancellor of New York State and a well-respected jurist and author of legal commentaries.

FOR PRESIDENT,
ANDREW JACKSON.
FOR VICE PRESIDENT,
JOHN C. CALHOUN.

"Magna est veritas et prevalebit."
Truth is mighty and will prevail.
JACKSON.

Names of Ohio Electors.
Ethan A. Brown, of Hamilton.
Robert Harper, of Ashtabula.
William Piatt, of Hamilton.
James Shields, of Butler.
Henry Barrington, of Miami,
Thomas Gillespie, of Green.
Thomas L. Hamer, of Brown.
Valentine Keffer, of Pickaway.
Robert Lucas, of Pike.
John M'Elvain, of Franklin.
Samuel Herrick, of Muskingum.
George Sharp, of Belmont.
Walter M. Blake, of Tuscarawas,
Benjamin Jones, of Wayne,
William Rayen, of Trumbull.
Hugh M'Fall, of Richland.

Jackson started out his professional life as a lawyer, as did many 19th century politicians. Accordingly, he had more than a passing knowledge of Latin, as did many of the educated class.

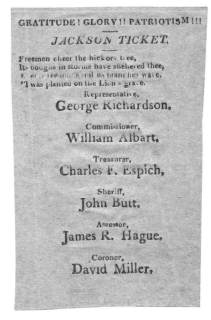

GRATITUDE ! GLORY !! PATRIOTISM !!!

JACKSON TICKET.

Freemen cheer the hickory tree,
Its boughs in storms have sheltered thee,
[...] tree its branches wave,
'Twas planted on the Lion's grave.

Representative,
George Richardson.

Commissioner,
William Albart.

Treasurer,
Charles F. Espich,

Sheriff,
John Butt.

Assessor,
James R. Hague.

Coroner,
David Miller,

Maryland [n.d.]. "Glory" is a word that was often used to criticize Andrew Jackson's assertive and unprecedented use of executive power. The Democratic politicians appearing on this ticket evidently did not see it that way and felt grateful that Jackson was their leader and role model.

JACKSON TICKET
Fifth Electoral District of Maryland.

"Freemen cheer the Hickory tree,
In storms its boughs have shelter'd thee."

FOR ELECTOR
Of President & Vice-President of the U. States,
WILLIAM BROWN.

Maryland, 1832. This ballot may be the only one picturing Andrew Jackson that was actually issued during one of his presidential campaigns. All others were issued after he left office.

" *The Union—It must be preserved.*"
FOR PRESIDENT,
ANDREW JACKSON,
OF TENNESSEE.
FOR VICE PRESIDENT,
MARTIN VAN BUREN,
OF NEW YORK.

ELECTORAL TICKET.
1. George Loyall, of Norfolk.
2. John Cargill, of Sussex.
3. James Jones, of Nottoway.
4. Thomas M. Nelson, of Mecklenburg.
5. Archibald Austin, of Buckingham.
6. Richard Logan, of Halifax.
7. Joseph Martin, of Henry.
8. William Jones, of Gloucester.
9. William H. Roane, of Hanover.
10. Samuel Carr, of Albemarle.
11. Lawrence T. Dade, of Orange.
12. Archibald R. Harwood, of King & Queen.
13. Samuel Blackwell, of Northumberland.
14. John Gibson, of Prince William.
15. Inman Horner, of Fauquier.
16. Hierome L. Opie, of Jefferson.
17. James M. Mason, of Frederick.
18. John McMillan, of Brooke.
19. Jacob D. Williamson, of Rockingham.
20. Charles Beale, of Botetourt.
21. Thomas Bland, of Lewis.
22. Andrew Russell, of Washington.

Virginia, 1832. Jackson's famous dinner toast, issued in response to John C. Calhoun's toast to states' rights, appears at the top of the ticket.

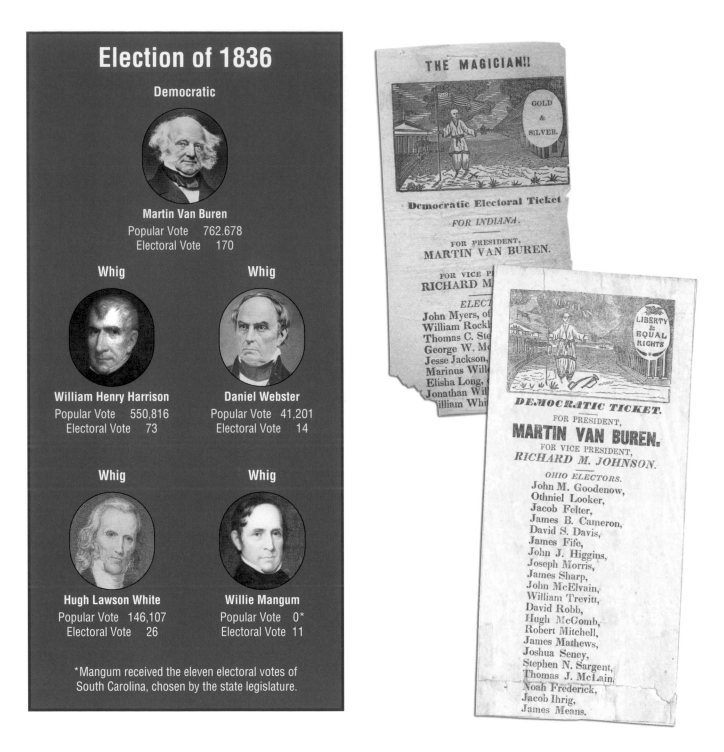

Election of 1836

Democratic

Martin Van Buren
Popular Vote   762.678
Electoral Vote   170

Whig

William Henry Harrison
Popular Vote   550,816
Electoral Vote   73

Whig

Daniel Webster
Popular Vote   41,201
Electoral Vote   14

Whig

Hugh Lawson White
Popular Vote   146,107
Electoral Vote   26

Whig

Willie Mangum
Popular Vote   0*
Electoral Vote   11

*Mangum received the eleven electoral votes of South Carolina, chosen by the state legislature.

THE MAGICIAN!!

GOLD & SILVER.

Democratic Electoral Ticket

FOR *INDIANA.*

FOR PRESIDENT,
MARTIN VAN BUREN.

FOR VICE P
RICHARD M

ELECT
John Myers, of
William Rockl
Thomas C. Ste
George W. Mc
Jesse Jackson,
Marinus Wille
Elisha Long,
Jonathan Wil
William Whi

LIBERTY & EQUAL RIGHTS

DEMOCRATIC TICKET.
FOR PRESIDENT,
MARTIN VAN BUREN.
FOR VICE PRESIDENT,
RICHARD M. JOHNSON.

OHIO ELECTORS.
John M. Goodenow,
Othniel Looker,
Jacob Felter,
James B. Cameron,
David S. Davis,
James Fife,
John J. Higgins,
Joseph Morris,
James Sharp,
John McElvain,
William Trevitt,
David Robb,
Hugh McComb,
Robert Mitchell,
James Mathews,
Joshua Seney,
Stephen N. Sargent,
Thomas J. McLain,
Noah Frederick,
Jacob Ihrig,
James Means.

By virtue of his keen political skills, Van Buren was nicknamed the "Little Magician." He was able to benefit when Vice President John C. Calhoun resigned in the wake of the Peggy Eaton Affair (a scandal involving the wife of the Secretary of War) and became Jackson's running mate and heir apparent in 1832. He appears on two 1836 ballots from Ohio and Indiana dressed in the Oriental manner, holding a lantern that projects the slogans "Liberty & Equal Rights" and "Gold & Silver." His political legerdemain did him little good when the nation fell into the depths of an economic depression, the Panic of 1837.

Ohio, 1836. Riding hogs, Democrat Van Buren is in the lead in the presidential race. The three runners-up are Hugh White, William Henry Harrison and Daniel Webster. The Whigs, who could not agree on a single candidate to oppose Jackson's chosen successor, hoped to win enough votes to deprive Van Buren of a majority and throw the election into the House of Representatives. In another variation, a Democratic partisan is truly "bringing home the bacon." He appears pleased that good times have resulted in pork selling for 10 cents a pound. Carrying a pig on his shoulder, he says he is "Going the whole hog."

North Carolina newspaper from 1836 containing multiple ballots which could be clipped and distributed.

Ohio, 1836. Jackson's veto of the Second Charter of the Bank of the United States in 1832 created a great deal of turmoil and uncertainty in the financial markets. Van Buren supported an "Independent Treasury" and payment of public debts in specie (gold and silver). Missouri's Thomas Hart Benton and Ohio's Thomas Ewing both weigh-in on the financial question on this rare ballot. "If the Deposites [sic] are not restored, the country will be ruined," Ewing warns, a prediction that came true in 1837.

ELECTORAL TICKET.

FOR PRESIDENT,
MARTIN VAN BUREN.
FOR VICE PRESIDENT,
RICHARD M. JOHNSON.

1st District.—*ARTHUR SMITH*, of Isle of Wight.
2d District.—*JOHN CARGILL*, of Sussex.
3d District.—*JAMES JONES*, of Nottoway.
4th District.—*WM. R. BASKERVILLE*, of Mecklenburg.
5th District.—*CHARLES YANCEY*, of Buckingham.
6th District.—*RICHARD LOGAN*, of Halifax.
7th District.—*ARCHIBALD STUART*, of Patrick.
8th District.—*WILLIAM JONES*, of Gloucester.
9th District.—*AUSTIN BROCKENBROUGH*, of Essex.
10th District.—*JOHN GIBSON*, of Prince William.
11th District.—*J. D HALYBURTON*, of New Kent.
12th District.—*THOMAS J. RANDOLPH*, of Albemarle.
13th District.—*WALLER HOLLADAY*, of Spottsylvania.
14th District.—*INMAN HORNER*, of Fauquier.
15th District.— *James Gibson of Hampshire*
16th District.—*WILLIAM A. HARRIS*, of Page.
17th District.—*JACOB D. WILLIAMSON*, of Rockingham.
18th District.—*WILLIAM TAYLOR*, of Rockbridge.
19th District.—*AUGUSTUS A. CHAPMAN*, of Monroe.
20th District.—*JAMES HOGE*, of Pulaski.
21st District.— *WILLIAM BYARS*, of Washington.
22d District.—*BENJAMIN BROWN*, of Cabell.
23d District.—*JOHN HINDMAN*, of Brooke.

Virginia, 1836. A replacement "paste-down" name has been substituted as candidate of the 15th district. (The original owner signed his name on the back when he cast his vote.)

Democratic Ticket.

For President.
MARTIN VAN BUREN,
of New York.

For Vice President.
RICHARD M. JOHNSON,
of Kentucky.

Electors.
1st. District.
ABRAHAM BIRD, *of Cape Girardeau.*
2d. District.
EDWARD DOBYNS, *of St. Louis.*
3d. District.
JAMES HOLMAN, *of Ray.*
4th. District.
W. G. MERRIWETHER, *of Pike.*

Missouri, 1836.

The People, against Official Dictation.

REPUBLICAN
WHIG TICKET.

FOR PRESIDENT,
HUGH LAWSON WHITE, *of Tennessee*,
OR
WILLIAM HENRY HARRISON, of Ohio,

As the vote for the one or the other may prevent an election by the House of Representatives, and secure a choice by the PEOPLE.

The first, a Republican of the Old Virginia School—of mature wisdom—upright, honest, inflexible—and of great experience in public affairs.

The second, a Virginian by birth and education; attached to her principles and institutions—a gallant defender of his country in the field, and an experienced statesman.

FOR VICE-PRESIDENT,
That tried Republican Statesman and Patriot,
JOHN TYLER, *of Virginia.*

"The recent demonstrations of public sentiment inscribe, on the list of Executive duties, in characters too legible to be overlooked, the task of REFORM; which will require, particularly, the correction of those abuses that have brought the *patronage of the Federal Government* in conflict with the *freedom of elections.*"
[*Jackson's Inaugural Address.*]

ELECTORS FOR PRESIDENT AND VICE-PRESIDENT.
WILLIAM R. JOHNSON, of Chesterfield,
JOHN URQUHART, of Southampton,
WILLIAM COLLINS, of Norfolk County,
MARK ALEXANDER, of Mecklenburg,
ALLEN WILSON, of Cumberland,
JAMES SAUNDERS, of Campbell,
JOSEPH MARTIN, of Henry,
ROBERT McCANDLISH, of York,
WILLIAM P. TAYLOR, of Caroline,
ROBERT W. CARTER, of Richmond County,
CHAPMAN JOHNSON, of Richmond City,
WILLIAM F. GORDON, of Albemarle,
JOHN L. MARYE, of Spottsylvania,
JOHN JANNEY, of Loudoun,
CHARLES J. FAULKNER, of Berkeley,
JOHN B. D. SMITH, of Frederick,
JOSEPH CRAVENS, of Rockingham,
BRISCOE G. BALDWIN, of Augusta,
HENRY ERSKINE, of Greenbrier,
JOHN P. MATTHEWS, of Wythe,
ROBERT BEATTIE, of Smyth,
JOEL SHREWSBURY, of Kanawha,
MOSES W. CHAPLINE, of Ohio.

Virginia, 1836. Various candidates are suggested on this ticket. Jackson is quoted, even though the slogan at the top of the ballot seems to refer negatively to his hand-picked successor, Martin Van Buren. Issued in Virginia, it supports Hugh White of Tennessee and William Henry Harrison and John Tyler of Virginia. It also asserts that a vote for White or Harrison would prevent the election from being thrown into the House of Representatives, although that is exactly what they had in mind. Tyler would be Harrison's running mate in 1840 and succeed to the Presidency following Harrison's death one month into his term of office.

Ohio, 1836. A German language ballot for one of the four Whig candidates, William Henry Harrison, but titled "Democratic Harrison Ticket."

Connecticut, 1836. (This ballot was preserved in a scrapbook – a souvenir of that important campaign.)

A second example of a German language ballot from 1836 promoting the Whig (or "Farmer's Ticket") of Harrison and Granger. Quotes favorable to General Harrison are reprinted, including one from Van Buren's running mate Richard Mentor Johnson, credited with killing the great Indian leader Tecumseh in the War of 1812.

Ohio, 1836.

Three

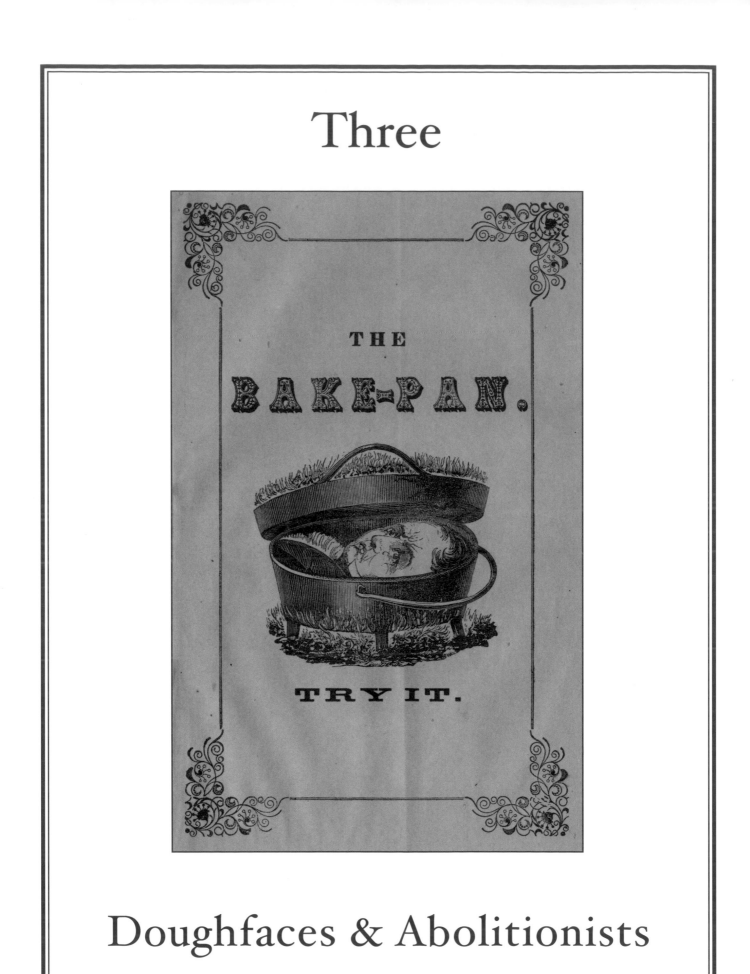

Doughfaces & Abolitionists

"Let each citizen remember at the moment he is offering his vote that he is not making a present or a compliment to please an individual — or at least that he ought not so to do; but that he is executing one of the most solemn trusts in human society for which he is accountable to God and his country."

–Samuel Adams

Ohio, 1840.

The years between 1840 and 1860 saw continued expansion of American territory, vastly increased immigration and anti-slavery agitation, issues that prompted both political actions and reactions.

Following Ireland's potato famine and various European revolutions, many German, Irish and Scandinavian immigrants entered the United States in the 1840's and 1850's. An anti-Catholic, xenophobic backlash took hold, manifested in the Native American or "Nativist" movement which birthed and nourished the American or Know Nothing Party between 1854 and 1860. President Millard Fillmore was their most prominent member and their standard bearer in the 1856 election, but finished a distant third to Democrat James Buchanan and Republican John Fremont.

Anti-slavery sentiment developed a head of steam in the 1840's, in large part due to such men as Owen Lovejoy, James Birney, William Lloyd Garrison and Frederick Douglass. The abolitionists ran presidential candidates in 1840 and 1844 under the Liberty Party banner. Like Whig candidate Henry Clay, they opposed the annexation of Texas because it would be admitted as a slave state. In 1848 and 1852 the Free Soil Party ran as their candidate former President Martin Van Buren and then John Parker Hale. In 1856 the newly-formed Republican Party – primarily composed of old-line Whigs – nominated John C. Fremont as their candidate. He ran on a campaign slogan of "Free Soil, Free Men, Free Speech and Fremont." Noted New York abolitionist Gerrit Smith, who bankrolled John Brown's raids, ran for president on the Radi-

Election of 1840

Whig

William Henry Harrison

Popular Vote 1,275,016
Electoral Vote 234

Democratic

Martin Van Buren

Popular Vote 1,129,102
Electoral Vote 60

Liberty

James Gillespie Birney

Popular Vote 6,797
Electoral Vote 0

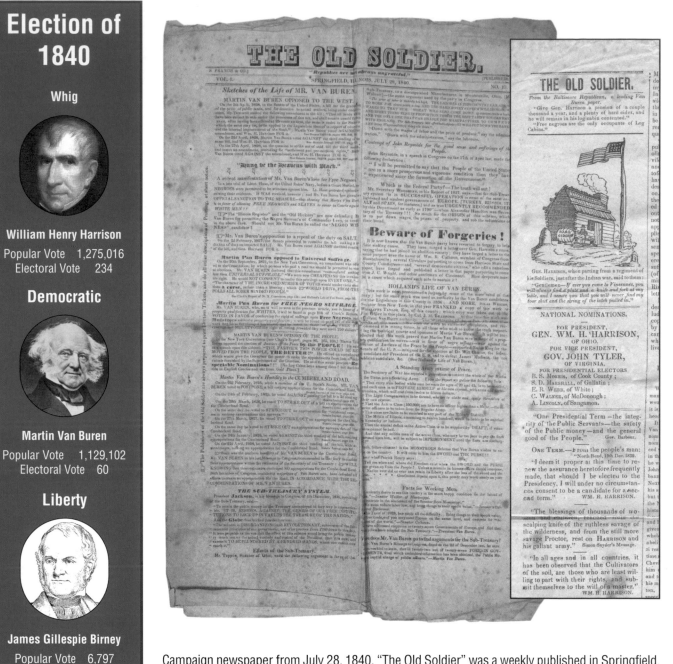

Campaign newspaper from July 28, 1840. "The Old Soldier" was a weekly published in Springfield, Illinois in support of William Henry Harrison. The publisher was Simeon Francis, but it is remembered because one of its five editors was Abraham Lincoln. The back page contains a ballot that lists Lincoln as a Presidential Elector. The front page has two items of note: a small ad announcing that: "The Publishers of The Old Soldier are always prepared to print Election Tickets, and do all other descriptions of Printing, at short notice" and a news item asserting that Democrat Martin Van Buren favors freeing the Negroes and – contrary to the so-called Black Laws of Illinois – allowing slaves and free blacks to testify in court against white men. Consequently the paper declares Van Buren "the Negro Witness Candidate." If Lincoln didn't write this story, he certainly approved the content. In contrast, the Democrats accused Harrison of promoting "white slavery," because as Governor of Indiana Territory he approved a bill that forced white debtors to work off their debts if they were unable to pay them off.

Harrison & the Bounty.

For Electors of President and Vice President,
Isaac C. Bates, of Northampton, } ELECTORS
Peleg Sprague, of Boston,   } at Large.
Districts.
No. 1—Richard Haughton, of Boston.
    2—Stephen C. Phillips, of Salem.
    3—Rufus Longley, of Haverhill.
    4—Sidney Willard, of Cambridge.
    5—Ira M. Barton, of Worcester.
    6—George Grennell, Jr. of Greenfield.
    7—Thaddeus Pomeroy, of Stockbridge.
    8—Samuel Mixter, of N. Braintree.
    9—Thomas French, of Canton.
   10—Wilkes Wood, of Middleboro'.
   11—Joseph Tripp, of Fairhaven.
   12—John B. Thomas, of Plymouth.

For Representative to Congress from the Second
District,
LEVERETT SALTONSTALL
OF SALEM.

FOR GOVERNOR,
JOHN DAVIS,
Of Worcester.

FOR LIEUT. GOVERNOR,
GEORGE HULL,
Of Sandisfield.

For Senators for Essex County,
DANIEL P. KING, of Danvers.
AMOS ABBOTT, of Andover.
DAVID CHOATE, of Essex.
STEPHEN OLIVER, of Lynn.
HENRY W. KINSMAN, of Newburyport.

For Representatives to the General Court,
WILLIAM PARSONS, JR.
GEORGE W. PEARCE.
WILLIAM DAVIS.

Massachusetts, 1840. A sailing ship seemed appropriate for maritime interests in the Bay State.

cal Abolition ticket. His effort attracted so little attention (and so few votes) it is seldom even mentioned in history books. (The exploits of his surrogate John Brown, however, are an entirely different story.)

Presidents John Tyler, James Polk and Zachary Taylor each haled from a Southern state and supported slavery. They were followed by three Northerners: Millard Fillmore (New York), Franklin Pierce (New Hampshire) and James Buchanan (Pennsylvania). The latter three were derisively known as "Doughfaces", that is, Northern politicians who were soft on the issue of slavery and deferred to or distinctly favored the South.

A long chain of key individuals made the 19th century's seminal event, the Civil War, inevitable. Polk sponsored annexation of Texas, a slave state, and engineered a war with Mexico and acquisition of Mexican territory (widely viewed as fertile ground for the expansion of slavery). Discovery of gold in California in 1848 fostered agitation for the introduction of slave labor into its gold fields, and its admission as a free state in 1850 – with agreement to actively enforce the Fugitive Slave Law (the Compromise of 1850) – encouraged further argument over slavery. The "peculiar institution" became national discourse two years later with the publication of Harriet Beecher Stowe's *Uncle Tom's Cabin*. The Kansas-Nebraska Act of 1854 effectively annulled the Missouri Compromise of 1820, and the Dred Scott decision of 1857 prevented Congressional regulation of slavery in the territories. This meant slaveholders could take their "property" almost anywhere in the Union without fear of loss. John Brown's raid at Harper's Ferry, Virginia in 1859 alerted Southerners to the threat of a "servile insurrection" which threatened their way of life. Into this maelstrom of emotion and conflicting interests walked a moderate politician who, while not an abolitionist, advocated a halt to the spread of slavery into newly acquired territories. His name was Abraham Lincoln. ∾

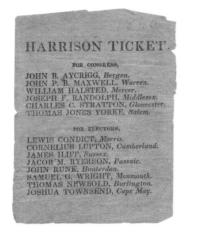

HARRISON TICKET.

FOR CONGRESS,

JOHN B. AYCRIGG, *Bergen.*
JOHN P. B. MAXWELL, *Warren.*
WILLIAM HALSTED, *Mercer.*
JOSEPH F. RANDOLPH, *Middlesex.*
CHARLES C. STRATTON, *Gloucester.*
THOMAS JONES YORKE, *Salem.*

FOR ELECTORS,

LEWIS CONDICT, *Morris.*
CORNELIUS LUPTON, *Cumberland.*
JAMES HUFF, *Sussex.*
JACOB M. RYERSON, *Passaic.*
JOHN RUNK, *Hunterdon.*
SAMUEL G. WRIGHT, *Monmouth.*
THOMAS NEWBOLD, *Burlington.*
JOSHUA TOWNSEND, *Cape May.*

New Jersey, 1840.

Harrison Ticket.

FOR ELECTORS.

Joseph Healy, of Washington,
George W. Nesmith, of Franklin,
Joseph Cilley, of Nottingham,
Andrew Peirce, of Dover,
William Bixby, of Francestown,
Thomas M. Edwards, of Keene,
Amos A. Brewster, of Hanover.

New Hampshire, 1840.

HARRISON TICKET.

HARRISON & REFORM

CONSTITUTION & LAWS

For Electors of President and Vice-President of the United States.

DAVID HOFFMAN,
JOHN LEEDS KERR,
THOMAS A. SPENCE,
THEODORE R. LOOCKERMAN,
GEORGE HOWARD,
JOHN P. KENNEDY,
RICHARD J. BOWIE,
JACOB A. PRESTON,
JAMES M. COALE,
WILLIAM T. WOOTTON.

Day of Election—Monday, 2d of November.

HARRISON TICKET.

FOR GOVERNOR,

JOHN DAVIS.

OF WORCESTER.

FOR LIEUT. GOVERNOR,

GEORGE HULL.

OF SANDISFIELD.

FOR SENATORS.

Joseph Grinnell, *of New Bedford.*
Seth Presbrey, *of Taunton,*
John Daggett, *of Attleborough.*

Massachusetts, 1840.

Maryland, 1840. The item in the middle is a large, slogan-inscribed leather ball that Harrison partisans pushed around from city to city. These unique campaign items spawned the expression "Keep the ball rolling!"

Ohio, 1840. Ballots with the exact same slate of candidates but different slogans appealed to different voters in that state.

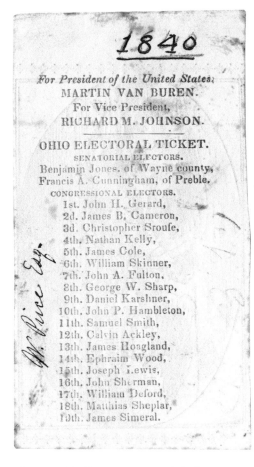

For President of the United States,
MARTIN VAN BUREN.
For Vice President,
RICHARD M. JOHNSON.

OHIO ELECTORAL TICKET.

SENATORIAL ELECTORS.

Benjamin Jones, of Wayne county,
Francis A. Cunningham, of Preble.

CONGRESSIONAL ELECTORS.

1st. John H. Gerard,
2d. James B. Cameron,
3d. Christopher Sroufe,
4th. Nathan Kelly,
5th. James Cole,
6th. William Skinner,
7th. John A. Fulton,
8th. George W. Sharp,
9th. Daniel Karshner,
10th. John P. Hambleton,
11th. Samuel Smith,
12th. Calvin Ackley,
13th. James Hoagland,
14th. Ephraim Wood,
15th. Joseph Lewis,
16th. John Sherman,
17th. William Deford,
18th. Matthias Sheplar,
19th. James Simeral.

Ohio, 1840. (Reverse at top right.)

1840 poll book leaf from Jacksonville, Illinois. Abraham Lincoln, listed here as "Abram Lincoln", is one of five Whig electoral candidates in the contest that pitted William Henry Harrison against Martin Van Buren. Stephen Douglas was chosen as a Van Buren elector.

POLL BOOK FOR *Jacksonville* PRECINCT, NOV. 1840.

Names.	ADAM W. SNYDER,	ISAAC P. WALKER,	JOHN W. ELDREDGE,	JAMES H. RALSTON,	JOHN A. McCLERNAND,	BUCKNER S. MORRIS,	SAMUEL D. MARSHALL,	EDWIN B. WEBB,	CYRUS WALKER,	ABRAM LINCOLN,
Joshua Cully	1	1	1	1	1					
Nathan Wells						1	1	1	1	1
Adam Pist	1	1	1	1	1					
Elijah Bacon	1	1	1	1	1					
Christopher Brink						1	1	1	1	1
J. Bardin	1	1	1	1	1					
George Killham						1	1	1	1	1
John B. Handy						1	1	1	1	1
Samuel Meredith						1	1	1	1	1
James H. Mellen						1	1	1	1	1
Wm. M. Patterson	1	1	1	1	1					
Alexander Sear	1	1	1	1	1					
Samuel Sear	1	1	1	1	1					
Joseph Dayton	1	1	1	1	1					
A. A. Austin	1	1	1	1	1					
N. H. Compton						1	1	1	1	1
Jno. Sample						1	1	1	1	1
M. Pitner						1	1	1	1	1
J. Reeves						1	1	1	1	1
Joseph Bowen	1	1	1	1	1					
James C. Sutton	1	1	1	1	1					
Wm. M. Harney						1	1	1	1	1
Jno. C. Wolfree						1	1	1	1	1
Wm. B. Newton						1	1	1	1	1
Thomas Emerson						1	1	1	1	1
Rodolph Miller	1	1	1	1	1					
S. C. Person						1	1	1	1	1
	14					13				

Election of 1844

Democratic

James Knox Polk

Popular Vote   1,337,243
Electoral Vote   170

Whig

Henry Clay

Popular Vote   1,229,062
Electoral Vote   105

Liberty

James Gillespie Birney

Popular Vote   62,300
Electoral Vote   0

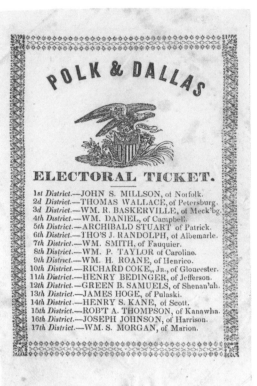

POLK & DALLAS

ELECTORAL TICKET.

1st District.—JOHN S. MILLSON, of Norfolk.
2d District.—THOMAS WALLACE, of Petersburg.
3d District.—WM. R. BASKERVILLE, of Meck'bg.
4th District.—WM. DANIEL, of Campbell.
5th District.—ARCHIBALD STUART of Patrick.
6th District.—THO'S J. RANDOLPH, of Albemarle.
7th District.—WM. SMITH, of Fauquier.
8th District.—WM. P. TAYLOR of Caroline.
9th District.—WM. H. ROANE, of Henrico.
10th District.—RICHARD COKE, Jr., of Gloucester.
11th District.—HENRY BEDINGER, of Jefferson.
12th District.—GREEN B. SAMUELS, of Shenan'ah.
13th District.—JAMES HOGE, of Pulaski.
14th District.—HENRY S. KANE, of Scott.
15th District.—ROB'T A. THOMPSON, of Kanawha.
16th District.—JOSEPH JOHNSON, of Harrison.
17th District.—WM. S. MORGAN, of Marion.

Virginia, 1844.

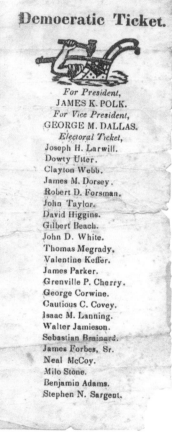

Democratic Ticket.

For President,
JAMES K. POLK.
For Vice President,
GEORGE M. DALLAS.
Electoral Ticket,
Joseph H. Larwill.
Dowty Utter.
Clayton Webb.
James M. Dorsey.
Robert D. Forsman.
John Taylor.
David Higgins.
Gilbert Beach.
John D. White.
Thomas Megrady.
Valentine Keffer.
James Parker.
Grenville P. Cherry.
George Corwine.
Cautious C. Covey.
Isaac M. Lanning.
Walter Jamieson.
Sebastian Brainard.
James Forbes, Sr.
Neal McCoy.
Milo Stone.
Benjamin Adams.
Stephen N. Sargent.

Ohio, 1844.

POLK, DALLAS AND VICTORY.

ELECTORS:

1 BENJAMIN F. BUTLER,
2 DANIEL S. DICKINSON,

3 Hugh Halsey,
4 John C. Thompson,
5 George Douglass,
6 Niel Gray,
7 William F. Havemeyer,
8 Jonathan I. Coddington,
9 Daniel Johnson,
10 John Crawford,
11 William Murray,
12 Jacobus Hardenbergh,
13 Tobias L. Hogeboom,
14 Nicholas M. Masters,
15 John K. Paige,
16 John Savage,
17 William Hedding,
18 John Fay,
19 John Nellis,
20 Clemence Whitaker,
21 Azariah Doane,
22 Thomas H. Hubbard,
23 Lemuel Pattengill,
24 William Mason,
25 Henry Potts,
26 Daniel Dana,
27 John Gillett,
28 Jacob E. Bogardus,
29 Jonathan Boynton,
30 Elisha Johnson,
31 John Lapham,
32 John D. Higgins,
33 Robert H. Shankland,
34 Jonathan Hascall, Jun.,
35 Rufus H. Smith,
36 John D. Perkins.

New York, 1844.

DEMOCRATIC TICKET.

FOR PRESIDENT
James K. Polk.
FOR VICE-PRESIDENT
George M. Dallas.
ELECTORS:
J. W. MATTHEWS,
JOSEPH BELL,
HENRY S. FOOTE,
JEFFERSON DAVIS,
ARTHUR FOX,
R. H. BOONE.

Mississippi, 1844. Future Confederate President Jefferson Davis is listed as a Polk elector. Like Polk, Davis was elected.

FOR PRESIDENT
JAMES K. POLK, OF TENNESSEE.
FOR VICE PRESIDENT,
GEO. M. DALLAS, OF PENNSYLVANIA.

ELECTORS FOR THE STATE AT LARGE.
LEVIN H. COE of FAYETTE.
H. L. TURNEY of FRANKLIN.

FOR CONGRESSIONAL DISTRICTS.
1st L. C. HAYNES,
2d T. A. ANDERSON,
3d G. W. ROWLES,
4th J. H. SAVAGE,
5th J. C. ROGERS,
6th J. H. THOMAS,
7th D. M. CURRIN,
8th J. C. GUILD,
9th L. B. CHASE,
10th F. P. STANTON,
11th T. EWELL.

Tennessee, 1844.

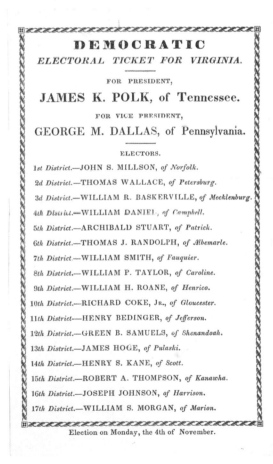

DEMOCRATIC
ELECTORAL TICKET FOR VIRGINIA.

FOR PRESIDENT,

JAMES K. POLK, of Tennessee.

FOR VICE PRESIDENT,

GEORGE M. DALLAS, of Pennsylvania.

ELECTORS.

1st District.—JOHN S. MILLSON, of Norfolk.

2d District.—THOMAS WALLACE, of Petersburg.

3d District.—WILLIAM R. BASKERVILLE, of Mecklenburg.

4th District.—WILLIAM DANIEL, of Campbell.

5th District.—ARCHIBALD STUART, of Patrick.

6th District.—THOMAS J. RANDOLPH, of Albemarle.

7th District.—WILLIAM SMITH, of Fauquier.

8th District.—WILLIAM P. TAYLOR, of Caroline.

9th District.—WILLIAM H. ROANE, of Henrico.

10th District.—RICHARD COKE, JR., of Gloucester.

11th District.—HENRY BEDINGER, of Jefferson.

12th District.—GREEN B. SAMUELS, of Shenandoah.

13th District.—JAMES HOGE, of Pulaski.

14th District.—HENRY S. KANE, of Scott.

15th District.—ROBERT A. THOMPSON, of Kanawha.

16th District.—JOSEPH JOHNSON, of Harrison.

17th District.—WILLIAM S. MORGAN, of Marion.

Election on Monday, the 4th of November.

Virginia, 1844.

Democratic Republican Ticket.

1844

"We must preserve our liberties or perish in the last ditch." JACKSON.

For Electors of President and Vice President.
William Badger,
John McNeil,
Elijah R. Currier,
Isaac Hale,
Elijah Sawyer,
John L. Putnam.

"Is it expedient to alter the Constitution?" Yes.

"Shall capital punishment be abolished?"

New Hampshire, 1844. This ballot also allowed voters to choose whether the state constitution would be amended to abolish capital punishment.

Abraham Lincoln is mentioned three times in this July 20, 1844 issue of "The Free Press" from Vandalia, Illinois. As a Whig Party organ, the paper was devoted to the election of Henry Clay. Lincoln is listed as a candidate for Presidential Elector on the second page. He is also mentioned as one of six speakers at a Clay rally held three days prior, and his name appears in the description of a banner made for that occasion: "The banner of the Marion delegation bore on one side: 'All for Clay and Frelinghuysen/ Protection to Home Industry', a hammer, a plow and a sheaf of wheat below, and on the other side a large U. S. Bank bill – J. J. Hardin, Cashier. Abraham Lincoln, President; and besides this, two national flags."

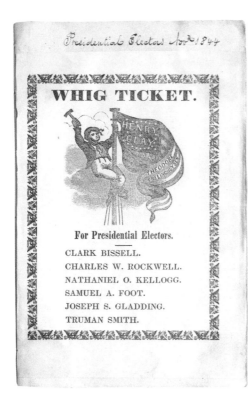

WHIG TICKET.

For Presidential Electors.

CLARK BISSELL.

CHARLES W. ROCKWELL.

NATHANIEL O. KELLOGG.

SAMUEL A. FOOT.

JOSEPH S. GLADDING.

TRUMAN SMITH.

Connecticut, 1844.

Für Präsident,
Henry Clay.
Für Vice Präsident,
Theodore Frelinghuysen.
Senatorial Erwähler,
Thomas Corwin, von Warren,
Peter Hitchcock, von Geauga,
Dist. Congressional Erwähler.
1—Bellamy Storer, von Hamilton,
2—William Bebb, von Butler,
3—Aaron Harlan, von Greene,
4—Samson Mason von Clark,
5—David J. Cory, von Henry,
6—Josiah Scott, von Crawford;
7—Reader W. Clarke von Clermont;
8—David Adams, von Roß;
9—Joseph Olds, von Pickaway;
10—Daniel S. Norton, von Knor,
11—Washington W. Concklin, v Marion
12—Samuel R. Holcomb, von Gallia;
13—Harlow Chapin, von Washington;
14—John Crooks, von Guernsey;
15—Samuel W. Bostwick, von, Harrison;
16—William R. Sapp, von Holmes;
17—John W. Gill, von Jefferson;
18—Cyrus Spink, von Wayne,
19—Jacob H. Baldwin, von Trumbull;
20—William L. Perkins, von Lake;
21—John Fuller, von Erie;

Ohio, 1844. German language ballot.

WHIG ELECTORAL TICKET.

FOR PRESIDENT OF THE UNITED STATES,

HENRY CLAY,

OF KENTUCKY,

The Glory of his Country, and the first Living Statesman.

FOR VICE PRESIDENT,

Theodore Frelinghuysen,

OF NEW JERSEY,

An Upright and Able Statesman, and Honest Man.

These men, if elected, will support American industry against the capital and pauper labor of Europe, which will lead to the creation of a steady and permanent HOME MARKET for the American Farmer. They will support the Distribution of the Proceeds of the Public Lands among the States, to whom they of right belong, thus securing annually to Virginia from a half million to a million of dollars, for educating her children ; and they are friendly to a sound National Currency, which will make money more plenty, and prevent its depreciation.

These are the measures to make the country great and prosperous, and to protect Liberty !

Whigs of Virginia ! Let each man now do his duty.

ELECTORS.

District 1. ROBERT H. WHITFIELD, of Isle of Wight.
2. JOHN E. SHELL, of Brunswick.
3. HENRY P. IRVING, of Cumberland.
4. JOSEPH K. IRVING, of Amherst.
5. GEORGE H. GILMER, of Pittsylvania.
6. VALENTINE W. SOUTHALL, of Albemarle.
7. JOHN JANNEY, of Loudoun.
8. EDWARD T. TAYLOE, of King George.
9. RALEIGH T. DANIEL, of Richmond City.
10. MOREAU BOWERS, of Williamsburg.
11. ANDREW HUNTER, of Jefferson.
12. ALEXANDER H. H. STUART, of Augusta.
13. WILLIAM B. PRESTON, of Montgomery.
14. ANDREW S. FULTON, of Wythe.
15. ALLEN T. CAPERTON, of Monroe.
16. AUGUSTINE J. SMITH, of Harrison.
17. JAMES M. STEPHENSON, of Tyler.

Richmond Whig Extra.

FOR PRESIDENT,
HENRY CLAY.
VICE PRESIDENT,
THEODORE FRELINGHUYSEN.

Electors of President and Vice President of the U. States,

THOMAS CORWIN,	PETER HITCHCOCK,
BELLAMY STORER,	WILLIAM BEBB,
AARON HARLAN,	SAMSON MASON,
DAVID J. CORY,	JOSIAH SCOTT,
READER W. CLARKE,	DAVID ADAMS,
JOSEPH OLDS,	DANIEL S. NORTON,
WASHINGTON W. CONCKLIN,	SAMUEL R. HOLCOMB,
HARLOW CHAPIN,	JOHN CROOKS,
SAMUEL W. BOSTWICK,	WILLIAM R. SAPP,
JOHN W. GILL,	CYRUS SPINK,
JACOB H. BALDWIN,	WILLIAM L. PERKINS,
	JOHN FULLER.

Ohio, 1844.

Virginia, 1844. Newspapers in the 19th century were highly partisan and made little effort at balanced journalism. The "Richmond Whig" issued this "Extra" in the form of a Henry Clay ballot with slogans and planks of the Whig platform.

Election of 1848

Whig

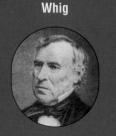

Zachary Taylor

Popular Vote 1,360,099
Electoral Vote 163

Democratic

Lewis Cass

Popular Vote 1,220,544
Electoral Vote 127

Free Soil

Martin Van Buren

Popular Vote 291,263
Electoral Vote 0

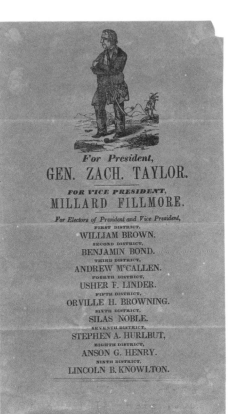

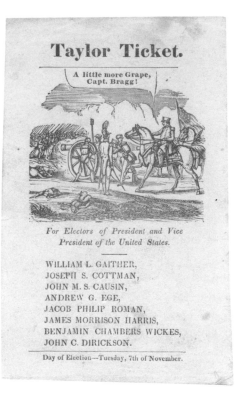

Illinois, 1848. Linder, Browning and Henry were all close Lincoln associates. All four barnstormed the state giving pro-Taylor speeches. At the time Lincoln was near the end of his one and only term in Congress.

Maryland, 1848. Taylor was but one of a long line of war heroes who sought the Presidency.

Ohio, 1848.

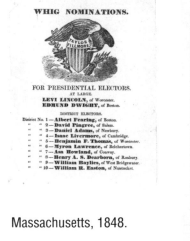

Massachusetts, 1848.

Connecticut, 1848.

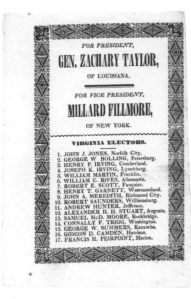

FOR PRESIDENT,
GEN. ZACHARY TAYLOR,
OF LOUISIANA.

FOR VICE PRESIDENT,
MILLARD FILLMORE,
OF NEW YORK.

VIRGINIA ELECTORS.

1. JOHN J. JONES, Norfolk City.
2. GEORGE W. BOLLING, Petersburg.
3. HENRY P. IRVING, Cumberland.
4. JOSEPH K. IRVING, Lynchburg.
5. WILLIAM MARTIN, Franklin.
6. WILLIAM C. RIVES, Albemarle.
7. ROBERT E. SCOTT, Fauquier.
8. HENRY T. GARNETT, Westmoreland.
9. JOHN A. MEREDITH, Richmond City.
10. ROBERT SAUNDERS, Williamsburg.
11. ANDREW HUNTER, Jefferson.
12. ALEXANDER H. H. STUART, Augusta.
13. SAMUEL McD. MOORE, Rockbridge.
14. CONNALLY F. TRIGG, Washington.
15. GEORGE W. SUMMERS, Kanawha.
16. GIDEON D. CAMDEN, Harrison.
17. FRANCIS H. PEIRPOINT, Marion.

Virginia, 1848.

"Rough & Ready" TICKET.

For Electors of President and Vice President.
Isaac V. Brown,
John Runk,
Joshua Brick,
Charles Burroughs,
Robert V. Armstrong,
Calvin Howell,
Peter I. Ackerman.

For a Member of the House of Representatives
William A. Newell.

For Members of Assembly.
Edward French,
Benjamin Kemble,
John S. Irick,
Samuel Stockton,
William R. Braddock.

For Sheriff,
Abraham Gaskill.

For Clerk,
Joseph F. Burr.

For Coroners,
Samuel Lowden,
Richard Dorell,
Nathan L. Mulliner.

New Jersey, 1848.

DEMOCRATIC
ELECTORAL TICKET FOR VIRGINIA.

FOR PRESIDENT,
LEWIS CASS, of Michigan.

FOR VICE PRESIDENT,
WILLIAM O. BUTLER, of Kentucky.

ELECTORS.

1st District—JOHN S. MILLSON, of Norfolk.
2d District—FRANCIS E. RIVES, of Petersburg.
3d District—HENRY L. HOPKINS, of Powhatan.
4th District—WILLIS P. BOCOCK, of Buckingham.
5th District—WILLIAM M. TREDWAY, of Pittsylvania.
6th District—SHELTON F. LEAKE, of Albemarle.
7th District—JOHN S. BARBOUR, Sr., of Culpeper.
8th District—HENRY A. WASHINGTON, of Westmoreland.
9th District—ROBERT G. SCOTT, of Richmond City.
10th District—HENRY A. WISE, of Accomac.
11th District—THOMAS SLOAN, of Hampshire.
12th District—GREEN B. SAMUELS, of Shenandoah.
13th District—JOHN LETCHER, of Rockbridge.
14th District—JOHN B. FLOYD, of Washington.
15th District—ALBERT G. PENDLETON, of Giles.
16th District—SAMUEL L. HAYS, of Gilmer.
17th District—OBADIAH W. LANGFITT, of Brooke.

Election on Tuesday, the 7th of November, 1848.

Virginia, 1848.

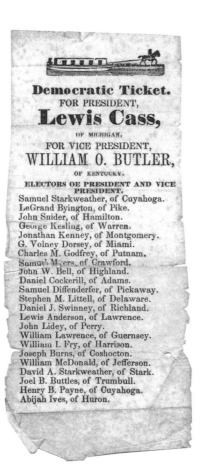

Democratic Ticket.
FOR PRESIDENT,
Lewis Cass,
OF MICHIGAN,
FOR VICE PRESIDENT,
WILLIAM O. BUTLER,
OF KENTUCKY.

ELECTORS OF PRESIDENT AND VICE PRESIDENT.

Samuel Starkweather, of Cuyahoga.
LeGrand Byington, of Pike.
John Snider, of Hamilton.
George Kesling, of Warren.
Jonathan Kenney, of Montgomery.
G. Volney Dorsey, of Miami.
Charles M. Godfrey, of Putnam.
Samuel Myers, of Crawford.
John W. Bell, of Highland.
Daniel Cockerill, of Adams.
Samuel Diffenderfer, of Pickaway.
Stephen M. Littell, of Delaware.
Daniel J. Swinney, of Richland.
Lewis Anderson, of Lawrence.
John Lidey, of Perry.
William Lawrence, of Guernsey.
William I. Fry, of Harrison.
Joseph Burns, of Coshocton.
William McDonald, of Jefferson.
David A. Starkweather, of Stark.
Joel B. Buttles, of Trumbull.
Henry B. Payne, of Cuyahoga.
Abijah Ives, of Huron.

Ohio, 1848. Future President James A. Garfield's 1880 campaign played up his youthful job as a canal "tow-path boy" in Ohio – as illustrated on this ballot.

DEMOCRATIC REPUBLICAN TICKET.

FOR PRESIDENT,
Lewis Cass.
FOR VICE PRESIDENT,
Wm. O. Butler.

1st Dist. Thomas Bragg, Jr.
2d " Asa Biggs
3d " Perrin Busbee.
4th " George S. Stevenson.
5th " William S. Ashe.
6th " Samuel J. Person.
7th " Cadwallader Jones, Sr.
8th " Junius L. Clemmons.
9th " Green W. Caldwell.
10th " W. W. Avery.
11th " Jesse R. Weaver.

North Carolina, 1848.

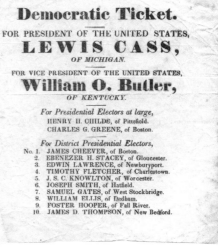

Democratic Ticket.
FOR PRESIDENT OF THE UNITED STATES,
LEWIS CASS,
OF MICHIGAN.
FOR VICE PRESIDENT OF THE UNITED STATES,
William O. Butler,
OF KENTUCKY.

For Presidential Electors at large,
HENRY H. CHILDS, of Pittsfield.
CHARLES G. GREENE, of Boston.

For District Presidential Electors,
No. 1. JAMES CHEEVER, of Boston.
2. EBENEZER H. STACEY, of Gloucester.
3. EDWIN LAWRENCE, of Newburyport.
4. TIMOTHY FLETCHER, of Charlestown.
5. J. S. C. KNOWLTON, of Worcester.
6. JOSEPH SMITH, of Hatfield.
7. SAMUEL GATES, of West Stockbridge.
8. WILLIAM ELLIS, of Dedham.
9. FOSTER HOOPER, of Fall River.
10. JAMES D. THOMPSON, of New Bedford.

Massachusetts, 1848.

Election of 1852

Democratic

Franklin Pierce

Popular Vote   1,601,274
Electoral Vote   254

Whig

Winfield Scott

Popular Vote   1,386,580
Electoral Vote   42

Free Soil

John Parker Hale

Popular Vote   155,825
Electoral Vote   0

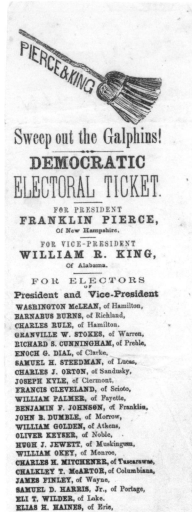

Ohio, 1852. "Galphins" refers to a controversy, lost in time, over whether a financial obligation incurred by Georgia should be paid by that state or the United States. A Senate committee decided against Georgia, precipitating charges of fraud. A viable campaign issue then, to modern eyes it ranks at the bottom of the electoral totem pole.

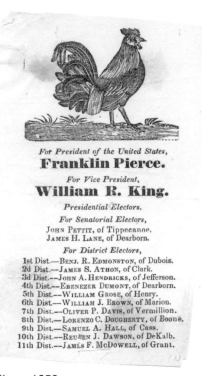

Indiana, 1852.

Massachusetts, 1852.

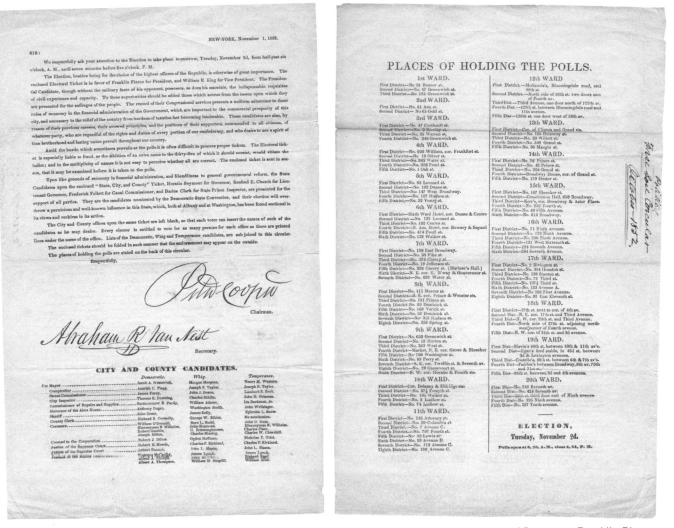

Although marked as a "Free Soil" circular, this piece of campaign ephemera was used in support of Democrat Franklin Pierce. It is signed by noted New York inventor, industrialist and philanthropist, Peter Cooper. It lists city and county candidates (Democratic, Whig and Temperance) and the locations of polling places in all twenty wards of the city. The polls opened at sunrise and closed at sundown.

New Hampshire, 1852. The New Hampshire native and Democratic nominee, Franklin Pierce, is quoted.

Virginia, 1852.

Indiana, 1852.

Vermont, 1852.

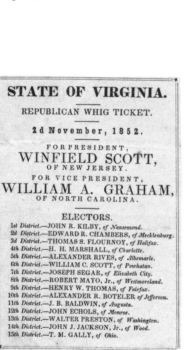

Virginia, 1852.

Virginia, 1852.

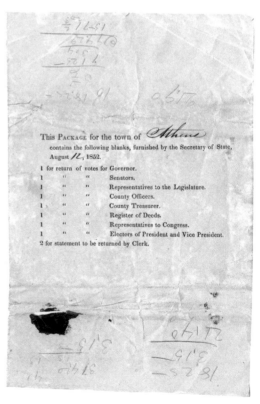

This circular from the Secretary of State to the town of Athens [Georgia?] transmits official forms for the recording of votes in the statewide and general election of 1852.

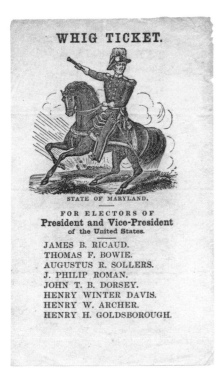

Maryland, 1852. Both presidential candidates this year had served in the Mexican War. In contrast to Pierce, Scott's record was exemplary, but not enough to assure his victory on the political battlefield.

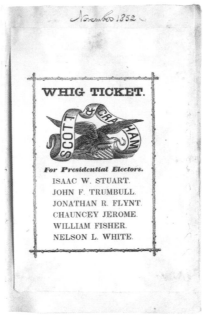

Connecticut, 1852. Chauncey Jerome was the owner of one of the nation's largest clock companies.

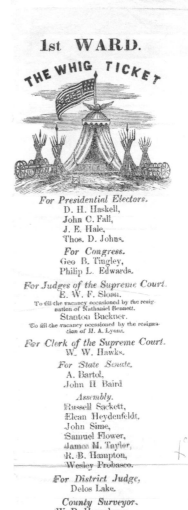

California, 1852. The "Bear Flag Republic" had just become a state in 1850. This is a souvenir of the first presidential election in which it participated. This ticket was sent home in a letter from a California gold miner, a "forty-niner."

Ohio, 1852.

New Hampshire, 1852.

Election of 1856

Democratic

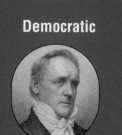

James Buchanan

Popular Vote 1,838,169
Electoral Vote 254

Republican

John Charles Fremont

Popular Vote 1,341,264
Electoral Vote 114

American

Millard Fillmore

Popular Vote 874,534
Electoral Vote 8

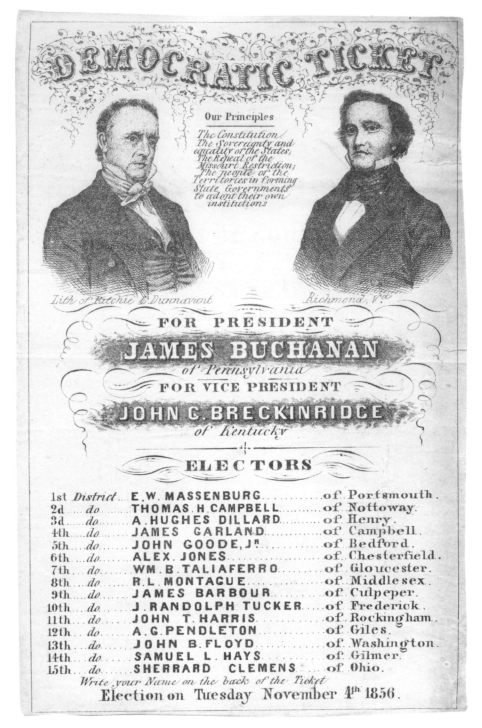

Virginia, 1856. The list of "Our Principles" (campaign planks), clearly reflect the views of slaveholders who favored unlimited expansion of slavery.

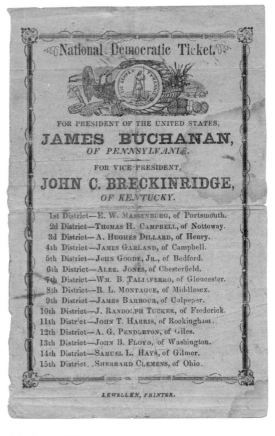

Virginia, 1856.

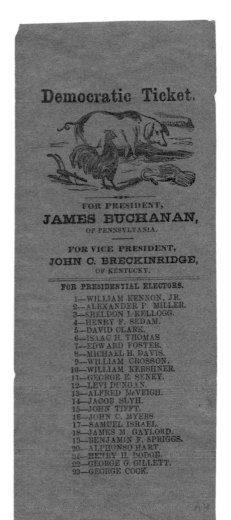

Ohio, 1856. The woodcut illustration doubtless appealed to those engaged in agriculture, Ohio's main industry.

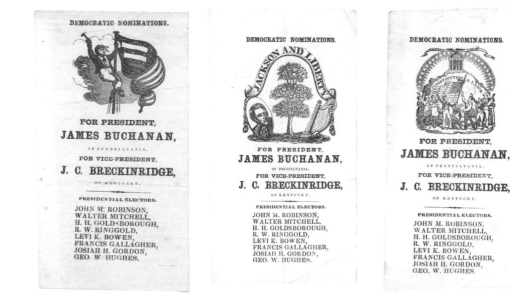

Maryland, 1856. Printers used a variety of woodcuts to decorate ballots, most of which saw use over multiple election cycles.

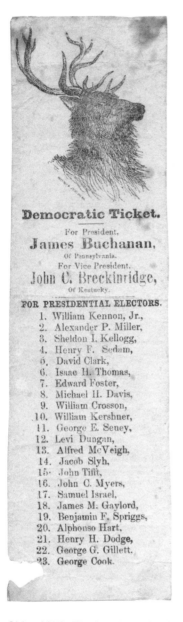

Ohio, 1856. The head of a buck was instantly recognizable as a symbol for James Buchanan.

Maryland, 1856.

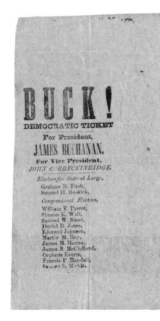

Indiana, 1856.

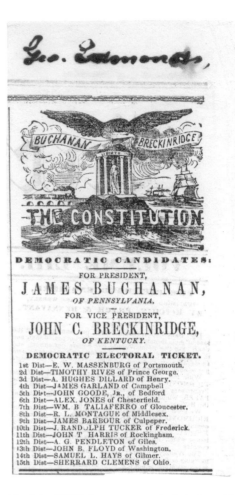

Virginia, 1856. A newspaper ballot signed by the voter. After tabulation, these were sewn together in bundles, after having been pierced in the center.

Connecticut, 1856.

Massachusetts, 1856.

Pennsylvania, 1856. Uncut sheet of eight ballots, four each for Fremont and Fillmore. Note that the Presidential Electors are the same for each candidate. This was part of a scheme by Kenneth Raynor of North Carolina who stumped the state for Fillmore. The Electors had pledged themselves to vote for the candidates based on the percentage of popular votes received by each. Their main goal was to deprive Pennsylvania native son James Buchanan of a majority of electoral votes, thereby throwing the election into the House of Representatives where Know Nothing Congressmen could influence the outcome.

Michigan, 1856. Three portraits of Fremont left no doubt as to the purpose of this ballot.

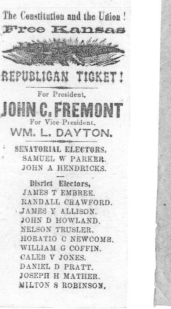

Indiana, 1856.

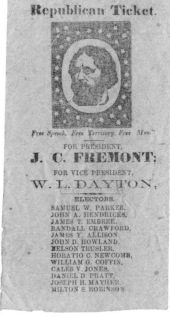

Indiana, 1856

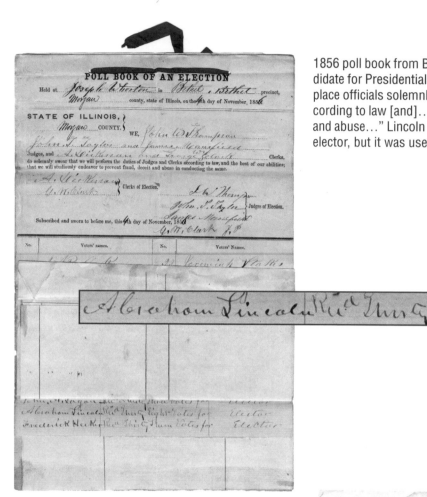

1856 poll book from Bethel, Illinois. Abraham Lincoln is listed as a candidate for Presidential Elector with 38 votes in his favor. The five polling place officials solemnly swore that they would perform their duties "according to law [and]… will studiously endeavor to prevent fraud, deceit and abuse…" Lincoln lost in all of his attempts to become a presidential elector, but it was useful experience for honing his political skills.

Illinois, 1856. Abraham Lincoln is listed as a Presidential Elector on both ballots. The Republican Party had been organized just two years earlier and there was no uniformity as to its name. Here, rather than "Republican," the ballots are headed "Fremont & Bissell Ticket" and "Anti-Nebraska Ticket." The Republicans opposed provisions of the Kansas-Nebraska Act of 1854 and Stephen Douglas' pernicious policy of "Popular Sovereignty" which had produced near civil war in Kansas.

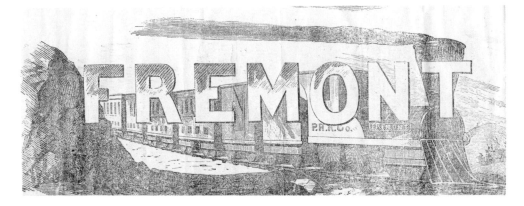

REPUBLICAN AND PEOPLE'S
REFORM TICKET.

SEVENTH DISTRICT.
STATE NOMINATIONS.

For Presidential Electors,
ALEXANDER BELL, of Los Angeles.
FREDERICK P. TRACY, of S. Francisco.
L. C. GUNN, of Tuolumne.
C. N. ORMSBY, of El Dorado.

For Members of Congress,
IRA P. RANKIN,
Of San Francisco.
J. N. TURNER,
Of Nevada.

For Clerk of the Supreme Court,
CORNELIUS COLE, of Sacramento.

For Superintendent of Public Instruction,
P. M. PUFFINGTON, of San Joaquin.
Henry B Janes, of San Francisco
For State Prison Director,
MOSES ARMS, of Sonoma.

COUNTY NOMINATIONS.

For State Senators,
SAMUEL SOULE.
EUGENE L. SULLIVAN.

For Members of the Assembly,
RICHARD M. JESSUP,   E MIRO,
W. W. SHEPARD,   CYRUS PALMER,
M. C. BLAKE,   RICHARD CHENERY,
DR. VICTOR J. FOURGEAUD,
T. G. PHELPS,
RUFUS MURPHY,   San Mateo.

President of the Board of Supervisors—E. W. BURR.
Auditor—ETTING MICKLE.
Police Judge—HENRY E. COON.
Chief of Police—JAMES F. CURTIS.
Superintendent of Streets and Highways—BENJ. O. DEVOE.
Assessor—CHARLES B. BOND.
Tax Collector—WILLIAM Y. PATCH.
Sheriff—CHRLES DOANE.
Coroner—DR. F. A. HOLMAN.
Dock Masters—Capt. HENRY J. CHEEVAR, Cont. AMOS NOYES
Public Administrator—ROBERT C. ROGERS.
Clerk of Superior Court—JOSEPH SIMPSON.

District Nominations.

SEVENTH DISTRICT.
Superior—HENRY A. GEORGE.
School Director—WILLIAM PEARSON.
Justice of the Peace—S. R. HARRIS.
Constable—JOHN WOOLAVER.
Judge of Election—JOHN B. PERRY.
Inspector of Election—ROBERT TURNER.

For the proposed Amendment to the Constitution.

California, 1856. The candidates listed are running under the "Republican and People's Reform Ticket." The use of the word "reform," a frequent occurrence on 19th century ballots, seems somewhat archaic in our day and age.

FREE SPEECH.   FREE PRESS.
FREE KANSAS.   FREMONT.

REPUBLICAN TICKET.

For Judge of the Supreme Court,—
Short Term.
Ozias Bowen
For Judge of the Supreme Court,—
Full Term.
Josiah Scott
For Attorney General,
Christopher P Wolcott
For Commissioner of Common Schools.
Anson Smyth
For Member of the Board of Public
Works.
John Waddle
For Representative in Congress.
John A Gurley
For Judges of Court of Common Pleas.
**William M Dickson
Warner M Bateman
John W Caldwell**
For Sheriff,
Enoch T Carson
For Auditor,
Joseph B Humphreys
For County Commissioners.
**Michael Goepper
Joseph Burgoyne**
For Prosecuting Attorney.
David P Lowe
For Director of the County Infirmary.
John Stoltz
For Coroner,
Dr. Levi M Rogers
For the Bank Charter
Against the Bank Charter.
**For Erection of the Lunatic
Asylum---Yea---Nay**

REPUBLICAN
FREE SPEECH.   FREE PRESS.
FREE KANSAS.   FREMONT.

NOMINATIONS.

FOR PRESIDENT,
JOHN C. FREMONT
OF CALIFORNIA,
FOR VICE PRESIDENT,
WM. L. DAYTON,
OF NEW JERSEY,

FOR ELECTORS
President and Vice President
OF THE UNITED STATES.
CALEB B. SMITH, of Hamilton Co.
JAUCB PERKINS, of Trumbull.
JOHN B. STALLO, of Hamilton.
RICHARD M. CORWINE, of Hamilton.
PETER ODLIN, of Montgomery.
JACOB S. CONKLIN, of Shelby.
WILLIAM TAYLOR, of Hancock.
EDWARD P. EVANS, of Adams.
WILLIAM H. P. DENNY, of Warren.
JAMES R. HUBBELL, of Delaware.
ROBERT G. PENNINGTON, of Seneca.
FRANCIS CLEVELAND, of Scioto.
JOHN WELCH, of Athens.
DANIEL HUMPHREY, of Licking.
HENRY D. COOKE, of Erie.
EUGENE PARDEE, of Wayne.
JOHN M. HODGE, of Tuscarawas.
DAVIS GREEN, of Washington.
MILLER PENNINGTON, of Belmont.
JOHN S. HERRICK, of Portage.
AARON WILCOX, of Lake.
JAMES DUMARS, of Mahoning.
AMOS E. BUSS, of Carroll.

Freie Rede   Freie Presse
Freies Kansas   Fremont

Republikanisches Ticket.

Für Richter der Supreme Court—erster Termin,
Ozias Bowen
Für Richter der Supreme Court—voller Termin,
Josiah Scott
Für General Staats-Anwalt,
Christopher P Wolcott
Für Commissär der Gemein-Schulen,
Anson Smyth
Für Mitglied des Board der öffentl. Werk,
John Waddle
Für Repräsentant im Congreß,
John A Gurley
Für Richter der Common Pleas Court.
**William M Dickson
Warner M Bateman
John W Caldwell**
Für Sheriff,
Enoch T Carson
Für Auditor,
Joseph B Humphreys
Für County Commissär,
**Michael Goepper
Joseph Burgoyne**
Für Staats-Anwalt,
David P Lowe
Für Director des County-Armenhauses,
John Stoltz
Für Coroner,
Dr. Levi M Rogers

**Für den Bank-Freibrief,
Gegen den Bank-Freibrief.
Für die Erbauung der Irren-Anstalt,
Gegen die Erbauung der Irren-Anstalt,**

REPUBLICAN TICKET.

Liberty and Union.

For President,
JOHN C. FREMONT.
For Vice President,
WILLIAM L. DAYTON.

Senatorial Electors,
CALEB B. SMITH.
JACOB PERKINS.

Representative Electors,
Dist.
1st—JOHN B. STALLO.
2d—RICHARD M. CORWINE.
3d—PETER ODLIN.
4th—JACOB S. CONKLIN.
5th—WILLIAM TAYLOR.
6th—EDWARD P. EVANS.
7th—WILLIAM H. P. DENNY.
8th—JAMES R. HUBBELL.
9th—ROBERT G. PENNINGTON.
10th—FRANCIS CLEVELAND.
11th—JOHN WELCH.
12th—DANIEL HUMPHREY.
13th—HENRY D. COOKE.
14th—EUGENE PARDEE.
15th—JOHN M. HODGE.
16th—DAVIS GREEN.
17th—MILLER PENNINGTON.
18th—JOHN S. HERRICK.
19th—AARON WILCOX.
20th—JAMES DUMARS.
21st—AMOS E. BUSS.

Ohio, 1856. "Liberty and Union" is a slogan that was also used by Lincoln in both of his runs for the White House.

Ohio, 1856. Statewide and general election ballots. The statewide ballot includes local initiatives such as the question of whether to build a lunatic asylum. All of these candidates ran under the Fremont banner.

Ohio, 1856. A statewide Fremont ballot printed in German.

Fremont Electoral Ticket.

FOR ELECTORS AT LARGE,
JULIUS ROCKWELL, of Pittsfield.
THOMAS COLT, of Pittsfield.
FOR DISTRICT ELECTORS,
Dist. 1—JOHN VINSON, of Edgartown.
" 2—AZARIAH B. WHEELER, of N. Bridgewater.
" 3—GEORGE R. RUSSELL, of West Roxbury.
" 4—GEORGE ODIORNE, of Boston.
" 5—LUCIUS B. MARSH, of Boston.
" 6—GEORGE H. DEVEREUX, of Salem.
" 7—JAMES M. USHER, of Medford.
" 8—JOHN NESMITH, of Lowell.
" 9—JOHN S. C. KNOWLTON, of Worcester.
" 10—CHARLES E. FORBES, of Northampton.
" 11—FRANKLIN RIPLEY, of Greenfield.

WHIG STATE TICKET.

FOR GOVERNOR,
LUTHER V. BELL,
OF CHARLESTOWN.
FOR LIEUTENANT GOVERNOR,
HOMER FOOT,
OF SPRINGFIELD.
For Attorney General,
JOHN H. CLIFFORD, of New Bedford.
For Secretary of State,
WILLIAM S. LINCOLN, of Worcester.
For State Treasurer,
JOHN SARGENT, of Cambridge.
For State Auditor,
JOSEPH MITCHELL, of Boston.
For Representative in Congress—District No. 2.
JAMES BUFFINGTON, of Fall River.
For Southeastern District Attorney,
EDWARD AVERY, of Braintree.
For Councillor,—District No. 3,
ABNER HOLBROOK, of Weymouth.
For State Senators,
JOSHUA B. TOBEY, of Wareham.
AMOS BATES, of Hingham.
For Clerk of Courts,
William H. Whitman, of Plymouth.
For Sheriff,
John Perkins, of Plymouth.
For County Commissioner,
Williams Latham, of Bridgewater.
For Special County Commissioners,
Soranus Standish, of Middleborough.
Seth Rose, of Hanover.
For Register of Probate,
Joseph S. Beal, of Kingston.
For Register of Insolvency,
Quincy Bicknell, of Hingham.
For Commissioners of Insolvency,
Jesse E. Keith, of Abington.
Welcome Young, of East Bridgewater.
Perez Simmons, of Hanover.
For Representative in General Court,
LUTHER STEPHENSON.

AMERICAN REPUBLICAN TICKET.

FOR PRESIDENT,
JOHN C. FREMONT,
OF CALIFORNIA.

FOR VICE PRESIDENT,
WILLIAM L. DAYTON,
OF NEW JERSEY.

FOR ELECTORS,
Edward W. Lawton,
Isaac Saunders,
William P. Bullock,
William D. Brayton.

REPUBLICAN TICKET.

FOR PRESIDENT,
JOHN C. FREMONT,
OF CALIFORNIA.

FOR VICE PRESIDENT,
WILLIAM L. DAYTON,
OF NEW JERSEY.

FOR ELECTORS,
Edward W. Lawton,
Isaac Saunders,
William P. Bullock,
William D. Brayton.

FREMONT & DAYTON People's Ticket.

ELECTION, TUESDAY, NOV. 4, 1856.
Polls open from 8, A. M. to 4, P. M.

PRESIDENTIAL ELECTORS.

AT LARGE.
Julius Rockwell of Pittsfield,
Thomas Colt of Pittsfield.

BY DISTRICTS.
1. John Vinson of Edgartown.
2. Azariah B. Wheeler of N. Bridgewater.
3. George R. Russell of West Roxbury.
4. George Odiorne of Boston.
5. Lucius B. Marsh of Boston.
6. George H. Devereux of Salem.
7. James M. Usher of Medford.
8. John Nesmith of Lowell.
9. John S. C. Knowlton of Worcester.
10. Charles E. Forbes of Northampton.
11. Franklin Ripley of Greenfield.

Rhode Island and Massachusetts, 1856. The Fremont ticket is designated by four different names: the Rhode Island tickets are titled "Republican Ticket" and "American Republican Ticket"; the Massachusetts ballots are titled "People's Ticket" and "Fremont Electoral Ticket/Whig State Ticket." The Whig Party had ceased to exist by this time; their last presidential candidate ran in 1852.

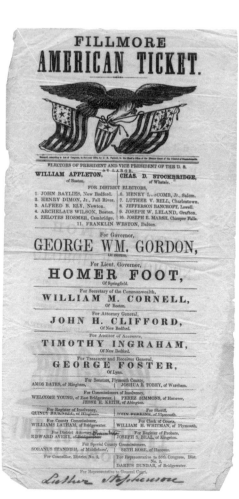

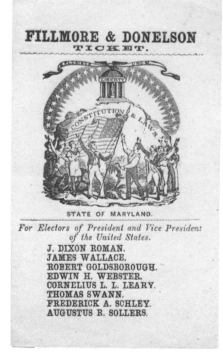

Maryland, 1856.

Massachusetts, 1856. The word "American" in the party designation was intended to appeal to both national pride and to prejudice against immigrants.

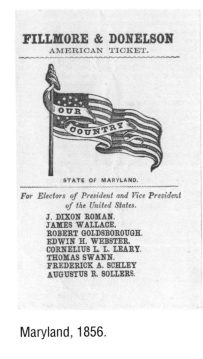

Maryland, 1856.

New Hampshire, 1856. Fillmore started out as a Whig, but aligned himself with the American or Know Nothing Party. The party designation was relatively unimportant: the main thing was the slate of Presidential Electors.

Ohio, 1856.

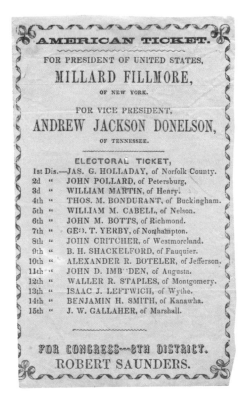

Virginia, 1856.

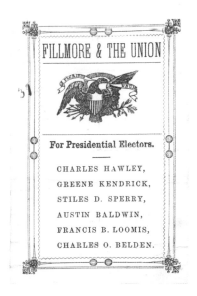

Connecticut, 1856.

Four

A Republican Army
Takes the Field

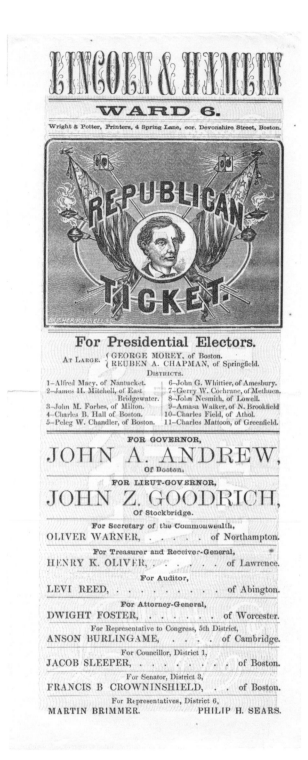

Massachusetts, 1860. Perhaps the most desirable of Lincoln presidential ballots. The folksy portrait surrounded by flags, lanterns and torches is quite evocative. There is a faint red overprint reading "National Republican Ticket".

"Down Fifth Avenue sways and surges this tide of earnest enthusiasm... [a] red canopy of smoke... traveling above... There some exuberant company again breaks into a circling war-dance, eighty or one hundred torches whirling around."

—*The New York Illustrated News*, October 3, 1860, reporting on a Wide Awake parade.

It remains a truism in politics: organization at the grassroots level is essential for victory at the polls. Getting out the vote and "energizing your base" was no less important in 1860 than it is today.

No records show what the campaign of 1860 cost. Candidate Lincoln did not attend fundraisers or solicit money from friends and prospective officeholders. Campaign buttons, medals and ribbons were made by specialty manufacturers and wholesaled to agents for resale. Local committees stood the cost of hiring speakers, printing posters and furnishing fireworks. Political clubs, the lifeblood of the campaign, had to buy or make their own uniforms, hire musicians and pay their own way to events. Urban centers such as New York and Washington had "executive committees" which centralized the printing and distribution of nearly all campaign literature.

One group contributing to Lincoln's success was the "Wide Awakes," formed two months before his nomination. Their avowed purpose was to promote the election and ensure the personal safety of Republican candidates. Members wore uniforms that consisted of a waterproof cape or "slicker" and a glazed kepi-style cap. Organized along military lines, they had manuals detailing drills and marching rules and

Election of 1860

Republican

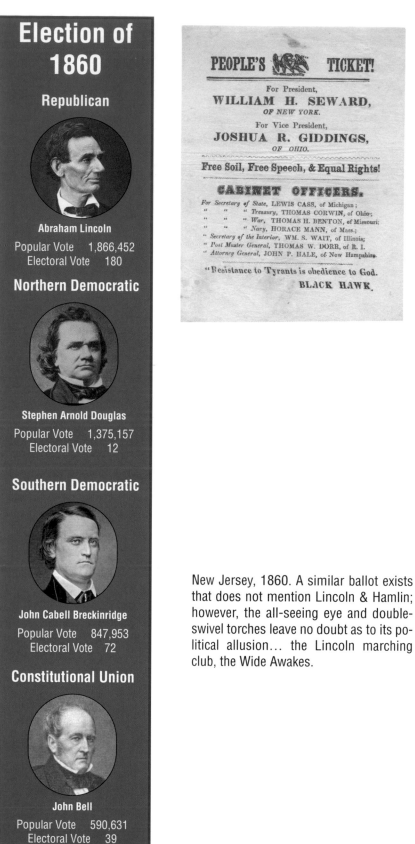

Abraham Lincoln

Popular Vote 1,866,452
Electoral Vote 180

Northern Democratic

Stephen Arnold Douglas

Popular Vote 1,375,157
Electoral Vote 12

Southern Democratic

John Cabell Breckinridge

Popular Vote 847,953
Electoral Vote 72

Constitutional Union

John Bell

Popular Vote 590,631
Electoral Vote 39

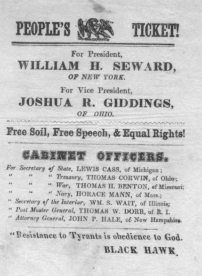

PEOPLE'S TICKET!

For President,
WILLIAM H. SEWARD,
OF NEW YORK.

For Vice President,
JOSHUA R. GIDDINGS,
OF OHIO.

Free Soil, Free Speech, & Equal Rights!

CABINET OFFICERS.

For Secretary of State, LEWIS CASS, of Michigan;
" " Treasury, THOMAS CORWIN, of Ohio;
" " War, THOMAS H. BENTON, of Missouri;
" " Navy, HORACE MANN, of Mass.;
" Secretary of the Interior, WM. S. WAIT, of Illinois;
" Post Master General, THOMAS W. DORR, of R. I.
" Attorney General, JOHN P. HALE, of New Hampshire.

"Resistance to Tyrants is obedience to God.
BLACK HAWK.

This pseudo-ballot was most likely distributed as a handbill at the Republican National Convention held in Chicago in 1860. William Seward was the front-runner. Here his supposed backers make a preemptive "close" and list his Vice President and Cabinet members. Although none of the parties named on the "ballot" achieved the offices indicated, Seward became Secretary of State in Lincoln's Cabinet. We do not think Black Hawk ever uttered Thomas Jefferson's quote. He did innocently provoke a war, named after him, in which Abraham Lincoln briefly served. He seems an unlikely role model for a political party.

New Jersey, 1860. A similar ballot exists that does not mention Lincoln & Hamlin; however, the all-seeing eye and double-swivel torches leave no doubt as to its political allusion… the Lincoln marching club, the Wide Awakes.

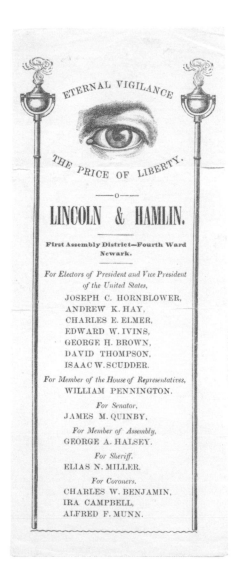

ETERNAL VIGILANCE
THE PRICE OF LIBERTY.

LINCOLN & HAMLIN.

First Assembly District—Fourth Ward
Newark.

For Electors of President and Vice President
of the United States,
JOSEPH C. HORNBLOWER,
ANDREW K. HAY,
CHARLES E. ELMER,
EDWARD W. IVINS,
GEORGE H. BROWN,
DAVID THOMPSON,
ISAAC W. SCUDDER.

For Member of the House of Representatives,
WILLIAM PENNINGTON.

For Senator,
JAMES M. QUINBY.

For Member of Assembly,
GEORGE A. HALSEY.

For Sheriff,
ELIAS N. MILLER.

For Coroners,
CHARLES W. BENJAMIN,
IRA CAMPBELL,
ALFRED F. MUNN.

REPUBLICAN TICKET.

For President,
ABRAHAM LINCOLN, *elected*
OF ILLINOIS.

For Vice President,
HANNIBAL HAMLIN, *elected*
OF MAINE.

For Presidential Electors at large,
FITZ HENRY WARREN, of the 1st Cong. Dis. *elected*
JOSEPH A. CHAPLINE, of the 2d Cong. Dis. *elected*

For District Electors,
M. L. McPHERSON, for the 1st Cong. Dis. *elected*
CHARLES POMEROY, for the 2d Cong. Dis. *elected*

For Member of Congress of the 1st Cong. Dis. *elected*
SAMUEL R. CURTIS. *elected*

For Judge of the Supreme Court,
GEORGE G. WRIGHT. *elected*

For Secretary of State,
ELIJAH SELLS. *elected*

For Auditor of State,
JONATHAN W. CATTELL, *elected*

For Treasurer of State,
JOHN W. JONES. *elected*

For Register of the State Land Office,
AMOS B. MILLER. *elected*

For Attorney General,
CHARLES C. NOURSE. *elected*

For Clerk of the District Court,
JAMES REYNOLDS. *beat*

County Supt. of Common Schools,
RUFUS HUBBARD. *elected*

For (County) Supervisors,
A. BRIDGMAN. *elected*
J. A. VIALL. *elected*

For Justices of the Peace,
THOMAS MARTIN. *elected*
O. LYMAN, *elected*
JAS. GRAHAM. *elected*

For Constables,
JOHN HENDRICKSON, *elected*
GEORGE R. NUNN, *elected*
GEORGE T. FRY. *elected*

For Township Trustees,
JAMES T. BLAIR, *elected*
GEORGE SCHAEFFER, *elected*
HAMILTON M. BLACK. *elected*

For Township Clerk,
HENRY C. LANDES. *elected*

For Assessor,
CHARLES HUBBELL. *elected*

For Road Supervisors, —— District,

Iowa, 1860. Lincoln the Rail Splitter appears as Uncle Sam, a.k.a. Brother Jonathan, dressed in striped pants. The ballot's owner has added the election results in the margin. Iowa was a good state for the Republicans that year.

carried torches in their parades, while the "captain" of each chapter carried a red glass lantern. Their quasi-military appeal brought in many recruits: chapters popped up in almost every small town and city ward, and even found expression in ethnic divisions such as the Lafayette (French) and Garibaldi (Italian) clubs. Once Lincoln was nominated the Wide Awakes campaigned tirelessly. Opponents tried to emulate them, but the "Breckinridge Minute Men," "Douglas Invincibles" and "Bell Ringers" paled by comparison. In 1860 the *New York Herald* estimated the total number of drilled and uniformed Wide Awakes at more than 400,000 nationwide.

Although Stephen Arnold Douglas is remembered as the continual rival of Abraham Lincoln, he nevertheless ardently supported the Union over secession and spoke in support of the new administration until his untimely death in June 1861. Even so, he shared responsibility for the war he deplored, not least because of his Kansas-Nebraska Act and its principle of "Popular Sovereignty," which allowed settlers to decide whether their territory would enter the Union as a free or slave state. This sounded simple and democratic, but in the absence of Federal restraints pro- and anti-slavery groups sought to outnumber and intimidate each other in the territories. The resulting violence foreshadowed the Civil War and made John Brown notorious – several years before his attempted slave uprising at Harper's Ferry – when he massacred a number of slavery proponents in Kansas. Regardless, Douglas clung to his "great principle" of popular sovereignty in the 1860 presidential campaign, while the Democratic Party itself split over a slavery plank in its platform. Northern Democrats nominated Douglas, Southern Democrats

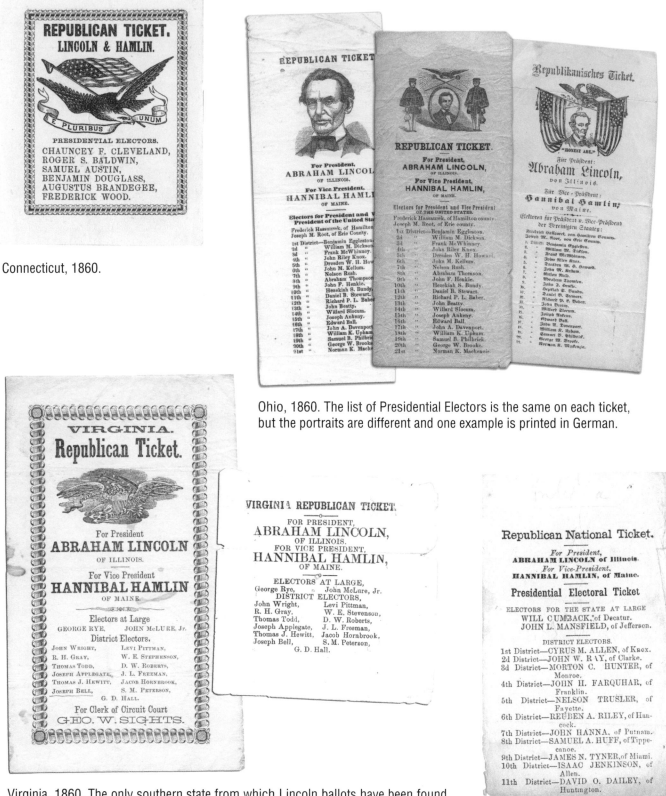

Connecticut, 1860.

Ohio, 1860. The list of Presidential Electors is the same on each ticket, but the portraits are different and one example is printed in German.

Virginia, 1860. The only southern state from which Lincoln ballots have been found is Virginia. Contrary to common belief that Lincoln received *no* southern votes, he in fact received 1,187 from Virginia. These most likely were cast in the western portion which was set off and admitted as the state of West Virginia in 1863.

Indiana, 1860.

nominated John Breckinridge; this split, with other votes going to John Bell of the Constitutional Union Party, resulted in the election of Abraham Lincoln by a plurality with less than 40% of the total vote. Southern states reacted to this "loathsome" result by seceding… and thus virtually ensured a civil war. ❦

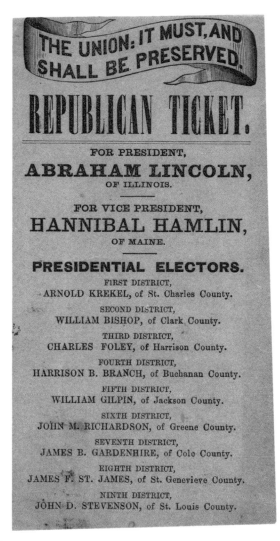

Missouri, 1860. Missouri was home to the wartime scourges Quantrill's Raiders and Jesse James.

New Hampshire, 1860.

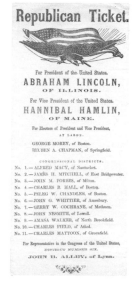

Massachusetts, 1860.

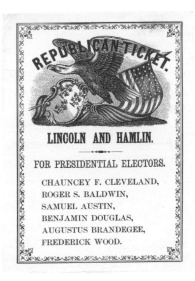

Connecticut, 1860.

Ohio, 1860.

Ohio, 1860.

The Election of President in Olden and Modern Times. Appearance of the Polls in New York City in Modern Times.

View of a New York City polling place as shown in the *New-York Illustrated News* of November 17, 1860. While he carried New York State, Lincoln came in second in New York City which gave a majority to a fusion ticket composed of Douglas, Bell and Breckinridge electors.

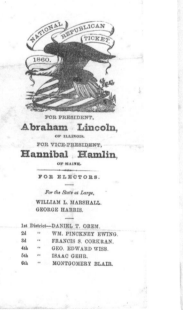

New York, 1860. Author, poet and newspaper publisher William Cullen Bryant appears as an Elector.

Maryland, 1860. Montgomery Blair would serve in Lincoln's Cabinet as Postmaster General.

Ohio, 1860. The woodcut highlights Lincoln's main campaign policy – restricting slavery to the states where it already existed.

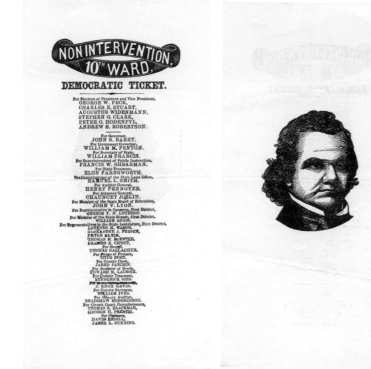

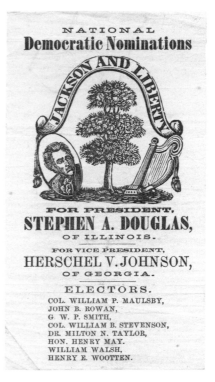

Michigan, 1860. Douglas favored a policy of non-intervention with the South and toleration of slavery.

Maryland, 1860.

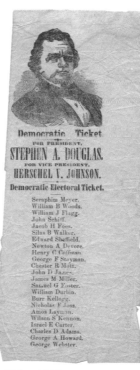

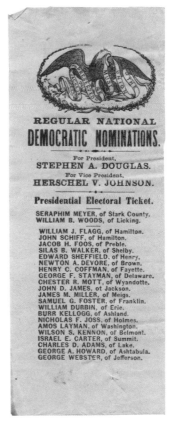

Illinois, 1860. John McClernand and Shelby Cullom were Lincoln associates. McClernand was a victorious Van Buren elector in 1840, while that same year Lincoln lost his bid to be a Harrison elector.

Ohio, 1860.

Ohio, 1860.

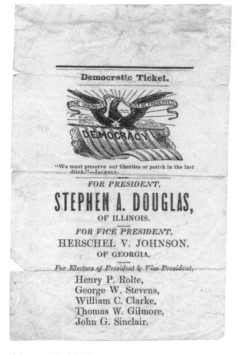

Vermont, 1860.

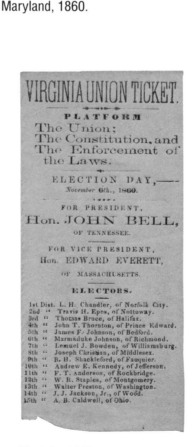

Maryland, 1860.

California, 1860.

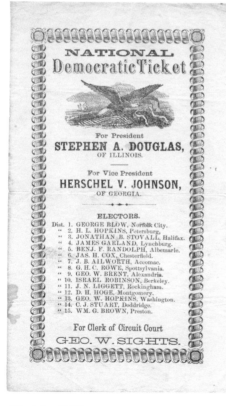

Virginia, 1860.

Virginia, 1860.

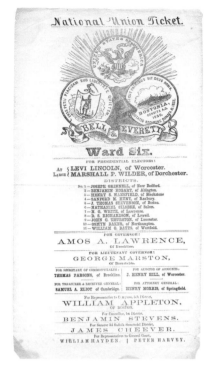

Massachusetts, 1860.

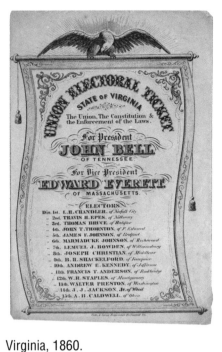

Virginia, 1860.

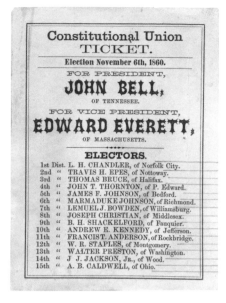

Virginia, 1860.

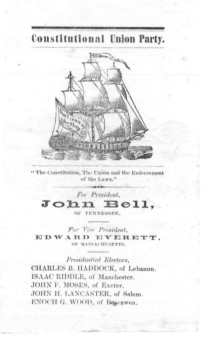

New Hampshire, 1860.

Virginia, 1860.

Regular Democratic Ticket.

FOR PRESIDENT,
JOHN C. BRECKINRIDGE

FOR VICE PRESIDENT.
JOSEPH LANE.

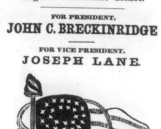

For Presidential Electors.

HENRY R. CAMPBELL,
EPHRAIM CHAMBERLAIN,
MARTIN ROBERTS,
EBEN M. STOCKER,
GEORGE W. AIKEN.

Vermont, 1860. The slogan "Equality of States" reflected the Southern view that northern and midwestern states imposed laws that failed to reflect Southern interests.

DEMOCRATIC TICKET.

FOR PRESIDENT
J. C. BRECKINRIDGE,
OF KENTUCKY.
FOR VICE PRESIDENT,
JOSEPH LANE,
OF OREGON.

ELECTORS.

1st Dist.—WM. LAMB, of Norfolk.
2d Dist.—THOMAS F. GOODE, of Mecklenburg.
3d Dist.—JOHN R. EDMUNDS, of Halifax.
4th Dist.—T. T. TREDWAY, of Prince Edward.
5th Dist.—JAMES L. KEMPER, of Madison.
6th Dist.—JAMES LYONS, of Henrico.
7th Dist.—R. A. CLAYBROOK, of Northumberland
8th Dist.—B. B. DOUGLAS, of King William.
9th Dist.—EPPA HUNTON, of Prince William.
10th Dist.—THOMAS M. ISBELL, of Jefferson.
11th Dist.—JAMES W. MASSIE, of Rockbridge.
12th Dist.—WM. H. ANTHONY, of Botetourt.
13th Dist.—ISAAC B. DUNN, of Washington.
14th Dist.—JOHN G. NEWMAN, of Kanawha.
15th Dist.—ZEDEKIAH KIDWELL, of Marion.

Virginia, 1860.

DEMOCRATIC TICKET

OUR PRINCIPLES
The Constitution
The Sovereignty & Equality of the States, The Repeal of the Missouri Restriction. The People of the Territories in forming State Governments to adopt their own Institutions. Equal protection to Citizens Native & Naturalised & to every species of Property

FOR PRESIDENT
JOHN C. BRECKINRIDGE
of Kentucky.
FOR VICE PRESIDENT
JOSEPH LANE
of Oregon

ELECTORS

1st District	William Lamb, of Norfolk City
2d do	Thomas F. Goode, of Mecklenburg
3d do	John R. Edmunds, of Halifax
4th do	Thomas T. Tredway, of Prince Edward
5th do	James L. Kemper, of Madison
6th do	James Lyons, of Henrico
7th do	Rich'd A. Claybrook, of Northumberland
8th do	Beverley B. Douglas, of King William
9th do	Eppa Hunton, of Prince William
10th do	Thomas M. Isbell, of Jefferson
11th do	James W. Massie, of Rockbridge
12th do	Wm. H. Anthony, of Botetourt
13th do	Isaac B. Dunn, of Washington
14th do	John G. Newman, of Kanawha
15th do	Zedekiah Kidwell, of Marion

Write your name on the back of this Ticket
Election on Tuesday November 6th 1860
Luther Hoyer & Ludwig Richmond Va

Virginia, 1860.

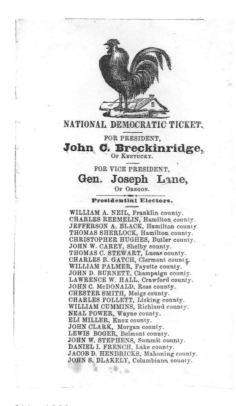

NATIONAL DEMOCRATIC TICKET.

FOR PRESIDENT,

John C. Breckinridge,
OF KENTUCKY.

FOR VICE PRESIDENT,

Gen. Joseph Lane,
OF OREGON.

Presidential Electors.

WILLIAM A. NEIL, Franklin county.
CHARLES REEMELIN, Hamilton county.
JEFFERSON A. BLACK, Hamilton county.
THOMAS SHERLOCK, Hamilton county.
CHRISTOPHER HUGHES, Butler county.
JOHN W. CAREY, Shelby county.
THOMAS C. STEWART, Lucas county.
CHARLES B. GATCH, Clermont county.
WILLIAM PALMER, Fayette county.
JOHN D. BURNETT, Champaign county.
LAWRENCE W. HALL, Crawford county.
JOHN C. McDONALD, Ross county.
CHESTER SMITH, Meigs county.
CHARLES FOLLETT, Licking county.
WILLIAM CUMMINS, Richland county.
NEAL POWER, Wayne county.
ELI MILLER, Knox county.
JOHN CLARK, Morgan county.
LEWIS BOGER, Belmont county.
JOHN W. STEPHENS, Summit county.
DANIEL I. FRENCH, Lake county.
JACOB D. HENDRICKS, Mahoning county.
JOHN S. BLAKELY, Columbiana county.

Ohio, 1860.

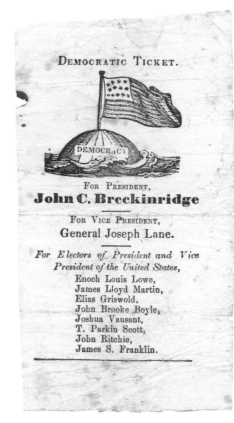

DEMOCRATIC TICKET.

FOR PRESIDENT,

John C. Breckinridge

FOR VICE PRESIDENT,

General Joseph Lane.

*For Electors of President and Vice
President of the United States,*

Enoch Louis Lowe,
James Lloyd Martin,
Elias Griswold,
John Brooke Boyle,
Joshua Vansant,
T. Parkin Scott,
John Ritchie,
James S. Franklin.

Maryland, 1860.

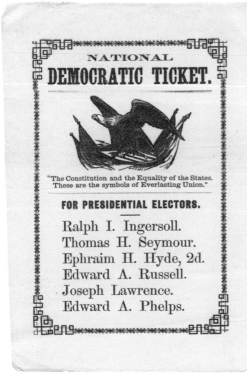

NATIONAL DEMOCRATIC TICKET.

"The Constitution and the Equality of the States.
These are the symbols of Everlasting Union."

FOR PRESIDENTIAL ELECTORS.

Ralph I. Ingersoll.
Thomas H. Seymour.
Ephraim H. Hyde, 2d.
Edward A. Russell.
Joseph Lawrence.
Edward A. Phelps.

Connecticut, 1860.

" The Constitution and the Equality of the States—these
are the symbols of everlasting Union ; let these be the rallying
cries of the people."—JOHN C. BRECKINRIDGE.

DEMOCRATIC TICKET.

For President,

HON. JOHN C. BRECKINRIDGE,
OF KENTUCKY.

For Vice President.

GEN. JOSEPH LANE,
OF OREGON.

Democratic Electors.

WILLIAM A. NEIL, Franklin County.
CHAS. REEMELIN, Hamilton County.

Congressional Electors.

1st District,	JEFF. A. BLACK, Hamilton,
2d	"	THOS. SHERLOCK, "
3d	"	CHRISTOPHER HUGHES, Butler,
4th	"	JOHN W. CAREY, Shelby,
5th	"	THOMAS C. STEWART, Lucas.
6th	"	JOHN G. ARMSTRONG, Clermont,
7th	"	WM. PALMER, Fayette,
8th	"	JOHN D. BURNETT, Champaign,
9th	"	LAWRENCE W. HALL, Crawford,
10th	"	JOHN C. McDONALD, Ross,
11th	"	C. E. SMITH, Meigs,
12th	"	CHARLES FOLLETT, Licking,
13th	"	WILLIAM CUMMINS, Richland,
14th	"	NEAL POWER, Wayne,
15th	"	ELI MILLER, Knox,
16th	"	JOHN CLARK, Morgan,
17th	"	LEWIS BOGER, Belmont,
18th	"	JOHN W. STEPHENS, Summit,
19th	"	DANIEL I. FRENCH, Lake,
20th	"	JACOB D. HENDRICKS, Mahoning,
21st	"	JOHN S. BLAKELY, Columbiana.

Ohio, 1860.

Five

The Confederate Election

Southern Rights Co-operation Ticket.

T. J. RUSSELL,
M. J. BULGER,
A. KIMBAL.

Election 24th December 1860.

Resolved, That we do not consider the election of any man to the Presidency, under the forms laid down and prescribed by the Constitution, a sufficient cause, within itself, to justify a dissolution of the Union.

Resolved, That we consider and believe, the right of the people to secede from the General Government to be an inherent and unalienable right, for grievances which they in their wisdom may determine are too insufferable to be borne ; but that such right, upon a question so momentous, should only be exercised when the burdens to be borne are more intolerable than the probable evils of separation.

Resolved, That the Constitution of the United States confers no power upon the President to coerce a seceding State into subjection.

Resolved, That we consider separate State action in the present emergency, as unwise and impolitic, and that Ala. should not withdraw without "an effort to secure" the co-operation of the entire South.

Resolved, That in order to secure the co-operation of the South as a unit, and justify ourselves in the eyes of a civilized world, we consider it wise and politic that a general Convention of all the Southern States should be called to adopt and present an *ultimatum* to the Northern Republicans, and that unless such *ultimatum* so presented be adopted, that then our own safety and the preservation of our rights demand that those rights should be maintained, even if it result in the secession of the State of Alabama and the rupture of the Union.

Resolved, That the sovereignty of Alabama remains with the people thereof, and that the result of the Convention called by the Governor, let it be what it may, should be referred back to the people for their rejection or ratification.

Alabama, 1860. This ballot calls for the election of three delegates to a statewide "Southern Rights Co-operation" convention, tasked to formulate an ultimatum to Northern Republicans and – barring its acceptance – put the question of secession before the voters. They were also trying to coordinate efforts with other Southern states and present a united front. Alabama seceded from the Union in the early months of 1861.

> "A vote is like a rifle: its usefulness depends upon the character of the user."
>
> *—Theodore Roosevelt*

> "Politics is the art of looking for trouble, finding it everywhere, diagnosing it incorrectly, and applying the wrong remedies."
>
> *—Groucho Marx*

Upon establishing the Confederate States of America, the C.S.A. Congress appointed a provisional President, Jefferson Davis, and Vice President, Alexander Stephens. The two assumed office and were sworn in at the provisional capital, Montgomery, Alabama. Southerners who refused to acquiesce to Lincoln's election and felt the need for an election of their own to validate the selection of Davis and Stephens voted in a general election on November 6, 1861 in which the two ran unopposed. Duly elected, they were inaugurated at the new official capital of Richmond, Virginia. The Confederates used the U. S. Constitution as a template for their own government, carrying over nearly all of its provisions, although it did limit the presidential term of office to a single six-year term.

For those interested in this period of our history, a variety of ballots and election ephemera remains extant. After the secession of South Carolina on December 20, 1860, several Southern states held elections for delegates to conventions convened for the purpose of deciding their future. In many cases these conventions chose a course of "watchful waiting," remaining in the Union for the time being. As the situation deteriorated and reconciliation efforts failed, state conventions were held to adopt ordinances of

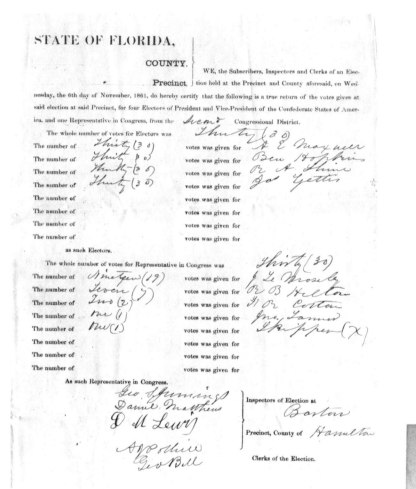

Polling place document from the Confederate election held November 6, 1861. This was issued for the Second Congressional District of Florida and lists the number of votes received by both Congressional candidates and "four Electors of President and Vice-President of the Confederate States of America."

Southern Rights Ticket.

FOR PRESIDENT.

JEFFERSON DAVIS,

FOR VICE-PRESIDENT,

ALEXANDER H. STEPHENS.

PRESIDENTIAL ELECTORS.

FOR STATE AT LARGE,
Charles Derbigny, of Orleans,
Albert G. Carter, of East Feliciana.

First District,
DONATIEN AUGUSTIN, Orleans,

Second District,
JAMES P. FRERET, Orleans.

Third District,
EDWARD DUFFEL, Ascension.

Fourth District,
WM. R. BARROW, West Feliciana.

Fifth District,
BART. EGAN, Sr. Bienville.

Sixth District,
S. L. CHAMBLISS, Carroll.

For Congress—2d District,
WILLIAM R. ADAMS.

Louisiana, 1861.

For President,
JEFFERSON DAVIS.
For Vice President,
ALEXANDER H. STEPHEHS.

Presidential Electors,
WM. B. ROSS, of East Florida.
JAMES GETTIS, of South Florida.
R. A. SHINE, of Middle Florida.
A. E. MAXWELL, of West Florida.

Florida, 1861. Florida saw little military action during the Civil War. The Union abandoned Fort Pickens prior to the start of the war but maintained a military prison in the Dry Tortugas of the Keys (where the surviving Lincoln assassination conspirators served their sentences). For electoral purposes in 1861, the state was divided into four districts.

North Carolina, 1861.

secession and authorize public elections to decide the question. Ballots are known from Tennessee and Virginia specifically related to this issue. However, in both cases, the Civil War had begun and the elections merely made official what had already transpired. Robert E. Lee waited until Virginia's election results were known (May 23, 1861) before resigning his U.S. Army commission and accepting command of Confederate forces. Tennesseeans voted for secession in June of 1861 but the capital, Nashville, remained in Unionist control, thwarting its implementation. In Maryland a vote on secession would have surely passed, but it never took place due to the occupation of Annapolis by General Butler and the arrest of numerous state legislators.

Virginia, 1861.

Virginia, 1861.

REGULATIONS
For the Election of Members of Congress and of Electors of President and Vice President of the Confederate States.

CONGRESSIONAL DISTRICTS.

[Broadside text of the Regulations for the Election of Members of Congress and of Electors of President and Vice President of the Confederate States, arranged in columns. Sections include: Congressional Districts; Electors of President and Vice President; Votes at Encampments for Presidential Electors; Votes at Encampments for Members of Congress; Laws of United States Substituted by Laws of Confederate States.]

EXTRACTS FROM ELECTION LAWS.

[Column text including: Qualification of Voters; How Votes Shall Be Received and Recorded, and Poll Books Authenticated and Delivered; How Long Poll Is To Be Open; Examination of Polls; Places of Voting; Appointment of Commissioners, Sub-Commissioners, &c.; Oaths of Officers, Who to Administer Them; Returns of Elections of Electors of President and Vice President for Counties and Corporations; Disposition of County and Corporation Tickets and Polls. Expense Defrayed.]

Virginia broadside detailing regulations for Congressional and Presidential elections to be held in the Confederate States of America. It also makes provision for voting by soldiers in the field.

FOR PRESIDENT,
JEFFERSON DAVIS, *Of Mississippi.*
FOR VICE PRESIDENT,
A. H. STEPHENS, *Of Georgia.*

Dist.		
1st Dist.	JOSEPH CHRISTIAN, of Middlesex.
2d "	CINCINNATUS NEWTON, of Norfolk city.
3d "	R. T. DANIEL, of Richmond city.
4th "	WM. F. THOMPSON, of Dinwiddie.
5th "	WOOD BOULDIN, of Charlotte.
6th "	WM. L. GOGGIN, of Bedford.
7th "	B. F. RANDOLPH, of Albemarle.
8th "	JAMES W. WALKER, of Madison.
9th "	ASA ROGERS, of Loudon.
10th "	SAM'L. C. WILLIAMS, of Shenandoah.
11th "	SAM'L. McD. REID, of Rockbridge.
12th "	H. A. EDMUNDSON, of Roanoke.
13th "	JAMES W. SHEFFEY, of Smythe.
14th "	HENRY J. FISHER, of Mason.
15th "	JOSEPH JOHNSON, of Harrison.
16th "	E. H. FITZHUGH, of Ohio.

FOR THE STATE AT LARGE.
JOHN R. EDMUNDS, of Halifax.
ALLEN T. CAPERTON, of Monroe.

FOR CONGRESS, *Jno. B. Baldwin*

Election, Wednesday, November 6th, 1861.
FOR PRESIDENT,
JEFFERSON DAVIS, OF MISSISSIPPI.
FOR VICE-PRESIDENT,
ALEXANDER H. STEPHENS, OF GEORGIA.

Electoral Ticket.
FOR THE STATE AT LARGE,
JOHN R. EDMUNDS, Halifax.
ALLEN T. CAPERTON, Monroe.

FOR THE DISTRICTS.

1st District	JOS. CHRISTIAN, Middlesex.
2d	CIN. W. NEWTON, Norfolk City.
3d	R. T. DANIEL, Richmond City.
4th	WM. F. THOMPSON, Dinwiddie.
5th	WOOD BOULDIN, Charlotte.
6th	WM. L. GOGGIN, Bedford.
7th	BEN. F. RANDOLPH, Albemarle.
8th	JAMES W. WALKER, Madison.
9th	ASA ROGERS, Loudoun.
10th	S. C. WILLIAMS, Shenandoah.
11th	SAMUEL McD. REID, Rockbridge.
12th	H. A. EDMUNDSON, Roanoke.
13th	JAMES W. SHEFFEY, Smyth.
14th	HENRY J. FISHER, Mason.
15th	JOS. JOHNSON, Harrison.
16th	E. H. FITZHUGH, Ohio.

FOR CONGRESS,
ROGER A. PRYOR.

Virginia, 1861.

The Confederate presidential election took place as planned on November 6, 1861. Ballots were issued in all rebel states, with those from Virginia among the most numerous. Confederate soldiers were afforded the opportunity to vote in the field in both the presidential election and the Congressional elections of their original state of residence. Ironically, Jefferson Davis, like Abraham Lincoln (but for a vastly different reason), never served out his full term of office. ❦

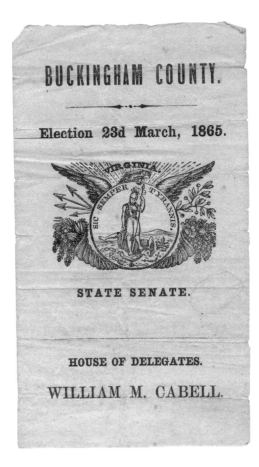

Virginia, 1865. A local ballot for an election held two weeks before the fall of Richmond. Despite war, privations and impending doom... politics as usual!

FOR PRESIDENT,
Jefferson Davis.
FOR VICE PRESIDENT,
Alex. H. Stephens.
Electors for the State at Large,
R. C. Foster, 3d, of Davidson.
William Wallace, of Blount.
For the Districts.
1. F. M. Fulkerson, of Hawkins.
2. W. G. McAdoo, of Knox.
3. W. L. Eakin, of Monroe.
4. S. D. Rowan, of Warren.
5. John F. Doak, of Wilson.
6. Geo. W. Buchanan, of Bedford.
7. Lucius J. Polk, of Maury.
8. G. A. Washington, of Robertson.
9. B. F. Lamb, of Henry.
10. Robt. B. Hurt, of Madison.
11. Joseph R. Mosby, of Fayette.

Tennessee, 1861.

SOUTHERN RIGHTS' TICKET.
FOR PRESIDENT,
JEFFERSON DAVIS.
FOR VICE PRESIDENT.
ALEX. H. STEPHENS.
Electoral Ticket.
FOR THE STATE AT LARGE.
ROBT. C. FOSTER, 3rd, of Davidson.
WILLIAM WALLACE, of Blount.
FOR THE DISTRICTS.
1st District, F. M. FULKERSON, *of Hawkins*
2nd " WM. G. McADOO, *of Knox.*
3rd " W. L. AIKEN, *of Monroe.*
4th " S. D. ROWAN, *of Warren.*
5th " JOHN F. DOAK, *of Wilson.*
6th " G. W. BUCHANAN, *of Bedford.*
7th " LUCIUS J. POLK, *of Maury.*
8th " G. A. WASHINGTON, *of Robertson.*
9th " B. F. LAMB, *of Henry.*
10th " ROBERT B. HURT, *of Madison.*
11th " JOSEPH R. MOSBY, *of Fayette.*
FOR CONGRESS.
WILLIAM G. SWAN. 2.5
1861 John Baxter — 00

Tennessee, 1861.

Army Congressional Ticket.
Nominated by the State Convention at Winchester.
1st District, J B HEISKELL, of Hawkins.
2nd District, WM. G. SWAN, of Knox.
3rd District, A. S. COLYAR of Franklin.
4th District, JOHN P. MURRAY, of Jackson.
5th District, H. S. FOOTE, of Davidson.
6th District, E. A. KEEBLE, of Rutherford.
7th District, JAMES McCULLOM, of Giles.
8th District, THOMAS MENEES, of Robertson.
9th District, J. D. C. ATKINS, of Henry.
10th District, JOHN V. WRIGHT, of McNairy.
11th District. D. M. CURRIN, of Shelby.

Tennessee, 1863. This war-time ballot was used by displaced Tennessee residents to vote for Congressional candidates endorsed by the State Convention held at Winchester. The state capital at Nashville had been occupied by Union forces, with Andrew Johnson serving as Military Governor.

Six

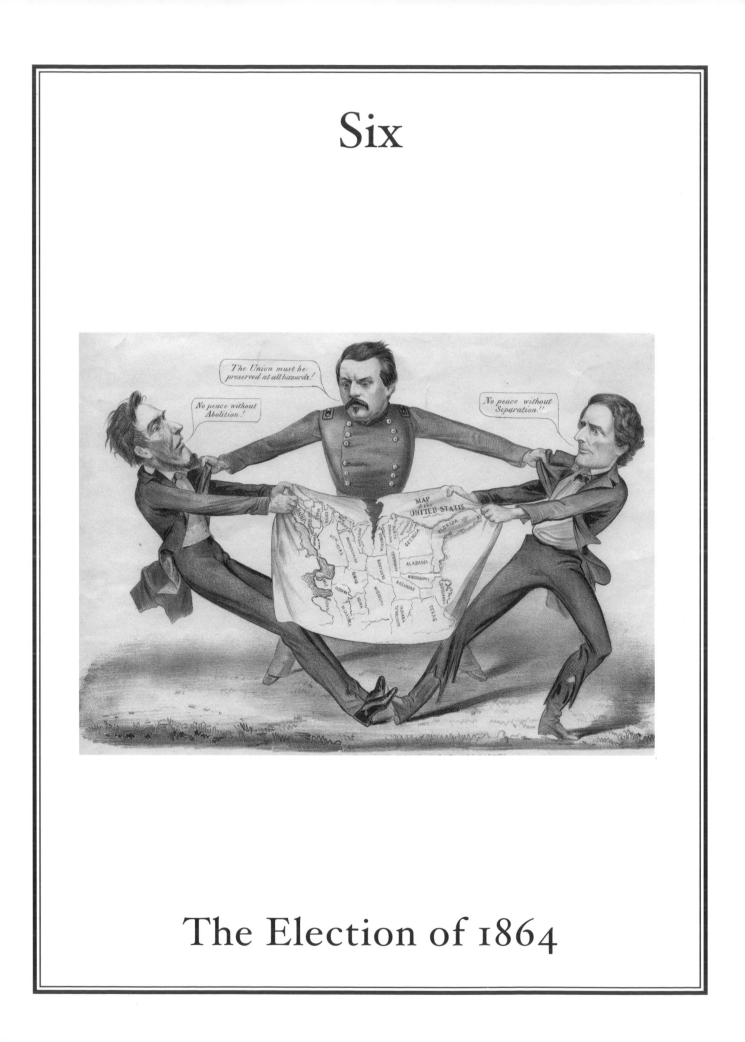

The Election of 1864

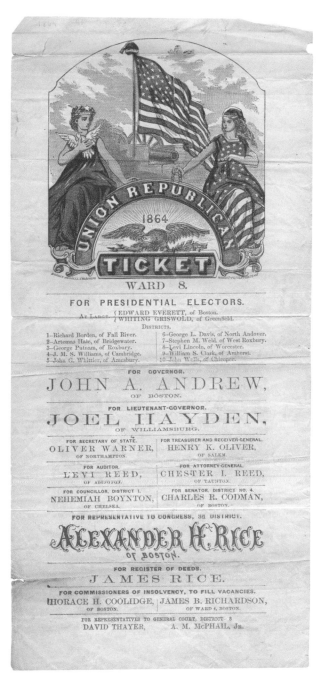

Massachusetts, 1864. Beloved New England poet John Greenleaf Whittier and Edward Everett, who spoke with Lincoln at Gettysburg, are listed as electors.

> "The election, along with its incidental and undesirable strife, has done good too. It has demonstrated that a people's government can sustain a national election in the midst of a great civil war."
>
> —*Abraham Lincoln*

> "It is not best to swap horses while crossing the river ... I'm not so poor a horse that they might not make a botch of it in trying to swap."
>
> —*Abraham Lincoln*

As the election of 1864 approached, Lincoln doubted that he would win a second term. Despite the crucial victories at Gettysburg and Vicksburg the previous year, Northerners were war-weary. It was feared that the conflict would continue indefinitely, or that the Confederacy would yet win European recognition and force a settlement. Some leading Republicans quietly sought to replace Lincoln with another candidate, such as Treasury Secretary Salmon P. Chase, or one of several popular generals, such as Benjamin Butler or Ulysses S. Grant. Grant, to his credit, disavowed any interest in running while the war continued. With opposition failing to coalesce, Lincoln was re-nominated in early June.

The Democrats, convening in late August in Chicago – where Lincoln had first been nominated in 1860 – chose the former commander of the Army of the Potomac, General George Mc-Clellan, as their standard bearer. The platform – influenced by Copperhead Congressman Clement Vallandigham from Ohio – criticized the suspension of the writ of habeas corpus and arbitrary arrest of civilians, called the war a failure and

Election of 1864

Republican, National Union

Abraham Lincoln

Popular Vote 2,213,635
Electoral Vote 212

Democratic

George McClellan

Popular Vote 1,805,237
Electoral Vote 21

Massachusetts, 1864.

Massachusetts, 1864.

California, 1864.

New Jersey, 1864.

California, 1864. Lincoln and Jackson, two defenders of the Union, appear on the reverse. Beardless portraits of Lincoln were used throughout his Presidency, even into the period of mourning following his assassination.

Connecticut, 1864. The stars in the flag's canton spell out "Free", referring to the Emancipation Proclamation and the impending end of all slavery.

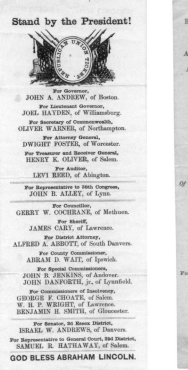

advocated a cessation of hostilities and a peace conference with the Confederacy. Although he was still quite popular among the military, McClellan lost respect for accepting the nomination of a party whose platform was seen as defeatist, which advocated "The Constitution As It Was," with or without slavery.

In September, with the election only weeks away, northern spirits were greatly buoyed when the Union army captured the rebel strongholds of Atlanta and Savannah. Voters — seeing that the "end was not far distant" — handed Lincoln an overwhelming victory, freeing him to pursue the task at hand and lay plans for reconstructing the Union. ❧

Massachusetts, 1864. The statewide candidates declare "Stand by the President!" and "God Bless Abraham Lincoln."

Maryland, 1864.

Michigan, 1864. Despite Lincoln's new running-mate, this ballot still included woodcut portraits from the 1860 ticket.

California, 1864. This design was printed on paper as a ballot and on silk as a lapel badge. The reverse depicts the sinking of the Confederate raider C.S.S. *Alabama* by the armor-clad U.S.S. *Kearsarge* outside Cherbourg, France on June 19, 1864 following a two-year pursuit.

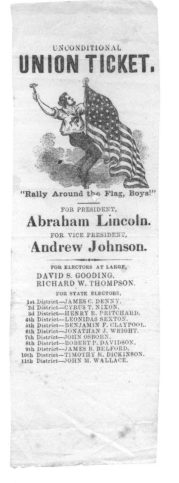

Indiana, 1864.

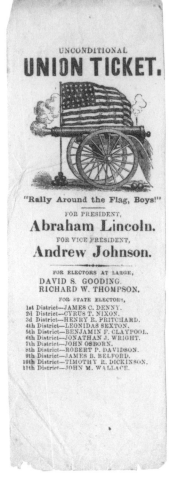

Indiana, 1864.

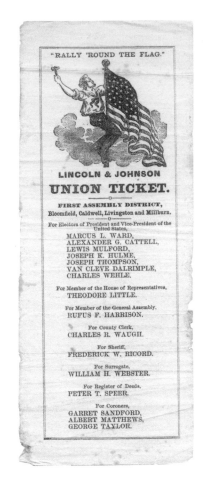

New Jersey, 1864.

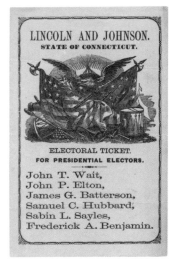

Connecticut, 1864.

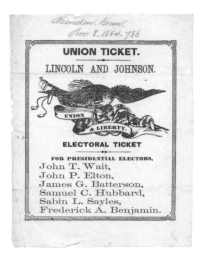

Connecticut, 1864.

New York, 1864. Lincoln's on-again, off-again (sometimes adversarial) "colleague," Horace Greeley, publisher of the *New York Tribune*, appears as an Elector.

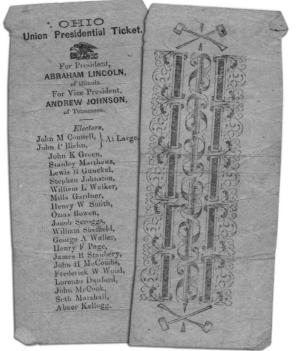

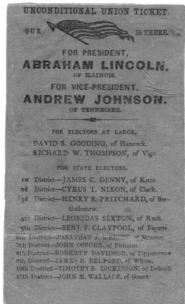

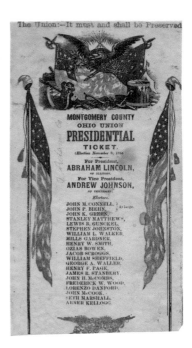

Ohio, 1864. Although Lincoln ran as the "Rail Splitter" in 1860, you can't keep a good slogan down. An ax, maul and wedge appear on the back of this ballot, just to remind voters of Lincoln's youthful credentials as a laborer and westerner.

Indiana, 1864. The word "Unconditional" possibly refers to the terms of surrender that the Union and General Ulysses S. Grant expected from vanquished rebels.

Ohio, 1864.

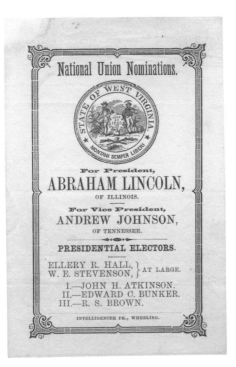

West Virginia, 1864. West Virginia had strong Union sentiments and was admitted to the Union in 1863, organized from Union-occupied and pro-Union territory on the western edge of old Virginia.

Missouri, 1864. Although Lincoln did not align himself with the Radical wing of the Republican Party, he is nevertheless listed here as the candidate of the "Radical Union Ticket" in Missouri.

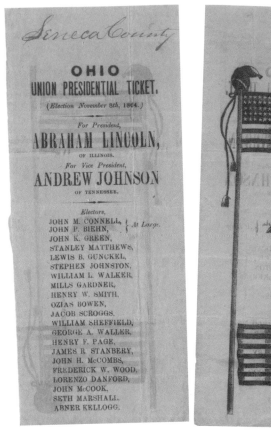

Ohio, 1864.

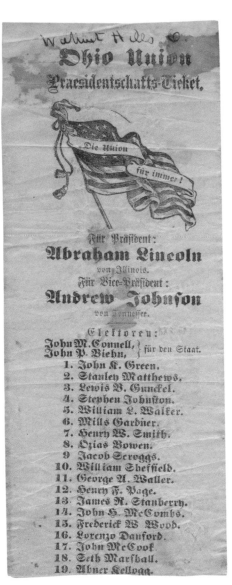

Ohio, 1864. German language ballot. "Die Union für immer!" or "The Union Forever!" *Sehr gut!*

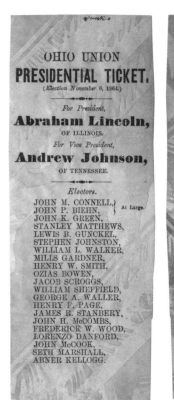

Ohio, 1864. There were paper shortages during the Civil War, primarily in the South, where items were often printed on "necessity" paper, including discarded scraps of wallpaper. Here we see a very unusual Lincoln ballot printed on necessity paper.

Ohio, 1864. One would think there would have been no shortage of printed Lincoln ballots, but here we see a hand-written one from Athens County.

Maryland, 1865. This ballot lists candidates for delegates to the Maryland State Constitutional Convention which decided that their state constitution needed revision, especially in regard to slavery. These staunch Unionists thought that the Emancipation Proclamation should not be annulled and that former slaveholders were not entitled to compensation for slaves freed as a result of the new constitution which made slavery illegal. Their position was subsequently affirmed.

Copperhead Ticket.

For President
GEO. B. McCLELLAN.

POISON.

For Vice President
GEO. H. PENDLETON.

Pennsylvania, 1864. A spoof or satiric item, this associates the Democrats with poison and the traitorous Copperhead faction of the Democratic Party. These scraps of paper are similiar in style to the popular "Salt River Tickets" which mocked unsuccessful candidates damned to travel to Hades on the River Styx – distributed primarily in the Philadelphia area, circa 1852-1880.

UNION DEMOCRATIC TICKET.

FOR PRESIDENT
Gen. GEO. B. McCLELLAN.

FOR VICE PRESIDENT
GEORGE H. PENDLETON.

For Electors at Large,
JOHN PETTIT,
SIMEON K. WOLFE,
District Electors,
SILAS M. HOLCOMB,
ELIJAH NEWLAND,
AMBROSE B. CARLTON,
BARTON W. WILSON,
JAMES BROWN,
FRANKLIN LANDERS,
ARCHIBALD JOHNSON,
JONATHAN C. APPLEGATE,
JOHN G. OSBORNE,
ROBERT LOWRY,
JAMES W. SANNSBERRY.

Indiana, 1864. The Republicans called themselves the "National Union Party" in 1864. Loyal Democrats, not to be outdone, here declare "We're for Union, too!" Hence the title "Union Democratic Ticket."

DEMOCRATIC & CONSERVATIVE TICKET.

FOR PRESIDENT,
GEO. B. McCLELLAN.
FOR VICE-PRESIDENT,
GEORGE H. PENDLETON.

FOR ELECTORS
Of the State of Maryland for President and Vice President of the United States,
WILLIAM SCHLEY,
JOHN R. FRANKLIN,
GEORGE VICKERS,
MILTON N. TAYLOR,
HENRY W. JENKINS,
THOMAS DEVECMON,
EDWARD W. BELT.

For Governor,
E. F. CHAMBERS.

For Lieutenant-Governor,
ODEN BOWIE.

For Judge of the Court of Appeals,
WM. P. MAULSBY.

For Attorney General,
BERNARD CARTER

For Comptroller,
A. LINGAN JARRETT.

For Congress,
WILLIAM KIMMEL.

For the State Senate,
WM. B. STEPHENSON.

For the House of Delegates,
JOSHUA R. WILSON,
ISAAC CAIRNS,
HENRY A. SILVER,
THOS. C. HOPKINS.

Ohio, 1864. McClellan partisans wanted to assure voters that they were not radicals, but conservatives, as indicated in the title.

THE UNION FOREVER!

ADAMS COUNTY, OHIO.
"The UNION is the one Condition of Peace."—*Ex. from McClellan's Letter of Acceptance.*

National Democratic Ticket.

[*Presidential Election, November 8th, 1864.*]

FOR PRESIDENT,
GEORGE B. McCLELLAN,
OF NEW JERSEY.
FOR VICE PRESIDENT,
GEORGE H. PENDLETON,
OF OHIO.

For Electors of President and Vice President of the United States,

ELECTORS AT LARGE,
CHARLES REEMELIN,
THOMAS W. BARTLEY.

CONGRESSIONAL ELECTORS,
JOHN L. VATTIER,
JOHN SCHIFF,
WILLIAM J. GILMORE,
LUTHER SMITH,
CHARLES N. LAMISON,
WILLIAM B. TELFAIR,
WILLIAM H. CREIGHTON,
JUDSON A. BEEBE,
EDWARD S. STOWE,
JAMES G. HALY,
HENRY C. MOORE,
JAMES EMMITT,
CHARLES H. JOHNSTON,
NEAL POWER,
ROBERT A. CONSTABLE,
OLIVER J. SWANEY,
CHARLES M. ATEN,
DAVID R. PAIGE,
SIMEON L. HUNT.

Ohio, 1864.

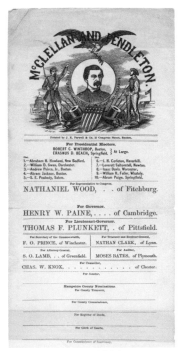

Massachusetts, 1864.

Ohio, 1864. Athens County, Ohio ballots on differently colored paper and in different languages.

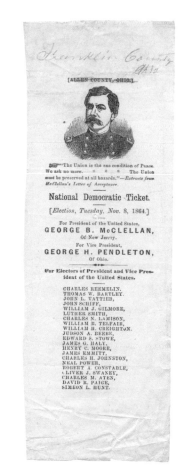

Connecticut, 1864.

Connecticut, 1864.

Massachusetts, 1864.

Ohio, 1864.

Seven

The Soldiers Get the Vote

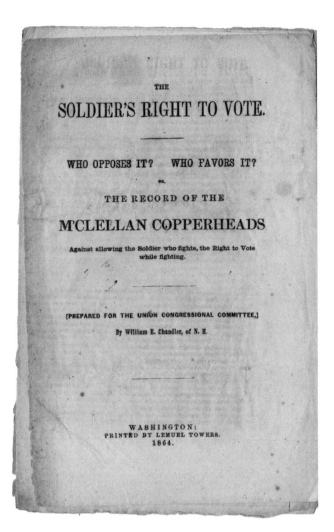

THE

SOLDIER'S RIGHT TO VOTE.

WHO OPPOSES IT?   WHO FAVORS IT?

or,

THE RECORD OF THE

M'CLELLAN COPPERHEADS

Against allowing the Soldier who fights, the Right to Vote
while fighting.

[PREPARED FOR THE UNION CONGRESSIONAL COMMITTEE,]

By William E. Chandler, of N. H.

WASHINGTON:
PRINTED BY LEMUEL TOWERS.
1864.

Pamphlet issued by the Union Congressional Committee in 1864 decrying the failure of Democratic-controlled state legislatures to pass laws that would allow soldiers absent from their respective states to vote. The committee asserted that anti-war Democrats ("Copperheads") were fearful that soldiers, if given the chance, would vote overwhelmingly for Lincoln.

"Impress upon children the truth that the exercise of the elective franchise is a social duty of as solemn a nature as man can be called to perform; that a man may not innocently trifle with his vote; that every elector is a trustee as well for others as himself and that every measure he supports has an important bearing on the interests of others as well as on his own. "

—Daniel Webster

"Democrats are the only reason to vote for Republicans."

—Will Rogers

With the outbreak of war, President Lincoln questioned whether an election "fairly won" could be repudiated, and whether any party could achieve goals through other means. After the close of the war Robert E. Lee commented that what could not be decided by the ballot *had* been decided on the field of battle. Along with slavery, it was a key issue, well-summarized in the simple question: "Bullets or ballots?"

As the war dragged on it became apparent that a final resolution would not take place until after the general election of 1864. Defeats on the battlefield and the seeming inability to deal a deathblow to the Confederate Army had observers giving little chance for Lincoln's reelection. Political heavyweight and *New York Tribune* publisher Horace Greeley sought an alternative candidate, one with greater appeal to the radical element of the party. He went so far as to propose a meeting between "Old Abe," New York Governor Edwin D. Morgan, Albany editor Thurlow Weed and himself to discuss options for a new ticket. But

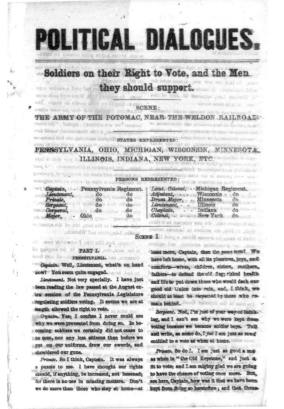

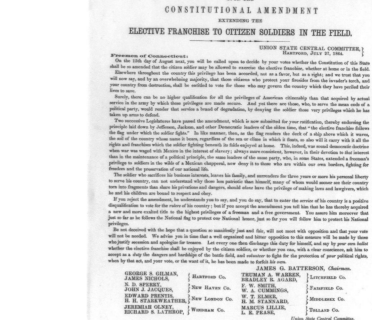

Pamphlet titled "Political Dialogues. Soldiers on their Right to Vote, and the Men they should support." The text consists of various imagined scenes of soldiers discussing the upcoming election by the campfire. It concludes with a private exclaiming: "… when the nation is battling for life, we all go for Lincoln and Johnston [sic], the Friends of Poor Men, The Champions of the Union, and the Firm Foes of All Treason."

Handbill issued by the Union State Central Committee of Connecticut urging voters to pass a constitutional amendment, in a special election on August 15, 1864, that would extend the "elective franchise to citizen soldiers in the field."

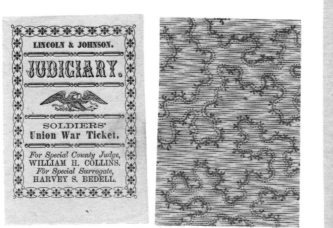

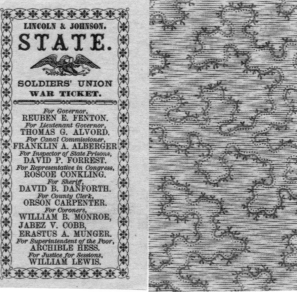

New York, 1864. Statewide office tickets used by soldiers. Though different in size, each has the same anti-counterfeiting pattern on the verso.

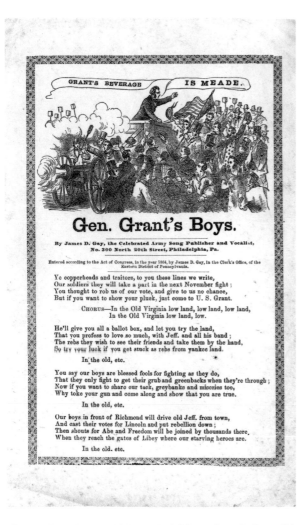

Song sheet from 1864 entitled "Gen. Grant's Boys." It depicts a political rally and has verses directed to anti-war partisans, making reference to the soldier vote: "Ye copperheads and traitors, to you these lines we write/ Our soldiers they will take a part in the next November fight/ You thought to rob us of our vote, and give to us no chance/ But if you want to show your pluck, just come to U. S. Grant."

the 1864 National Union Convention held in Baltimore re-nominated Lincoln. To bolster support for the ticket, Vice President Hannibal Hamlin of Maine was tossed aside for the "War Democrat" military governor of Tennessee, Andrew Johnson, as Lincoln's running-mate. Dissatisfied with the President's seeming moderation, the radical wing of his party nominated its own ticket, Union generals John C. Fremont and John Cochrane; they however withdrew from the race in September, with Fremont endorsing Lincoln.

The Civil War marks the first time in American history soldiers in the field could vote in a national election. And, holding an election during civil war was without precedent. Although there were those who felt the 1864 election should be postponed, the idea was generally repudiated, not least because violation of the principle of the sanctity of elections had been a cause of the war itself. Nothing that might undermine that sanctity was countenanced.

A huge number of potential voters were in the military, many stationed across the South and far from their homes. Most state laws dictated that voters had to personally cast their ballots in their hometown. Soldiers could do so only if granted furloughs, but wartime exigencies precluded their widespread use. Several states remedied this by amending their constitutions to allow absent soldiers to vote off-site via absentee ballot or through agents granted power-of-attorney; New York, Ohio, Pennsylvania and Connecticut passed such enabling legislation. Others, including Indiana and New Jersey, did not. New Jersey had a Democratic-controlled legislature that feared its soldiers would vote for Lincoln over native son and Orange resident General George McClellan.

Much surviving paperwork attests to the soldier vote. Poll books were printed so their votes could be recorded: individual books inscribed for each state and county. The number of election clerks and

ELECTION DAY IN THE ARMY OF THE SHENANDOAH.

Our illustrations of life in camp this week are ample, graphic and interesting. On page 165 we present a sketch illustrative of Election Day in the Army of the Shenandoah. The prominent incident delineated is the voting of Gen. Sheridan and Gen. Crook. The scene must have been at once romantic and solemnly impressive. The weather, on the occasion, was dim and drizzly; but the woods wore their beautiful autumnal foliage, and cast abroad the sombre spell of their shadows and their silence. The polls, constructed of an ambulance wagon and an old cartridge-box, are seen to occupy a commodious position among the trees.

From *Frank Leslie's Illustrated Newspaper*, December 3, 1864: "Scene at the Polls – Gen. Sheridan, Gen. Crook, and other officers casting their votes."

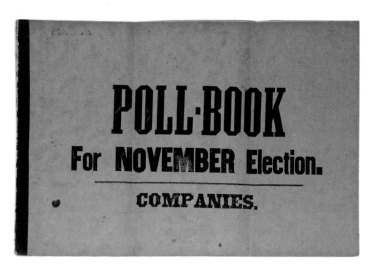

Poll book used to record the votes of just two soldiers from Columbia County, Pennsylvania, members of companies H & K, 7th Regiment, Pennsylvania Volunteers, at Thompson Station, Tennessee. Both men voted for Lincoln!

Tintype photograph of a Union soldier in a studio pose proudly wearing his 1864 campaign badge.

judges sometimes outnumbered the number of soldiers voting! Also still to be found are power-of-attorney documents assigning a soldier's voting rights, related affidavits, and pre-printed ballots shipped to the various theaters of war. Many of the tickets were imprinted "Union Soldier's Vote."

Not surprisingly there were accusations of fraud. It was said that Secretary of War Edwin Stanton and certain Union generals, friendly to the administration, had granted furloughs to soldiers likely to vote for Lincoln. Soldiers likely to vote for McClellan "whistled Dixie." Officials in Republican-held states were accused of sending Republican ballots to the war zone while withholding information necessary for Democratic

"Soldier's Vote" transmittal envelope and affidavit of David Hartwell, a member of Company D of the 120th New York Volunteer Infantry stationed near Petersburg, Virginia. The soldier affirms that he is a U.S. citizen over 21 years of age, has resided in New York for at least one year preceding the election, is a member of the armed forces and has not made any wagers on the outcome of the election. This affidavit and a ballot were sent to a relative back home who was assigned the task of presenting the paperwork to officials on election day.

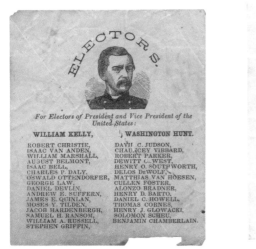

Transmittal envelope that contained tally sheets for the presidential election of 1864 sent to election officials in Ohio.

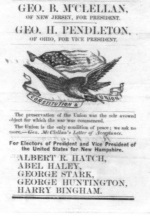

New York, 1864. Ballot issued specifically for the use of soldiers.

New Hampshire, 1864.

Michigan, 1864. The reverse of this ballot indicates it was cast by a Michigan soldier and returned to Berrien County to be tabulated, but the vote was never counted because the State Supreme Court ruled the soldiers' voting law invalid.

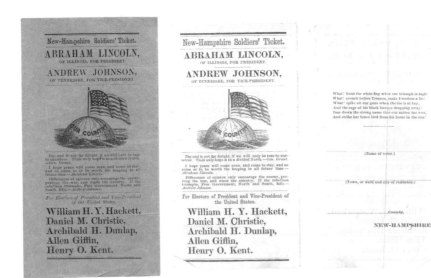

New Hampshire, 1864. In addition to quotes from Grant, Lincoln and Vice President Johnson, assuring voters the war would ostensibly end soon, the reverse of these ballots include a patriotic poem.

McCLELLAN AND THE UNION !
ABSENT ELECTOR'S TICKET.
DIRECTIONS TO SOLDIERS AND SAILORS.—There
are THREE tickets or ballots to be voted ; they must
be cut at each dotted line, and then folded so as to show
only the heading of the ticket, as—
ELECTORS—STATE—ASSEMBLY.
These are the only words to be seen when the tickets
are folded. They should then be enclosed in the envelopes, with the accompanying power of attorney, and
directed to some friend in the district where you reside
who is a voter, and who will deliver your vote to the
Inspector.

ELECTORS.

For Electors of
President and Vice President
of the United States.
WILLIAM KELLY,
WASHINGTON HUNT.

ROBERT CHRISTIE,	STEPHEN GRIFFIN,
ISAAC VAN ANDEN,	DAVID C. JUDSON,
WILLIAM MARSHALL,	CHAUNCEY VIBBARD,
AUGUST BELMONT,	ROBERT PARKER,
ISAAC BELL,	DEWITT C. WEST,
CHARLES P. DALY,	HENRY O. SOUTHWORTH,
OSWALD OTTENDORFER,	DELOS DeWOLF,
GEORGE LAW,	MATTHIAS VAN HOESEN,
DANIEL DEVLIN,	CULLEN FOSTER,
ANDREW E. SUFFERN,	ALONZO BRADNER,
JAMES E. QUINLAN,	HENRY D. BARTO,
MOSES Y. TILDEN,	DANIEL C. HOWELL,
JACOB HARDENBURGH,	THOMAS CORNES,
SAMUEL H. RANSOM,	HENRY J. GLOWACKI,
WILLIAM A. RUSSELL,	SOLOMON SCHEU,
BENJAMIN CHAMBERLAIN.	

STATE.

For Governor,
HORATIO SEYMOUR.
For Lieutenant Governor,
DAVID R. FLOYD JONES.
For Canal Commissioner,
JARVIS LORD.
For Inspector of State Prisons,
DAVID B. McNEIL.
For Representative in Congress,
WILLIAM RADFORD.
For Sheriff,
DARIUS LYON.
For Register,
STEPHEN S. MARSHALL.
For County Clerk,
HIRAM P. ROWEL.
For Superintendent of the Poor,
ABRAHAM R. STRANG.
For Coroners,
T. MASON OLIVER,
STEPHEN BILLINGS,
ISAAC COVERT.
For Justice of the Sessions,
THOMAS J. BYRNE.

ASSEMBLY.

For Member of Assembly—First District.
PIERRE C. TALMAN.

ASSEMBLY.

For Member of Assembly—Second District,
ALSOP H. LOCKWOOD.

ASSEMBLY.

For Member of Assembly—Third District,
JACOB T. COCKS.

The following Towns comprise the First Assembly
District : *Eastchester, Morrisania, Westchester, West
Farms, Yonkers.*
Second Assembly District : *Greenburgh, Harrison,
Mamaroneck, Mount Pleasant, Pelham, Poundridge,
Rye, New Rochelle, North Castle, Scarsdale, White
Plains.*
Third Assembly District : *Bedford, Cortlandt, Ossin-
ing, North Salem, Lewisboro, New Castle, Somers
Yorktown.*

ballots to be delivered. Lincoln ballots might reach sailors at sea, while McClellan ballots mysteriously remained on the dock. Incredible as it may seem, only recently a number of soldier ballots sent to Ohio were discovered unopened, still in sealed envelopes and never counted. These originated with soldiers predominantly from Democratic southern districts of Ohio. An innocent oversight? Not likely. It was also alleged that the War Department sent high ranking officers to polling places in an effort to intimidate Democratic voters. Notorious General and later presidential aspirant Benjamin "Beast" Butler went to New York City for the election. Upon arrival he was given an enthusiastic welcome at the train depot and escorted to a key polling station where his mission was to prevent Southern agents from somehow casting illegal ballots. According to a witness, reporting to Washington's War Department, Butler – who was known for being cross-eyed – was able to "keep an eye on" *two* groups of suspicious characters in different parts of the room at the same time!

Even allowing some credence to claims of voter fraud, of which both sides were likely guilty, it had little effect on the outcome. Significant numbers of Union soldiers voted in the Presidential election of 1864 – the vast majority of them for "Old Abe"– but while substantial, their numbers were not crucial to his re-election. ﷼

New York, 1864. Multiple general election and statewide tickets. There are instructions at the top for their use by soldiers and sailors. They had to be cut and folded in a certain manner, sealed in the envelopes provided, and sent to an agent of the voter in his hometown, together with a completed power-of-attorney form.

Eight

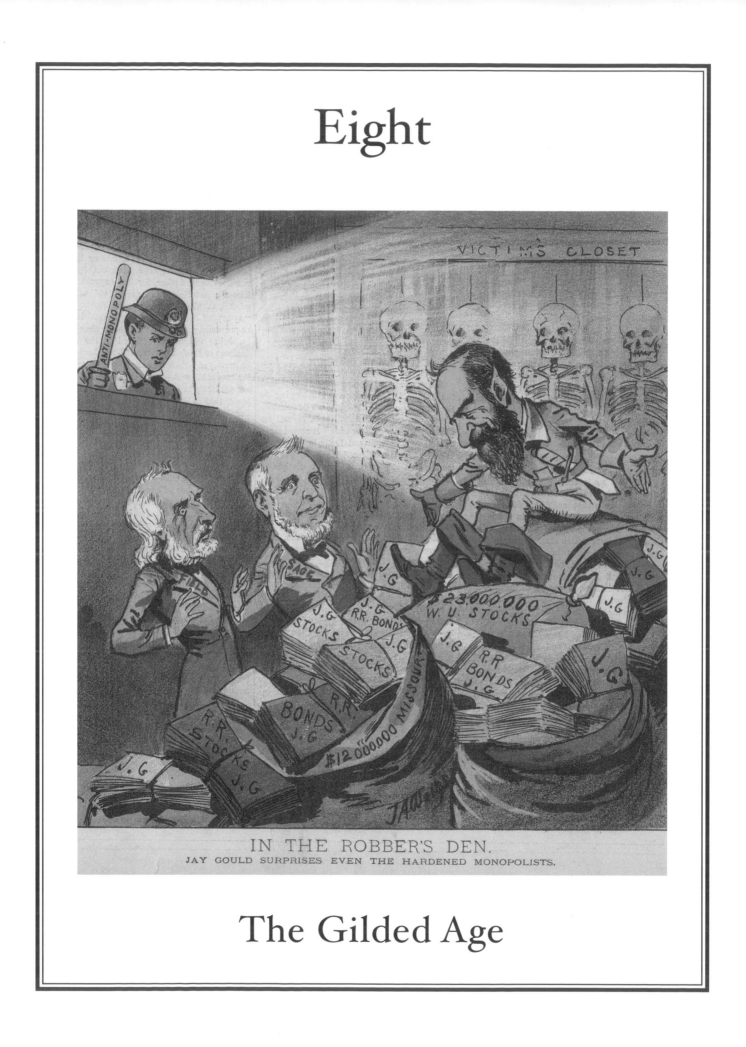

The Gilded Age

For Electors of President and Vice President of the United States,
CHARLES M. CROSWELL, JOHN BURT,
WILLIAM DOELTZ. CHARLES W. CLISBEE,
CHARLES T. GORHAM, BYRON M. CUTCHEON,
GILES HUBBARD. MICHAEL C. T. PLESSNER.
For Governor,
HENRY P. BALDWIN.
For Lieutenant Governor,
MORGAN BATES.
For Secretary of State,
OLIVER L. SPAULDING.
For State Treasurer,
EBENEZER O. GROSVENOR.
For Auditor General,
WILLIAM HUMPHREY.
For Commissioner of the State Land Office,
BENJAMIN D. PRITCHARD.
For Attorney General,
DWIGHT MAY.
For Superintendent of Public Instruction,
ORAMEL HOSFORD.
For Member of the State Board of Education,
DANIEL E. BROWN
For Representative in Congress—Fifth District,
OMAR D. CONGER.
For Senator in the State Legislature Fifth District,
P. DEAN WARNER.
For Representative in the State Legislature—Second District,
ROBERT GARNER.
For Judge of Probate,
ALFRED CRAWFORD.
For Sheriff,
WILLIAM SATTERLEE.
For County Clerk,
JOHN FITZPATRICK.
For County Treasurer,
LYSANDER WOODWARD.
For Register of Deeds,
THOMAS F. GERLS,
For Prosecuting Attorney,
CHARLES DRAPER.
For Circuit Court Commissioners,
BYRON L. RANSFORD.
MARK S. BREWER.
For County Surveyor,
HORATIO MERRYWEATHER.
For Coroners,
CURTIS BABCOCK.
JOHN CAMPBELL.

Michigan, 1868. The individual running for Commissioner of the State Land Office, Benjamin D. Pritchard, commanded the cavalry regiment that captured fugitive Confederate President Jefferson Davis in 1865.

"No amount of charters, direct primaries, or short ballots will make a democracy out of an illiterate people."

—Walter Lippmann

"Suffrage, noun. Expression of opinion by means of a ballot. The right of suffrage (which is held to be both a privilege and a duty) means, as commonly interpreted, the right to vote for the man of another man's choice, and is highly prized."

—Ambrose Bierce

While the Democrats enjoyed great success throughout the antebellum period, they fell on hard times following the Civil War. The only Democrat to reach the White House in the latter decades of the 19th century was Grover Cleveland. The period was beset by issues such as Reconstruction of the South, stock market scandals, industrialization, the rise of monopolies and the greed of the "robber barons" including personalities such as William "The Public Be Damned!" Vanderbilt, Jay Gould, Jim Fisk, John D. Rockefeller, J. Pierpont Morgan and Andrew Carnegie. Financial panics in 1873 and 1893 spawned the Greenback, Union Labor, People's and Socialist parties. Labor unrest, a phenomenon rare in the antebellum period, became a regular feature on the American scene, sometimes manifested in violence like that perpetrated by the "Molly Maguires" in Pennsylvania and bomb-throwing anarchists in Chicago.

In presidential politics, an attractive war record had always been an asset; it now became a virtual requisite for office. "Waving the bloody shirt" was a

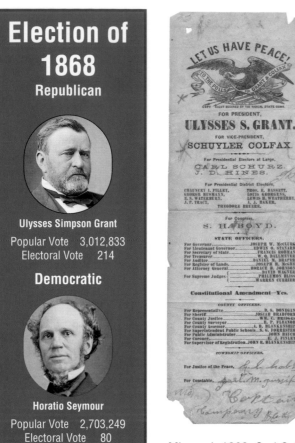

Election of 1868

Republican

Ulysses Simpson Grant

Popular Vote 3,012,833
Electoral Vote 214

Democratic

Horatio Seymour

Popular Vote 2,703,249
Electoral Vote 80

Missouri, 1868. Carl Schurz, a German immigrant and popular Republican speaker, had been a strong Lincoln supporter beginning in 1860.

Pennsylvania, 1868. This handbill from Philadelphia urges all qualified voters to participate in the general election to "crush under foot, Fraud, Corruption and the Spirit of Rebellion." It also alerts voters to the dissemination of spurious tickets and prints an example of the official Republican ballot for comparison purposes.

California, 1868.

Massachusetts, 1868.

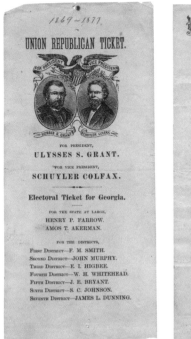

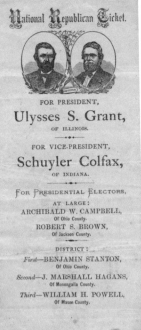

Georgia, 1868. Republican ballots from the Reconstruction South are rare. After the 1877 withdrawal of federal troops the South went solidly Democratic.

West Virginia, 1868.

common tactic of candidates great and small. Union veterans, the "Boys in Blue," mobilized into marching clubs. Their endorsement and their power as a voting bloc proved invaluable to many a presidential hopeful.

The highlight of the period (or nadir depending upon one's perspective) was the so-called "stolen election" of 1876. Accepted history has the Republicans pulling a "fast one" to deprive Democrat Samuel J. Tilden of the Presidency. Hayes and his partisans challenged electoral results in five Southern states, claiming widespread voter intimidation; Democrats in fact intimidated and suppressed the black vote in these states. As with the disputed election of 2000, Florida was a center of controversy and attention. Eventually the electoral votes of the five disputed states were awarded to Hayes, a result declared just two days prior to his inauguration. Supposedly as recompense for his election, Hayes agreed to withdraw federal troops from the South formally ending Reconstruction. While this did

North Carolina, 1868. On one ballot former slaves are shown baling cotton. Under Reconstruction they received wages and could – theoretically – vote in elections.

California, 1868.

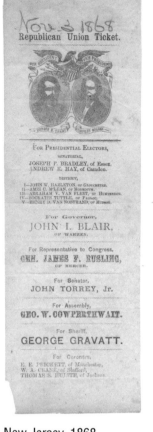

New Jersey, 1868.

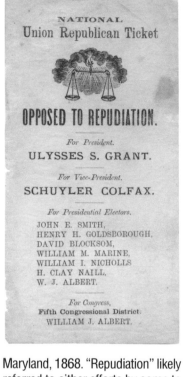

Maryland, 1868. "Repudiation" likely referred to either efforts by some to reverse the policies of President Lincoln and the Radical Republicans or the suspension of war debts.

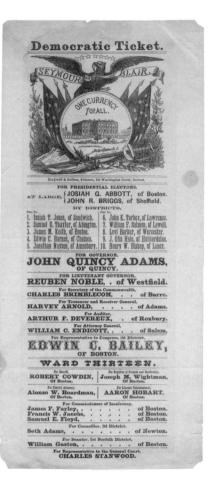

Massachusetts, 1868.

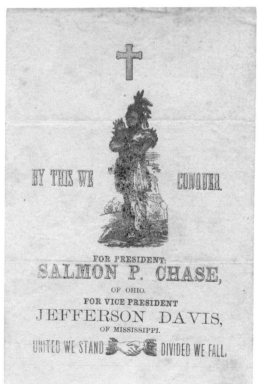

Ohio, 1868. In German.

This pseudo-ballot likely dates from 1868. Although Salmon P. Chase and Jefferson Davis were Democrats, Chase was consistent in his abolitionist views. He later switched to the Republican Party and was a presidential hopeful in 1860. He was touted as a possible replacement for Lincoln as the Republican standard bearer in 1864 and in 1868 sought the nomination despite serving as Chief Justice of the Supreme Court. The association with Confederate President Jefferson Davis and the inclusion of the cross (associated with Catholicism) indicates this was a piece of negative campaigning and not a sincere expression of support.

give a free hand to discrimination and mistreatment of African Americans, Reconstruction, as a policy, had become untenable. Hayes most likely would have withdrawn Federal troops in any event. One lasting result of this election was the establishment of the "Solid South" – a geographic bloc that uniformily voted Democratic from 1880 until 1964, when it supported Barry Goldwater's run for the Presidency and began a swing toward the Republicans. In politics the pendulum swings both ways – sometimes it does so very slowly! ∝

Illinois, 1868.

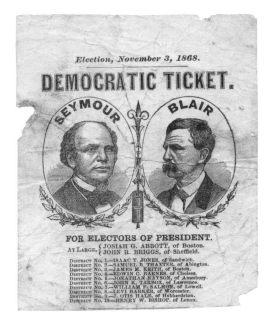

Massachusetts, 1868.

New Jersey, 1868. Montclair, New Jersey was the site of a "Republican Wigwam" at which numerous Grant and Colfax rallies were held, including one addressed by Horace Greeley.

Election of 1872

Republican

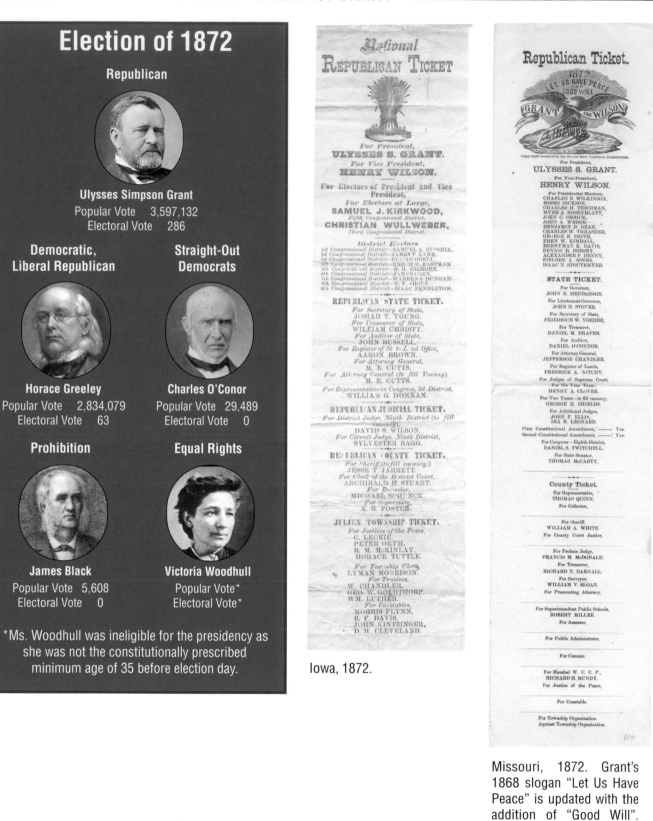

Ulysses Simpson Grant
Popular Vote   3,597,132
Electoral Vote   286

Democratic, Liberal Republican

Horace Greeley
Popular Vote   2,834,079
Electoral Vote   63

Straight-Out Democrats

Charles O'Conor
Popular Vote   29,489
Electoral Vote   0

Prohibition

James Black
Popular Vote   5,608
Electoral Vote   0

Equal Rights

Victoria Woodhull
Popular Vote*
Electoral Vote*

*Ms. Woodhull was ineligible for the presidency as she was not the constitutionally prescribed minimum age of 35 before election day.

Iowa, 1872.

Missouri, 1872. Grant's 1868 slogan "Let Us Have Peace" is updated with the addition of "Good Will". Peace and Good Will… that's the ticket!

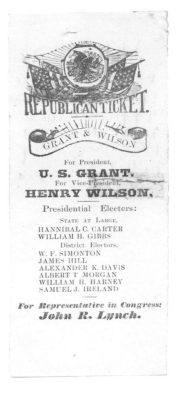

Mississippi, 1872. Rare Reconstruction era ballot. The candidate for Congress, John Roy Lynch, was a former slave. He was elected as a Republican to the 43rd and 44th Congresses.

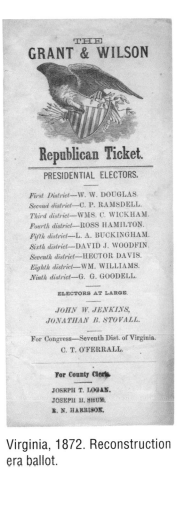

Virginia, 1872. Reconstruction era ballot.

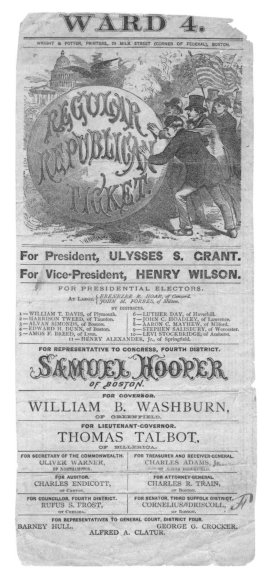

Massachusetts, 1872. Various segments of society "Keep the ball rolling" on this oversized ballot.

Reverse of the Massachusetts ballot above.

New Hampshire, 1872.

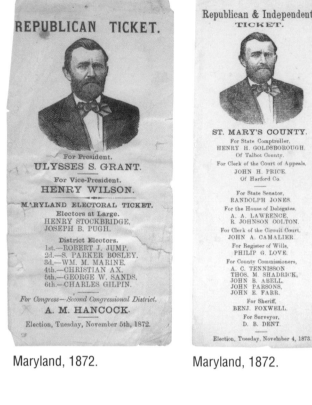

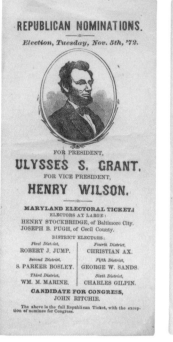

Maryland, 1872.

Maryland, 1872.

Maryland, 1872.

Maryland, 1872.

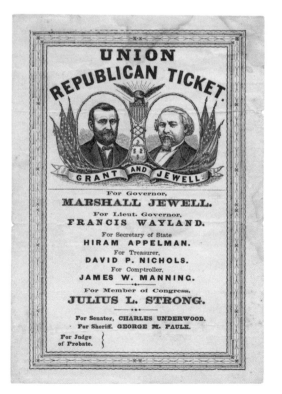

Connecticut, 1872. A "coattail" ballot with presidential and gubernatorial candidates.

Massachusetts, 1872. Greeley was the standard bearer for both the Democratic and Liberal Republican Parties. The slate of Presidential Electors was also the same for both parties… a potential "win-win" situation, but it didn't work out that way for publisher Greeley. The problem? Grant got too many votes!

LIBERAL REPUBLICAN
AND
DEMOCRATIC TICKET.

GREELEY AND BROWN.

For Presidential Electors,
AT LARGE { CHESTER W. CHAPIN, of Springfield.
JOSIAH G. ABBOTT, of Boston.

District.   District.
1—George Delano, of New Bedford.   6—John A. Bassett, of Salem.
2—James E. Carpenter, of Foxboro'. 7—William H. Clemence of Lowell.
3—Charles A. B. Shephard, of Boston. 8—Henry W. Muzzey, of Cambridge.
4—Joseph Everdean, of Chelsea.   9—Isaac Davis of Worcester.
5—Richard Frothingham, of Charlestown. 10—C. R. B. Snow, of Fitchburg.
                                    11—Charles W. Knox, of Chester.

For Governor,
FRANCIS W. BIRD, - - - of Walpole.
For Lieutenant Governor,
WILLIAM L. SMITH, of Springfield,

For Secretary of State,   For Treasurer and Receiver-General,
Geo. H. Monroe, of Boston.   Levi Heywood, of Gardner.

For Auditor,   For Attorney-General,
Patrick A. Collins, of Boston. Waldo Colburn, of Dedham.

For Representative to Congress, (First District).
JOSEPH M. DAY, of Barnstable.
For Councillor, (First District).
SIDNEY TUCKER, of Middleborough.
For County Commissioner,
HORATIO N. RICHARDSON, of Attleborough.
For Senator, (Second District).
PARDON DEVOLL,
For Representatives to the General Court,
TENTH BRISTOL DISTRICT,
RODNEY FRENCH,
DAVID A. SNELL.

Massachusetts, 1872.

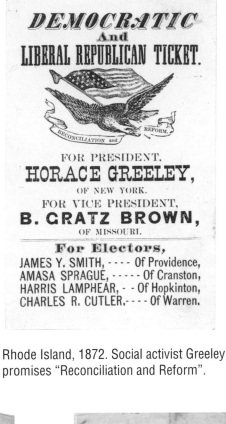

DEMOCRATIC
And
LIBERAL REPUBLICAN TICKET.

RECONCILIATION and REFORM.

FOR PRESIDENT.
HORACE GREELEY,
OF NEW YORK.
FOR VICE PRESIDENT,
B. GRATZ BROWN,
OF MISSOURI.

For Electors,
JAMES Y. SMITH, - - - - Of Providence,
AMASA SPRAGUE, - - - - - Of Cranston,
HARRIS LAMPHEAR, - - Of Hopkinton,
CHARLES R. CUTLER. - - - - Of Warren.

Rhode Island, 1872. Social activist Greeley promises "Reconciliation and Reform".

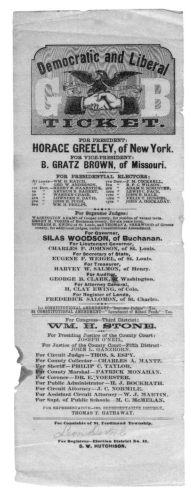

Democratic and Liberal
G B
TICKET.

FOR PRESIDENT:
HORACE GREELEY, of New York.
FOR VICE-PRESIDENT:
B. GRATZ BROWN, of Missouri.

FOR PRESIDENTIAL ELECTORS:
AT LARGE—WM. H. HATCH,   7TH DIST.—F. M. COCKRELL,
"   GEO. W. ANDERSON,   8TH   " R. P. C. WILSON,
1ST DIST.—HENRY F. ILARRICK, 9TH   " ADAM N. SCHUSTER,
2D   "   ARTHUR B. BARRET,   10TH   " LEWIS C. PACK,
3D   "   WARREN CHASE,   11TH   " JOHN B. HALE,
4TH "   LOWNDES H. DAVIS,   12TH   " FELIX T. HUGHES,
5TH "   JOHN H. PUGH,   13TH   " JOHN A. HOCKADAY.
6TH "   WM. H. PHELPS,

For Supreme Judges:
WASHINGTON ADAMS of Cooper county, for residue of vacant term.
HENRY M. VORIES of Buchanan county, for six years term.
EPHRAIM B. EWING of St. Louis, and THOMAS A. SHERWOOD of Greene
county, for additional judges, under Constitutional Amendment.

For Governor,
SILAS WOODSON, of Buchanan.
For Lieutenant Governor,
CHARLES P. JOHNSON, of St. Louis.
For Secretary of State,
EUGENE F. WEIGEL, of St. Louis.
For Treasurer,
HARVEY W. SALMON, of Henry.
For Auditor,
GEORGE B. CLARK, of Washington.
For Attorney General,
H. CLAY EWING, of Cole.
For Register of Lands,
FREDERICK SALOMON, of St. Charles.

1st CONSTITUTIONAL AMENDMENT—"Supreme Judges"—Yes.
2d CONSTITUTIONAL AMENDMENT—"Investment of School Funds"—Yes.

For Congress—Third District:
WM. H. STONE.

For Presiding Justice of the County Court:
JOSEPH O'NEIL.
For Justice of the County Court—Fifth District·
JOHN L. GANZHORN.
For Circuit Judge—THOS. S. ESPY.
For County Collector—CHARLES A. MANTZ.
For Sheriff—PHILIP C. TAYLOR.
For County Marshal—PATRICK MONAHAN.
For Coroner—DR. E. VOERSTER.
For Public Administrator—H. J. BOCKRATH.
For Circuit Attorney—J. C. NORMILE.
For Assistant Circuit Attorney—W. J. MARTIN.
For Supt. of Public Schools—M. C. McMELAN.

FOR REPRESENTATIVE—12th REPRESENTATIVE DISTRICT,
THOMAS T. HATHAWAY.

For Constable of St. Ferdinand Township,

For Register—Election District No. 43,
S. W. HUTCHISON.

Missouri, 1872.

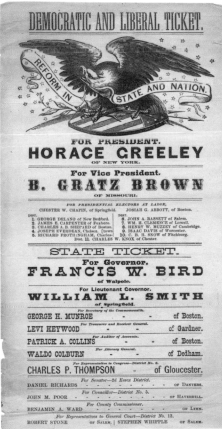

DEMOCRATIC AND LIBERAL TICKET.

REFORM IN STATE AND NATION.

FOR PRESIDENT.
HORACE GREELEY
OF NEW YORK
For Vice President.
B. GRATZ BROWN
OF MISSOURI

FOR PRESIDENTIAL ELECTORS AT LARGE,
CHESTER W. CHAPIN, of Springfield.   JOSIAH G. ABBOTT, of Boston.

DIST.   DIST.
1. GEORGE DELANO of New Bedford.   6. JOHN A. BASSETT of Salem.
2. JAMES E. CARPENTER of Foxboro. 7. WM. H. CLEMENCE of Lowell.
3. CHARLES A. B. SHEPARD of Boston. 8. HENRY W. MUZZEY of Cambridge.
4. JOSEPH EVERDEAN, Chelsea. [town 9. ISAAC DAVIS of Worcester.
5. RICHARD FROTHINGHAM, Charles-   10. C. R. B. SNOW of Fitchburg.
   Dist. 11. CHARLES W. KNOX of Chester.

STATE TICKET.
For Governor.
FRANCIS W. BIRD
of Walpole.
For Lieutenant Governor.
WILLIAM L. SMITH
of Springfield

For Secretary of the Commonwealth.
GEORGE H. MUNROE - - of Boston.
For Treasurer and Receiver General.
LEVI HEYWOOD - - of Gardner.
For Auditor of Accounts.
PATRICK A. COLLINS - - of Boston.
For Attorney General.
WALDO COLBURN - - of Dedham.
For Representative to Congress—District No. 6.
CHARLES P. THOMPSON - of Gloucester.
For Senator—2d Essex District.
DANIEL RICHARDS - - - OF DANVERS.
For Councillor—District No. 5.
JOHN M. POOR - - - OF HAVERHILL.
For County Commissioner.
BENJAMIN A. WARD - - OF LYNN.
For Representatives to General Court—District No. 13.
ROBERT STONE   OF SALEM. | STEPHEN WHIPPLE   OF SALEM.

Massachusetts, 1872.

REGULAR DEMOCRATIC AND LIBERAL REPUBLICAN.
Nominations.

FOR ELECTORS OF
PRESIDENT & VICE-PRESIDENT,
George B. McClellan.
Abraham Browning.
Robert Newell.
John S. Noble.
Charles F. Davenport.
Charles Sitgreaves.
John Kyle.
John A. Boppe.
Sidney B. Bevans.

For Representative in Congress,
7th DISTRICT.
Noah D. Taylor.

For Member of Assembly,
7th DISTRICT.
John A. O'Neill.

For Sheriff,
John Reinhardt.

For Coroners,
Jacob Reinhardt.
William N. Parslow.
John Mahan.

New Jersey, 1872. Democrat George B. McClellan, presidential candidate in 1864, is listed here as an elector. He was elected Governor of New Jersey in 1877.

LIBERAL-DEMOCRATIC
TICKET.

For President—
HORACE GREELEY.
For Vice President—
B. GRATZ BROWN.

For Presidential Electors,
AT LARGE—MONS. ANDERSON.
JOHN BLACK.
FIRST DISTRICT—WYMAN SPOONER.
SECOND DISTRICT—A. G. COOK.
THIRD DISTRICT—GEO. H. KING.
FOURTH DISTRICT—S. BINDSKOPF.
FIFTH DISTRICT—R. H. HUTCHKISS.
SIXTH DISTRICT—ANTON KLAUS.
SEVENTH DISTRICT—M. MONTGOMERY.
EIGHTH DISTRICT—M. WADLEIGH.

For Congress—
2d Dist.—GEORGE B. SMITH.
For Senator—
A. R. CORNWALL.
For Assembly—
2d Dist.—LEVI B. VILAS.
For Sheriff—
JOHN ADAMS.
For Treasurer—
C. W. HEYL.
For County Clerk—
PHILIP BARRY.
For Clerk of Court—
WM. P. ATWELL.
For Register of Deeds—
L. J. GRINDE.
For District Attorney—
SINCLAIR W. BOTKIN.
For Surveyor—
GEO. P. HARRINGTON.
For Coroner—
J. P. SWITZER.

Wisconsin, 1872.

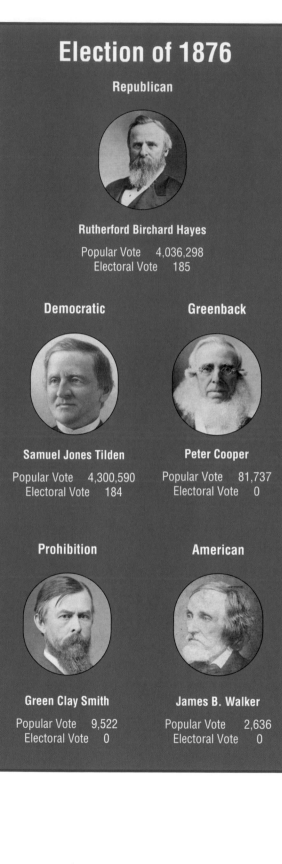

Election of 1876

Republican

Rutherford Birchard Hayes

Popular Vote 4,036,298
Electoral Vote 185

Democratic

Samuel Jones Tilden

Popular Vote 4,300,590
Electoral Vote 184

Greenback

Peter Cooper

Popular Vote 81,737
Electoral Vote 0

Prohibition

Green Clay Smith

Popular Vote 9,522
Electoral Vote 0

American

James B. Walker

Popular Vote 2,636
Electoral Vote 0

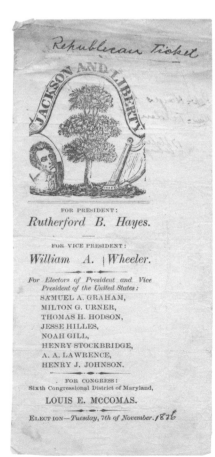

Connecticut, 1876.

Maryland, 1876. Democrat Andrew Jackson appears at the head of this ticket for Republican Hayes. That's bipartisanship for you!

New Hampshire, 1876. The nation's centennial is duly noted and celebrated.

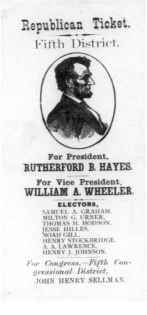

Maryland, 1876.

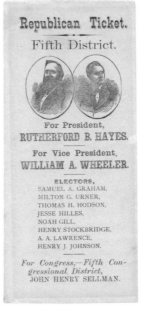

Maryland, 1876.

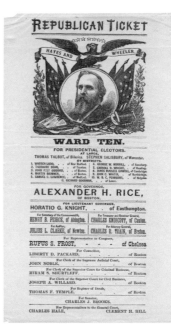

Massachusetts, 1876.

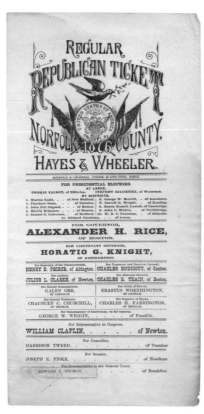

Massachusetts, 1876. A dove and $20 gold piece symbolize "Peace and Prosperity".

Massachusetts, 1876. "Equality for all Men Under the Law" is promised. The printer, located on Arch Street in Boston, uses an arch in the woodcut illustration – a subliminal advertisement?

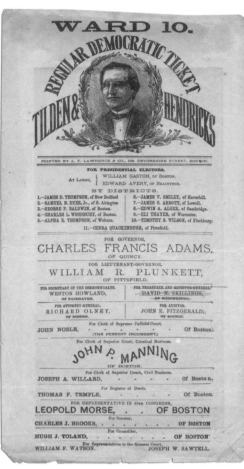

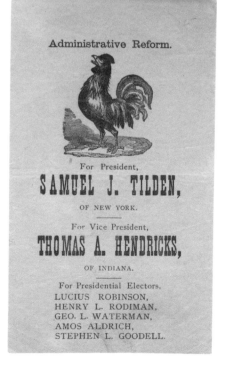

Massachusetts, 1876. The reverse has a printed script excerpt from a campaign statement by the candidate in which he hopes that the "evils of the past be forgotten" urging "let by-gones be by-gones." Sounds nice... on paper.

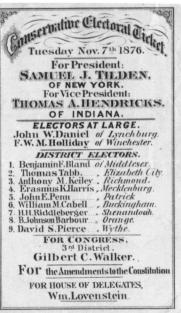

In Iowa Tilden ran on the "Democratic Liberal Ticket," while in Virginia it was the "Conservative Electoral Ticket." He still lost.

Vermont, 1876.

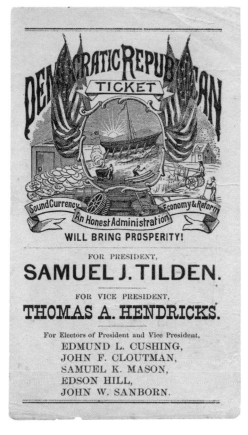

New Hampshire, 1876.

REGULAR
DEMOCRATIC TICKET.

For President,
SAMUEL J. TILDEN,
OF NEW YORK.

For Vice President,
THOMAS A. HENDRICKS,
OF INDIANA.

FOR PRESIDENTIAL ELECTORS.

AT LARGE.
WILLIAM GASTON, of Boston.   EDWARD AVERY, of Braintree.

BY DISTRICTS.

1. JAMES D. THOMPSON, of New Bedford.
2. SAMUEL N. DYER, Jr., of So. Abington.
3. GEORGE P. BALDWIN, of Boston.
4. CHAS. LEVI WOODBURY, of Boston.
5. ALPHA E. THOMPSON, of Woburn.
6. JAMES V. SMILEY, of Haverhill.
7. JAMES C. ABBOTT, of Lowell.
8. EDWIN A. ALGER, of Cambridge.
9. ELI THAYER, of Worcester.
10. TIMOTHY S. WILSON, of Fitchburg.
11. CEBRA QUACKENBUSH, of Pittsfield.

For Representative to Congress, Dist. No. 2.
EDWARD AVERY, - - - of Braintree.

FOR GOVERNOR,
CHAS. FRANCIS ADAMS, of Quincy.

FOR LIEUT. GOVERNOR,
WILLIAM R. PLUNKETT, of Pittsfield.

For Secretary of the Commonwealth, WESTON HOWLAND, Of Fairhaven.	For Treasurer, DAVID N. SKILLINGS, Of Winchester.
For Auditor, JOHN E. FITZGERALD, Of Boston.	For Attorney General, RICHARD OLNEY, Of Boston.
For Councillor, District No. 1, S. B. PHINNEY, Of Barnstable.	For Senator 2d Plymouth Dist., HENRY A. FORD, Of Brockton.
For County Commissioner, JOHN S. LORING, Of Duxbury.	For Special Commissioner, BENJAMIN WILDER, Of Scituate.
For Clerk of the Courts, JOHN F. SIMMONS, Of Hanover.	For County Treasurer, ANDREW GRIFFITH, Of Green.
For Register of Deeds, WILLIAM T. HOLLIS, Of Plymouth.	For Sheriff, ALPHEUS K. HARMON, Of Plymouth.

For Representation to General Court, First Plymouth District,
GEORGE CUSHING, 2d, of Hingham.

Massachusetts, 1876.

TILDEN & HENDRICKS
Reform Ticket.
1776.   1876.

Electoral Ticket.

For Electors of President and Vice President of the
United States.

At Large—GEORGE V. N. LOTHROP.
AUSTIN BLAIR.
First District—JAMES HEINTZEN.
Second District—ALFRED L SAWYER.
Third District—JAMES S. UPTON.
Fourth District—MARSHALL L. HOWELL.
Fifth District—FREDERICK HALL.
Sixth District—HUGH McCURDY.
Seventh District—JAMES B. ELDREDGE.
Eighth District—ALBERT MILLER.
Ninth District—MICHAEL FINNEGAN.

State Ticket.

For Governor,
WILLIAM L. WEBBER.
For Lieutenant Governor,
JULIUS HOUSEMAN.
For Secretary of State,
GEORGE H. HOUSE.
For State Treasurer,
JOHN G. PARKHURST.
For Auditor General,
FREDERICK M. HOLLOWAY.
For Commissioner of the State Land Office,
JOSEPH BRUSH FENTON.
For Attorney-General,
MARTIN MORRIS.
For Superintendent of Public Instruction,
ZELOTES TRUESDEL.
For Member of the State Board of Education,
CHARLES I. WALKER.

Congressional Ticket.

For Representative in Congress, Third District,
FIDUS LIVERMORE.

Legislative Ticket.

For Senator, Eighth District,
CAMPBELL G. WALDO.
For Representative, Third District,
ELLIOTT W. HOLLINGSWORTH.

County Ticket.

For Sheriff,
CHARLES A. GARDANIER.
For County Clerk,
WILLIAM S. MARSH.
For Register of Deeds,
JEHIEL WISNER.
For County Treasurer,
WILLIAM A. POWELL.
For Judge of Probate,
BENJAMIN F. WITHEE.
For Prosecuting Attorney,
HENRY H. BROWN.
For Circuit Court Commissioners,
CYRUS M. ALWARD.
BYRON SMITH.
For County Surveyor,
CYRUS ROBERTSON.
For Coroners,
WILLIAM M. BARNES.
DEVILLO HUBBARD.

Michigan, 1876.

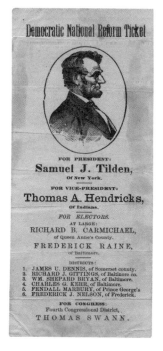

Maryland, 1876.

Election of 1880

Republican

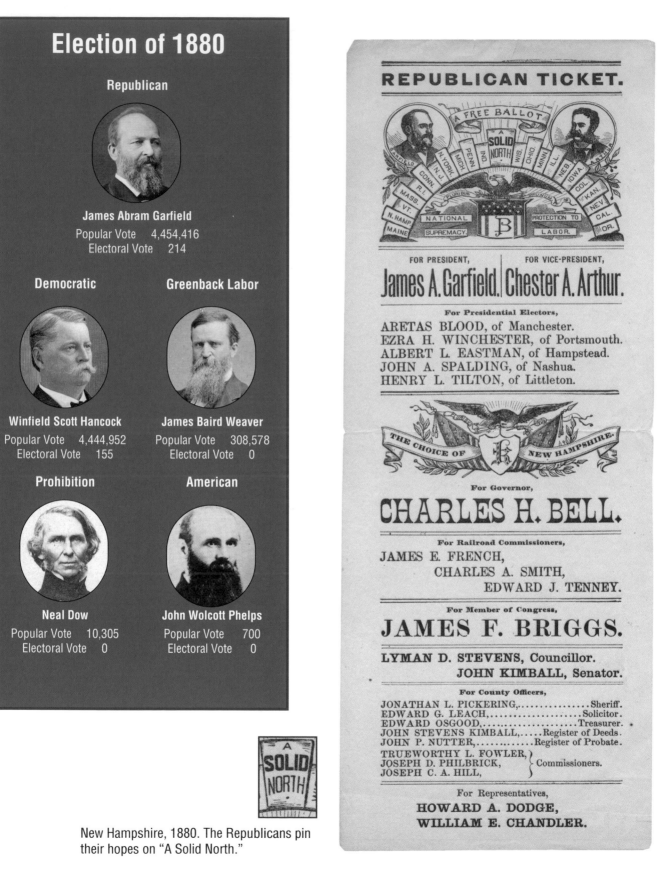

James Abram Garfield

Popular Vote 4,454,416
Electoral Vote 214

Democratic

Winfield Scott Hancock

Popular Vote 4,444,952
Electoral Vote 155

Greenback Labor

James Baird Weaver

Popular Vote 308,578
Electoral Vote 0

Prohibition

Neal Dow

Popular Vote 10,305
Electoral Vote 0

American

John Wolcott Phelps

Popular Vote 700
Electoral Vote 0

New Hampshire, 1880. The Republicans pin their hopes on "A Solid North."

REPUBLICAN TICKET.

A FREE BALLOT
A SOLID NORTH
E PLURIBUS UNUM
NATIONAL SUPREMACY.
PROTECTION TO LABOR.

FOR PRESIDENT,
James A. Garfield.

FOR VICE-PRESIDENT,
Chester A. Arthur.

For Presidential Electors,
ARETAS BLOOD, of Manchester.
EZRA H. WINCHESTER, of Portsmouth.
ALBERT L. EASTMAN, of Hampstead.
JOHN A. SPALDING, of Nashua.
HENRY L. TILTON, of Littleton.

THE CHOICE OF NEW HAMPSHIRE.

For Governor,

CHARLES H. BELL.

For Railroad Commissioners,
JAMES E. FRENCH,
CHARLES A. SMITH,
EDWARD J. TENNEY.

For Member of Congress,

JAMES F. BRIGGS.

LYMAN D. STEVENS, Councillor.
JOHN KIMBALL, Senator.

For County Officers,
JONATHAN L. PICKERING,................Sheriff.
EDWARD G. LEACH,....................Solicitor.
EDWARD OSGOOD,.....................Treasurer.
JOHN STEVENS KIMBALL,.....Register of Deeds.
JOHN P. NUTTER,............Register of Probate.
TRUEWORTHY L. FOWLER,
JOSEPH D. PHILBRICK,   } Commissioners.
JOSEPH C. A. HILL,

For Representatives,
HOWARD A. DODGE,
WILLIAM E. CHANDLER.

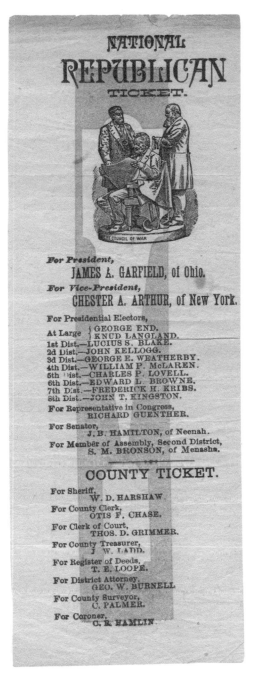

NATIONAL REPUBLICAN TICKET.

For President,
JAMES A. GARFIELD, of Ohio.
For Vice-President,
CHESTER A. ARTHUR, of New York.

For Presidential Electors,
At Large { GEORGE END.
{ KNUD LANGLAND.
1st Dist.—LUCIUS S. BLAKE.
2d Dist.—JOHN KELLOGG.
3d Dist.—GEORGE E. WEATHERBY.
4th Dist.—WILLIAM P. McLAREN.
5th Dist.—CHARLES P. LOVELL.
6th Dist.—EDWARD L. BROWNE.
7th Dist.—FREDERICK H. KRIBS.
8th Dist.—JOHN T. KINGSTON.

For Representative in Congress,
RICHARD GUENTHER.
For Senator,
J. B. HAMILTON, of Neenah.
For Member of Assembly, Second District,
S. M. BRONSON, of Menasha.

COUNTY TICKET.

For Sheriff,
W. D. HARSHAW.
For County Clerk,
OTIS F. CHASE.
For Clerk of Court,
THOS. D. GRIMMER.
For County Treasurer,
J. W. LADD.
For Register of Deeds,
T. E. LOOPE.
For District Attorney,
GEO. W. BURNELL.
For County Surveyor,
C. PALMER.
For Coroner,
C. R. HAMLIN.

Wisconsin, 1880. This unique ballot shows a well-known work by sculptor John Rogers, "The Council of War", a modestly-priced table-top plaster statue with Lincoln, Grant, and Stanton in consultation. These wildly popular "dust-catchers" adorned numerous Victorian homes. There appears to be an exclamation point in the background of the design.

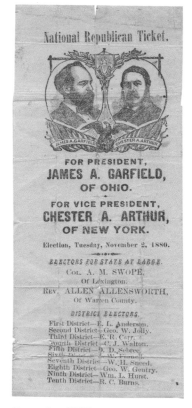

National Republican Ticket.

FOR PRESIDENT,
JAMES A. GARFIELD,
OF OHIO.

FOR VICE PRESIDENT,
CHESTER A. ARTHUR,
OF NEW YORK.

Election, Tuesday, November 2, 1880.

ELECTORS FOR STATE AT LARGE.
COL. A. M. SWOPE,
Of Lexington.
REV. ALLEN ALLENSWORTH,
Of Warren County.

DISTRICT ELECTORS.

First District—E. L. Anderson.
Second District—Geo. W. Jolly.
Third District—E. R. Carr.
Fourth District—C. J. Walton.
Fifth District—D. D. Sebree.
Sixth District—W. P. Powell.
Seventh District—W. H. Sneed.
Eighth District—Geo. W. Gentry.
Ninth District—Wm. L. Hurst.
Tenth District—R. C. Burns.

Kentucky, 1880.

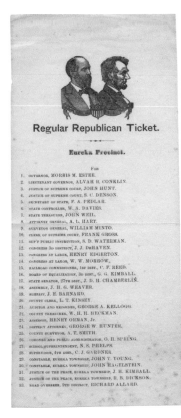

Regular Republican Ticket.

Eureka Precinct.

For
1. GOVERNOR, MORRIS M. ESTEE.
2. LIEUTENANT GOVERNOR, ALVAH R. CONKLIN.
3. JUSTICE OF SUPREME COURT, JOHN HUNT.
4. JUSTICE OF SUPREME COURT, S. C. DENSON.
5. SECRETARY OF STATE, F. A. PEDLAR.
6. STATE CONTROLLER, W. A. DAVIES.
7. STATE TREASURER, JOHN WEIL.
8. ATTORNEY GENERAL, A. L. HART.
9. SURVEYOR GENERAL, WILLIAM MINTO.
10. CLERK OF SUPREME COURT, FRANK GROSS.
11. SUP'T PUBLIC INSTRUCTION, S. D. WATERMAN.
12. CONGRESS 3D DISTRICT, J. J. DEHAVEN.
13. CONGRESS AT LARGE, HENRY EDGERTON.
14. CONGRESS AT LARGE, W. W. MORROW.
15. RAILROAD COMMISSIONER, 1ST DIST., C. F. REED.
16. BOARD OF EQUALIZATION, 3D DIST., G. G. KIMBALL.
17. STATE SENATOR, 27TH DIST., J. D. H. CHAMBERLIN.
18. ASSEMBLY, J. H. G. WEAVER.
19. SHERIFF, J. E. BARNARD.
20. COUNTY CLERK, L. T. KINSEY.
21. AUDITOR AND RECORDER, GEORGE A. KELLOGG.
22. COUNTY TREASURER, W. H. H. BECKMAN.
23. ASSESSOR, HENRY ORMAN, JR.
24. DISTRICT ATTORNEY, GEORGE W. HUNTER.
25. COUNTY SURVEYOR, A. T. SMITH.
26. CORONER AND PUBLIC ADMINISTRATOR, O. H. SPRING.
27. SCHOOL SUPERINTENDENT, N. S. PHELPS.
28. SUPERVISOR, 4TH DIST., C. J. GARDNER.
29. CONSTABLE, EUREKA TOWNSHIP, JOHN T. YOUNG.
30. CONSTABLE, EUREKA TOWNSHIP, JOHN HAGELSTEIN.
31. JUSTICE OF THE PEACE, EUREKA TOWNSHIP, J. H. KIMBALL.
32. JUSTICE OF THE PEACE, EUREKA TOWNSHIP, R. B. DICKSON.
33. ROAD OVERSEER, 9TH DISTRICT, RICHARD ALLARD.

California, 1880.

GARFIELD AND ARTHUR
TEMPERANCE TICKET.

For President,
JAMES A. GARFIELD,
OF OHIO.
For Vice President,
CHESTER A. ARTHUR,
OF NEW YORK.

For Presidential Electors,
AT LARGE,
PAUL A. CHADBOURNE, of Williamstown.
JOHN M. FORBES, of Milton.
1st District, MARSHALL S. UNDERWOOD, of Dennis.
2d " WILLIAM C. LOVERING, of Taunton.
3d " MOODY MERRILL, of Boston.
4th " RUFUS S. FROST, of Chelsea.
5th " AMOS F. BREED, of Lynn.
6th " AUGUSTUS N. CLARK, of Beverly.
7th " FRANCIS JEWETT, of Lowell.
8th " JAMES M. W. HALL, of Cambridge.
9th " CHARLES E. WHITIN, of Northbridge.
10th " WILLIAM B. C. PEARSONS, of Holyoke.
11th " WILLIAM C. PLUNKETT, of Adams.

For Governor,
CHARLES ALMY, of New Bedford.
For Lieutenant-Governor,
TIMOTHY K. EARLE, of Worcester.
For Secretary of the Commonwealth,
SOLOMON F. ROOT, of Dalton.
For Treasurer and Receiver General,
THOMAS J. LOTHROP, of Taunton.
For Auditor,
JONATHAN BUCK, of Harwich.
For Attorney General,
SAMUEL M. FAIRFIELD, of Malden.
For Representative to Congress. First District,
RODNEY FRENCH, of New Bedford.

Massachusetts, 1880. Garfield and Arthur were the Republican nominees. The statewide slate of candidates were supporters of the temperance movement.

REGULAR
CONSERVATIVE DEMOCRATIC TICKET

Election Tuesday November 2nd 1880.

For President
WINFIELD S. HANCOCK
OF PENNSYLVANIA
For Vice President
WILLIAM H. ENGLISH
OF INDIANA

ELECTORS AT LARGE
JOHN ECHOLS of Staunton.
P. W. McKINNEY of Farmville

DISTRICT ELECTORS
1ST THOMAS CROXTON of Essex
2ND LEIGH R. WATTS of Portsmouth
3RD HILL CARTER of Hanover
4TH SAMUEL F. COLEMAN of Cumberland
5TH JAMES S. REDD of Henry
6TH SAMUEL GRIFFIN of Bedford
7TH FRANCIS M. McMULLAN of Greene
8TH J. Y. MENEFEE of Rappahannock
9TH ROBERT R. HENRY of Tazewell

FOR CONGRESS
9TH DISTRICT
CONNALLY F. TRIGG.

Virginia, 1880.

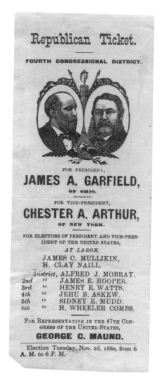

Maryland, 1880.

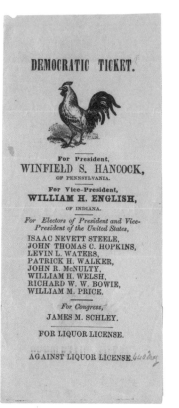

Maryland, 1880. 440 folks voted against the liquor license – a sober group of voters.

New Jersey, 1880. The reverse of a Morgan-style silver dollar indicates "good times ahead."

ELECTORS.

For Electors of President and Vice-President,

CLARENCE A. SEWARD,   JOHN C. CHURCHILL,

DE WITT STAFFORD,   ANDREW WILLIAMS,
WILLIAM H. BEARD,   LESLIE W. RUSSELL,
JOSEPH C. HOAGLAND,   WILLIAM W. WORDEN,
DITMAS JEWELL,   CYRUS B. MARTIN,
WILLIAM B. DINSMORE,   JOHN C. KNOWLTON,
FRANK WORK,   PATRICK H. COSTELLO,
SAMUEL M. SCHAFER,   CHARLES NORTH,
GEORGE F. MERKLEE,   DAVID A. MUNRO,
LE GRAND B. CANNON,   WILLIAM KREUTZER,
JOHN JACOB ASTOR,   ZARA H. BLAKE,
EDWIN D. MORGAN,   WILLIAM H. WAIT,
JOHN B. TREVOR,   AMORY HOUGHTON, JR.,
ALBERT J. AKIN,   HENRY S. HEBARD,
CHARLES ST. JOHN,   HENRY F. TARBOX,
JAMES HARROWAY,   SHERMAN S. JEWETT,
FREDERICK TOWNSEND,   ORSINO E. JONES.
JAMES A. BURDEN,

New York, 1880. This appears to be a ballot and handbill registered with the U.S. Chief Supervisor of Elections in Brooklyn just prior to the election. The flyer criticizes the Democratic nominee, Winfield Hancock, and predicts his election will mean "free trade and low wages, or none at all."

Massachusetts, 1880.

DEMOCRATIC TICKET.

For Electors of President and Vice-President of the United States:
PETER WHITE.
ARCHIBALD McDONELL.
WILLIAM FOXEN.
HIRAM J. BEAKES.
JAMES S. UPTON.
GERMAIN H. MASON.
HORACE B. PECK.
JEROME EDDY.
WILDMAN MILLS.
WILLIAM R. MARSH.
JAMES DEMPSEY.

CONGRESSIONAL TICKET.
For Representative in Congress, Fifth District,
LEONARD H. RANDALL.

STATE TICKET.
For Governor,
FREDERICK M. HOLLOWAY.
For Lieutenant-Governor,
EDWARD H. THOMSON.
For Secretary of State,
WILLARD STEARNS.
For State Treasurer,
ISAAC M. WESTON.
For Auditor-General,
RICHARD MOORE.
For Commissioner of the State Land Office,
JAMES I. DAVID.
For Attorney-General,
HENRY P. HENDERSON.
For Superintendent of Public Instruction,
ZELOTES TRUESDEL.
For Member of the State Board of Education,
ALBERT CRANE.

LEGISLATIVE TICKET.
For State Senator—Twenty-Fifth District,
SAMUEL TOBY.

Michigan, 1880.

Democratic Republican Ticket.

FOR PRESIDENT,
WINFIELD S. HANCOCK
For Vice President,
WILLIAM H. ENGLISH
For Electors of President and Vice President,
GEORGE B. CHANDLER,
JOHN C. MOULTON,
DANIEL MARCY,
FRANK A. McKEAN,
DON H. WOODWARD.
FOR GOVERNOR,
FRANK JONES.
For Railroad Commissioners,
JOSEPH W. GOODWIN,
JOHN W. DODGE,
WILLIAM H. D. COCHRANE.
For Representative in Congress,
JOHN W. SANBORN.
For Councilor—GEORGE W. TASH.
For Senator—JAMES FARRINGTON.
For County Officers,
FRANK P. HODGDON, Register of Deeds.
CHARLES K. HARTFORD, Register of Probate.
CHARLES E. HOITT, Treasurer.
STEPHEN NUTTER, Sheriff.
RUFUS W. NASON, Solicitor.
WILLIAM R GARVIN,
ICHABOD P. BERRY, Commissioners.
JOHN ROBERTS,

New Hampshire, 1880.

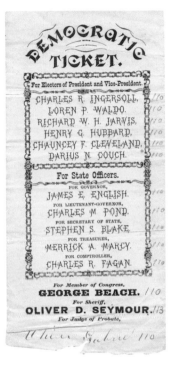

DEMOCRATIC TICKET.

For Electors of President and Vice-President.
CHARLES R. INGERSOLL,
LOREN P. WALDO.
RICHARD W. H. JARVIS,
HENRY G. HUBBARD,
CHAUNCEY F. CLEVELAND,
DARIUS N. COUCH.

For State Officers.
FOR GOVERNOR,
JAMES E. ENGLISH.
FOR LIEUTENANT-GOVERNOR,
CHARLES M POND.
FOR SECRETARY OF STATE,
STEPHEN S. BLAKE.
FOR TREASURER,
MERRICK A. MARCY.
FOR COMPTROLLER,
CHARLES R. FAGAN.

For Member of Congress,
GEORGE BEACH.
For Sheriff,
OLIVER D. SEYMOUR.
For Judge of Probate,

Connecticut, 1880. Darius Couch was a Civil War general and former Governor of Massachusetts who had relocated to the Nutmeg State.

Election of 1884

Democratic

Grover Cleveland
Popular Vote   4,874,986
Electoral Vote   219

Republican

James Gillespie Blaine
Popular Vote   4,851,981
Electoral Vote   182

Greenback / Anti-Monopoly / People's

Benjamin Franklin Butler
Popular Vote   175,370
Electoral Vote   0

Prohibition

John Pierce St. John
Popular Vote   150,369
Electoral Vote   0

Democratic Ticket.

For President of the United States,

Grover Cleveland,
OF NEW YORK.

For Vice-President of the United States,

THOMAS A. HENDRICKS,
OF INDIANA.

For Electors of President and Vice-President,

THOMAS J. KEATING,
BRADLEY T. JOHNSON,
CLEMENT SULIVANE,
PATRICK H. WALKER,
HARRY E. MANN,
SKIPWITH WILMER,
HENRY F. SPALDING,
HENRY H. KEEDY.

For Representative in Congress—Sixth Congressional District,

FREDERICK J. NELSON,
OF FREDERICK COUNTY.

Election—Tuesday, November 4th, 1884.—
Polls open from 8 a. m. till 6 p. m

Maryland, 1884. A dog guarding a safe was an image first used on political items during the administration of Martin Van Buren. During Cleveland's Presidency the government actually accumulated a surplus.

REGULAR DEMOCRATIC TICKET

KILEY, PRINTER, 7 SPRING LANE, BOSTON.

For President, GROVER CLEVELAND, of NEW YORK.
For Vice-President, THOMAS A. HENDRICKS, of INDIANA.

FOR PRESIDENTIAL ELECTORS.   AT LARGE.
JONAS H. FRENCH, of Gloucester. | REUBEN NOBLE, of Westfield. *377*

1 GEORGE DELANO, NEW BEDFORD.
2 BUSHROD MORSE, OF SHARON.
3 FRANCIS A. PETERS, OF BOSTON.
4 HUGH A. MADDEN, OF BOSTON.
5 CHRISTOPHER E. RYMES, OF SOMERVILLE.
6 KNOWLES FREEMAN, CHELSEA.
7 CHARLES P. THOMPSON, OF GLOUCESTER.
8 JOHN C. SANBORN, OF LAWRENCE.
9 JAMES E. COTTER, HYDE PARK.
10 WALDO LINCOLN, OF WORCESTER.
11 FESTUS C. CURRIER, FITCHBURG.
12 ELISHA B. MAYNARD, OF SPRINGFIELD

For Governor,
WILLIAM C. ENDICOTT,   of Salem. *375*
For Lieutenant Governor,
JAMES S. GRINNELL,   of Greenfield. *375*
For Secretary of State,
JEREMIAH CROWLEY,   of Lowell. *370*
For Attorney General,
JOHN W. CUMMINGS,   of Fall River. *373*
For Treasurer and Receiver General,
CHARLES MARSH,   of Springfield. *372*
For Auditor,
JOHN HOPKINS,   of Millbury. *372*
For Representative to Congress,
WILLIAM EVERETT,   of Quincy. *370*
For Councillor,
AUGUSTUS B. ENDICOTT, of Dedham. *375*
For County Commissioner,
JAMES MACKINTOSH,   of Needham. *376*
For Senator,
WILLIAM A. HODGES,   of Quincy. *347*
For Representative,
THOMAS F. LYONS,   of Canton. *338*

Massachusetts, 1884.

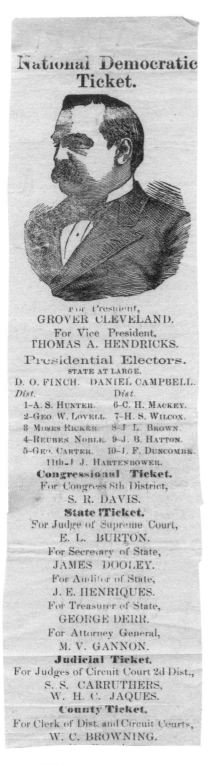

National Democratic Ticket.

For President,
GROVER CLEVELAND.
For Vice President,
THOMAS A. HENDRICKS.

Presidential Electors.
STATE AT LARGE.
D. O. FINCH. DANIEL CAMPBELL.
Dist.   *Dist.*
1–A. S. HUNTER.   6–C. H. MACKEY.
2–GEO. W. LOVELL. 7–H. S. WILCOX.
3–MOSES RICKER   8–J. L. BROWN.
4–REUBEN NOBLE.   9–J. B. HATTON.
5–GEO. CARTER.   10–J. F. DUNCOMBE.
11th–J. J. HARTENBOWER.

Congressional Ticket.
For Congress 8th District,
S. R. DAVIS.

State Ticket.
For Judge of Supreme Court,
E. L. BURTON.
For Secretary of State,
JAMES DOOLEY.
For Auditor of State,
J. E. HENRIQUES.
For Treasurer of State,
GEORGE DERR.
For Attorney General,
M. V. GANNON.

Judicial Ticket.
For Judges of Circuit Court 2d Dist.,
S. S. CARRUTHERS,
W. H. C. JAQUES.

County Ticket.
For Clerk of Dist. and Circuit Courts,
W. C. BROWNING.

Iowa, 1884.

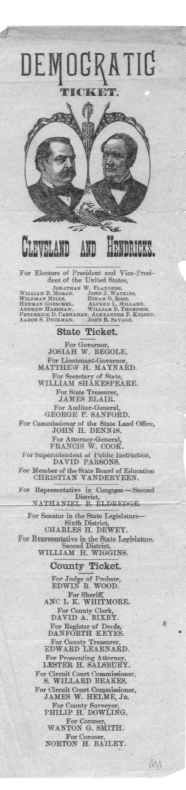

DEMOCRATIC
TICKET.

CLEVELAND AND HENDRICKS.

For Electors of President and Vice-President of the United States,
JONATHAN W. FLANDERS.
WILLIAM B. MORAN.   JOHN J. WATKINS.
WILDMAN MILLS.   HIRAM O. ROSE.
HERMAN GOESCHEL.   ALFRED L. MILLARD.
ANDREW HARSHAW.   WILLIAM D. THOMPSON.
FREDERICK D. CARNAHAN. ALEXANDER F. KELSEY.
AARON S. DYCKMAN.   JOHN R. SAVAGE.

State Ticket.
For Governor,
JOSIAH W. BEGOLE.
For Lieutenant-Governor,
MATTHEW H. MAYNARD.
For Secretary of State,
WILLIAM SHAKESPEARE.
For State Treasurer,
JAMES BLAIR.
For Auditor-General,
GEORGE P. SANFORD.
For Commissioner of the State Land Office,
JOHN H. DENNIS.
For Attorney-General,
FRANCIS W. COOK.
For Superintendent of Public Instruction,
DAVID PARSONS.
For Member of the State Board of Education
CHRISTIAN VANDERVEEN.

For Representative in Congress — Second
District,
NATHANIEL B. ELDREDGE.

For Senator in the State Legislature—
Sixth District,
CHARLES H. DEWEY.
For Representative in the State Legislature,
Second District,
WILLIAM H. WIGGINS.

County Ticket.
For Judge of Probate,
EDWIN B. WOOD.
For Sheriff,
ANC L K. WHITMORE.
For County Clerk,
DAVID A. BIXBY.
For Register of Deeds,
DANFORTH KEYES.
For County Treasurer,
EDWARD LEARNARD.
For Prosecuting Attorney,
LESTER H. SALSBURY.
For Circuit Court Commissioner,
S. WILLARD BEAKES.
For Circuit Court Commissioner,
JAMES W. HELME, JR.
For County Surveyor,
PHILIP H. DOWLING.
For Coroner,
WANTON G. SMITH.
For Coroner,
NORTON H. BAILEY.

Michigan, 1884.

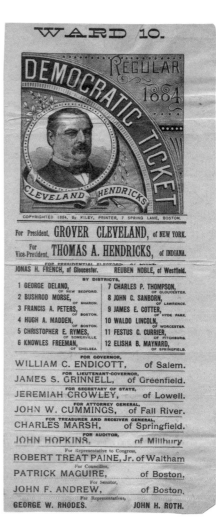

WARD 10.

DEMOCRATIC REGULAR TICKET 1884
CLEVELAND   HENDRICKS

COPYRIGHTED 1884. By KILEY, PRINTER, 7 SPRING LANE, BOSTON.

For President, GROVER CLEVELAND, of NEW YORK.
For Vice-President, THOMAS A. HENDRICKS, of INDIANA.

FOR PRESIDENTIAL ELECTORS AT LARGE,
JONAS H. FRENCH, of Gloucester.   REUBEN NOBLE, of Westfield.

BY DISTRICTS,
1 GEORGE DELANO, OF NEW BEDFORD.   7 CHARLES P. THOMPSON, OF GLOUCESTER.
2 BUSHROD MORSE, OF SHARON.   8 JOHN C. SANBORN, OF LAWRENCE.
3 FRANCIS A. PETERS, OF BOSTON.   9 JAMES E. COTTER, OF HYDE PARK.
4 HUGH A. MADDEN, OF BOSTON.   10 WALDO LINCOLN, OF WORCESTER.
5 CHRISTOPHER E. RYMES, OF SOMERVILLE. 11 FESTUS C. CURRIER, OF FITCHBURG.
6 KNOWLES FREEMAN, OF CHELSEA.   12 ELISHA B. MAYNARD, OF SPRINGFIELD.

FOR GOVERNOR,
WILLIAM C. ENDICOTT,   of Salem.
FOR LIEUTENANT-GOVERNOR,
JAMES S. GRINNELL,   of Greenfield.
FOR SECRETARY OF STATE,
JEREMIAH CROWLEY,   of Lowell.
FOR ATTORNEY GENERAL,
JOHN W. CUMMINGS,   of Fall River.
FOR TREASURER AND RECEIVER GENERAL,
CHARLES MARSH,   of Springfield.
FOR AUDITOR,
JOHN HOPKINS,   of Millbury.
For Representative to Congress,
ROBERT TREAT PAINE, Jr. of Waltham
For Councillor,
PATRICK MAGUIRE,   of Boston.
For Senator,
JOHN F. ANDREW,   of Boston.
For Representatives,
GEORGE W. RHODES.   JOHN H. ROTH.

Massachusetts, 1884.

New Hampshire, 1884.

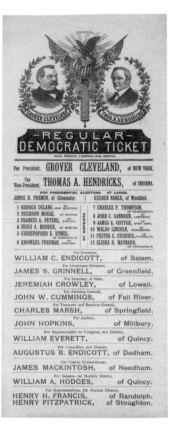

Massachusetts, 1884.

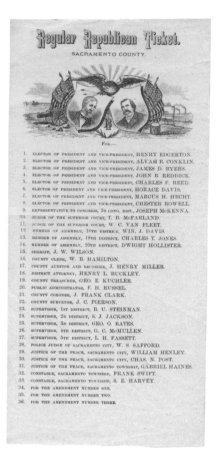

California, 1884.

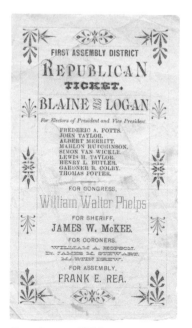

New Jersey, 1884.

Maryland, 1884. This ballot employs a very old woodcut dating back to the Mexican-American War.

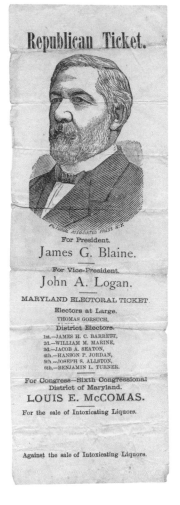

Maryland, 1884.

Kansas, 1884.

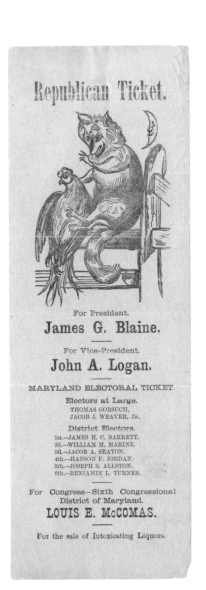

Maryland, 1884. The Republicans saw themselves as the heirs to the old Whig principles and used this circa 1844 woodcut as their motif. It depicts the Whig racoon mascot choking the Democratic rooster.

Election of 1888

Republican

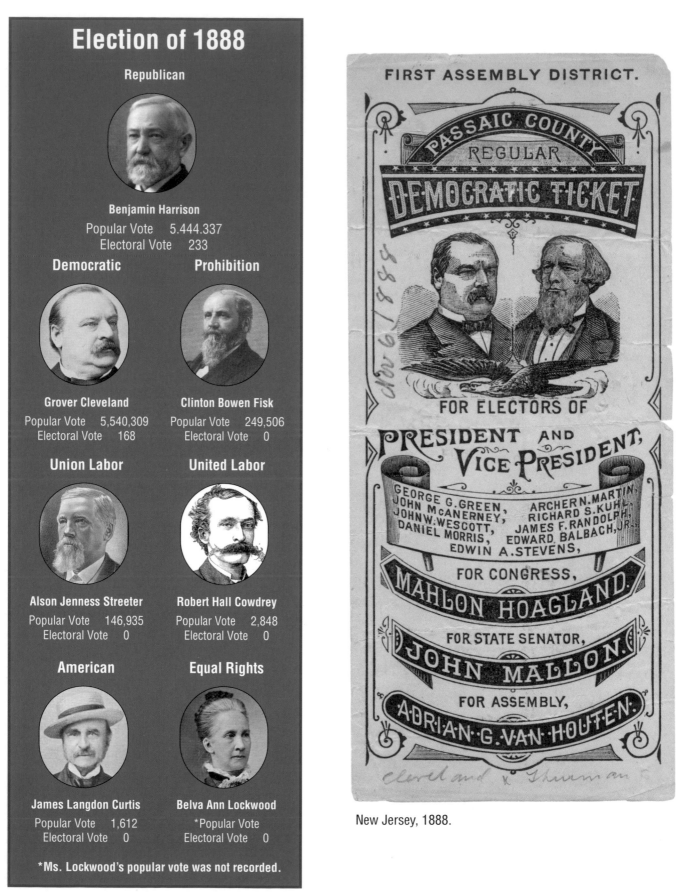

Benjamin Harrison

Popular Vote   5.444.337
Electoral Vote   233

Democratic

Grover Cleveland

Popular Vote   5,540,309
Electoral Vote   168

Prohibition

Clinton Bowen Fisk

Popular Vote   249,506
Electoral Vote   0

Union Labor

Alson Jenness Streeter

Popular Vote   146,935
Electoral Vote   0

United Labor

Robert Hall Cowdrey

Popular Vote   2,848
Electoral Vote   0

American

James Langdon Curtis

Popular Vote   1,612
Electoral Vote   0

Equal Rights

Belva Ann Lockwood

*Popular Vote
Electoral Vote   0

*Ms. Lockwood's popular vote was not recorded.

New Jersey, 1888.

REGULAR Democratic TICKET

JP.KEEN·CO.INC

SALEM, Nov. 6, 1888.
We hereby certify that this is the regular ballot of the Democratic Party of the City of Salem.

JAMES F. DEAN, Chairman.
JOHN O'REGAN, Secretary.
NATHAN R. MORSE, Treasurer.

CLEVELAND AND THURMAN.

FOR PRESIDENTIAL ELECTORS, AT LARGE,
JOHN BOYLE O'REILLY, of Boston ‖ GEORGE M. STEARNS, of Chicopee

BY DISTRICTS,

1 THOMAS C. DAY,	OF BARNSTABLE.	7 JAMES F. DEAN,	OF SALEM.
2 BUSHROD MORSE,	OF SHARON.	8 JOHN C. SANBORN,	OF LAWRENCE.
3 NATHAN MATTHEWS, Jr.,	OF BOSTON.	9 WILLIAM ASPINWALL,	OF BROOKLINE.
4 MATTHEW KEANEY,	OF BOSTON.	10 EDWARD W. LINCOLN,	OF WORCESTER.
5 CHARLES H. TAYLOR,	OF BOSTON.	11 FREDERIC S. COOLIDGE,	OF ASHBURNHAM.
6 HENRY BRADLEE,	OF MEDFORD.	12 WALTER CUTTING,	PITTSFIELD.

FOR GOVERNOR,
WILLIAM E. RUSSELL, of Cambridge

FOR LIEUTENANT-GOVERNOR,
JOHN W. CORCORAN, of Clinton

FOR SECRETARY OF THE COMMONWEALTH,
WILLIAM N. OSGOOD, of Boston

FOR TREASURER AND RECEIVER GENERAL,
HENRY C. THACHER, of Yarmouth

FOR AUDITOR,
WILLIAM A. WILLIAMS, of Worcester

FOR ATTORNEY GENERAL,
SAMUEL O. LAMB, of Greenfield

FOR REGISTER OF DEEDS,
CHARLES S. OSGOOD, of Salem

FOR REGISTER OF PROBATE AND INSOLVENCY,
JEREMIAH T. MAHONEY, of Salem

FOR COUNTY TREASURER,
JAMES F. GWINN, of Hamilton

FOR COUNTY COMMISSIONER,
CHARLES A. MAXWELL, of Haverhill

FOR REPRESENTATIVE TO CONGRESS—SEVENTH DISTRICT,
SAMUEL ROADS, Jr., of Marblehead

FOR COUNCILLOR—FIFTH DISTRICT,
WILLIAM STOPFORD, of Beverly

FOR SENATOR—SECOND ESSEX DISTRICT,
LAWRENCE E. MILLEA, of Salem

FOR REPRESENTATIVE TO THE GENERAL COURT—FOURTEENTH DISTRICT,
WILLIAM PERRY, of Salem

Massachusetts, 1888.

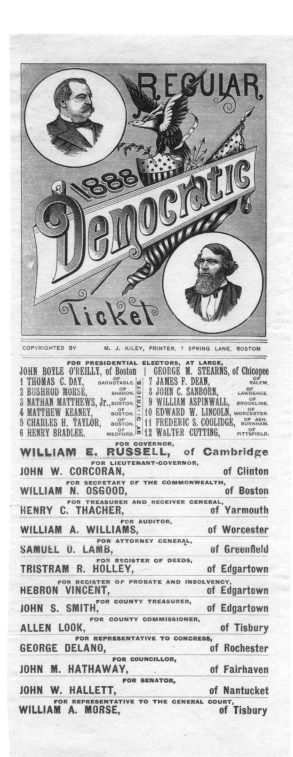

REGULAR 1888 Democratic Ticket

COPYRIGHTED BY M. J. KILEY, PRINTER, 7 SPRING LANE, BOSTON

FOR PRESIDENTIAL ELECTORS, AT LARGE,
JOHN BOYLE O'REILLY, of Boston ｜ GEORGE M. STEARNS, of Chicopee

1 THOMAS C. DAY,	OF BARNSTABLE.	7 JAMES F. DEAN,	OF SALEM.
2 BUSHROD MORSE,	OF SHARON.	8 JOHN C. SANBORN,	OF LAWRENCE.
3 NATHAN MATTHEWS, Jr.,	OF BOSTON.	9 WILLIAM ASPINWALL,	OF BROOKLINE.
4 MATTHEW KEANEY,	OF BOSTON.	10 EDWARD W. LINCOLN,	OF WORCESTER.
5 CHARLES H. TAYLOR,	OF MEDFORD.	11 FREDERIC S. COOLIDGE,	OF ASHBURNHAM.
6 HENRY BRADLEE,	OF MEDFORD.	12 WALTER CUTTING,	PITTSFIELD.

FOR GOVERNOR,
WILLIAM E. RUSSELL, of Cambridge

FOR LIEUTENANT-GOVERNOR,
JOHN W. CORCORAN, of Clinton

FOR SECRETARY OF THE COMMONWEALTH,
WILLIAM N. OSGOOD, of Boston

FOR TREASURER AND RECEIVER GENERAL,
HENRY C. THACHER, of Yarmouth

FOR AUDITOR,
WILLIAM A. WILLIAMS, of Worcester

FOR ATTORNEY GENERAL,
SAMUEL O. LAMB, of Greenfield

FOR REGISTER OF DEEDS,
TRISTRAM R. HOLLEY, of Edgartown

FOR REGISTER OF PROBATE AND INSOLVENCY,
HEBRON VINCENT, of Edgartown

FOR COUNTY TREASURER,
JOHN S. SMITH, of Edgartown

FOR COUNTY COMMISSIONER,
ALLEN LOOK, of Tisbury

FOR REPRESENTATIVE TO CONGRESS,
GEORGE DELANO, of Rochester

FOR COUNCILLOR,
JOHN M. HATHAWAY, of Fairhaven

FOR SENATOR,
JOHN W. HALLETT, of Nantucket

FOR REPRESENTATIVE TO THE GENERAL COURT,
WILLIAM A. MORSE, of Tisbury

Massachusetts, 1888.

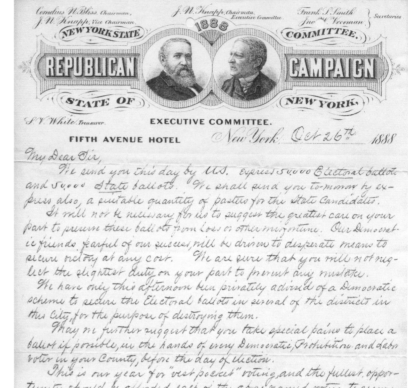

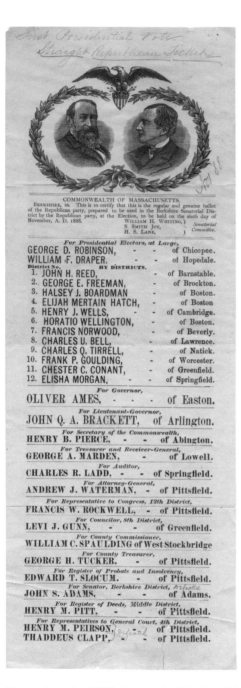

Massachusetts, 1888. As noted at the top, this was retained as a souvenir by a first-time voter. The first Presidential Elector listed, George D. Robinson, was for the defense counsel who won an aquittal for the infamous Lizzie Borden.

This communique from the Republican Executive Committee of New York, transmitting "50,000 Electoral ballots and 50,000 State ballots," accuses the Democrats of attempting to destroy Republican ballots and otherwise disrupt the election. It also suggests that the recipient engage in "vest pocket voting" – that is, handing out Republican ballots to prospective opposition voters before they reach the polls.

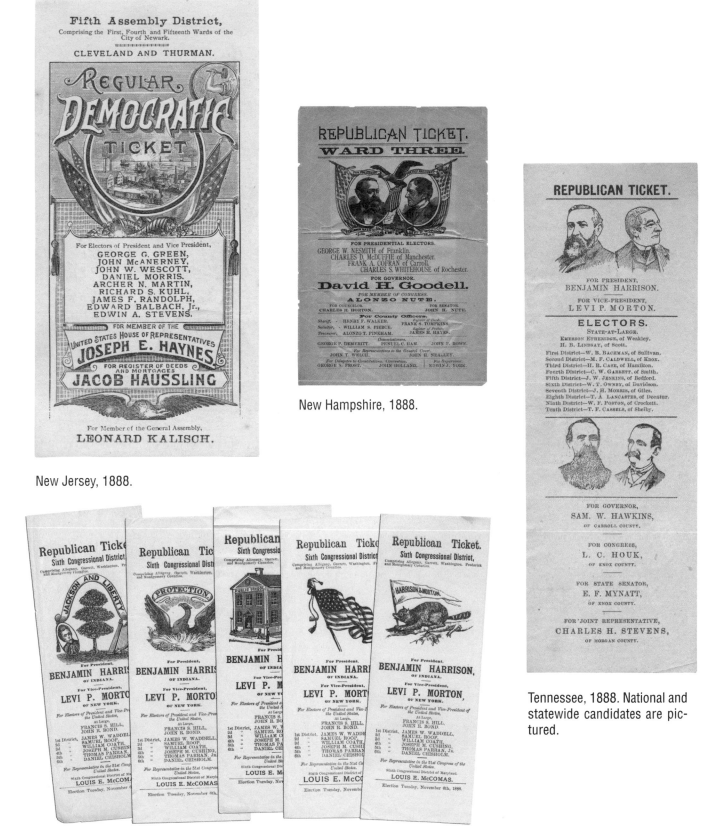

Fifth Assembly District,
Comprising the First, Fourth and Fifteenth Wards of the
City of Newark.

CLEVELAND AND THURMAN.

REGULAR DEMOCRATIC TICKET

For Electors of President and Vice President,
GEORGE G. GREEN,
JOHN McANERNEY,
JOHN W. WESCOTT,
DANIEL MORRIS,
ARCHER N. MARTIN,
RICHARD S. KUHL,
JAMES F. RANDOLPH,
EDWARD BALBACH, Jr.,
EDWIN A. STEVENS.

FOR MEMBER OF THE
UNITED STATES HOUSE OF REPRESENTATIVES
JOSEPH E. HAYNES,

FOR REGISTER OF DEEDS
AND MORTGAGES
JACOB HAUSSLING

For Member of the General Assembly,
LEONARD KALISCH.

New Jersey, 1888.

REPUBLICAN TICKET.
WARD THREE.

FOR PRESIDENTIAL ELECTORS.
GEORGE W. NESMITH of Franklin.
CHARLES D. McDUFFIE of Manchester.
FRANK A. COFRAN of Carroll.
CHARLES S. WHITEHOUSE of Rochester.
FOR GOVERNOR,
David H. Goodell.
FOR MEMBER OF CONGRESS,
ALONZO NUTE.

New Hampshire, 1888.

REPUBLICAN TICKET.

FOR PRESIDENT,
BENJAMIN HARRISON.

FOR VICE-PRESIDENT,
LEVI P. MORTON.

ELECTORS.
STATE-AT-LARGE.
EMERSON ETHERIDGE, of Weakley.
H. B. LINDSAY, of Scott.

First District—W. B. BACHMAN, of Sullivan.
Second District—M. F. CALDWELL, of Knox.
Third District—H. B. CASE, of Hamilton.
Fourth District—C. W. GARRETT, of Smith.
Fifth District—J. W. JENKINS, of Bedford.
Sixth District—W. T. OWNBY, of Davidson.
Seventh District—J. H. MORRIS, of Giles.
Eighth District—T. A. LANCASTER, of Decatur.
Ninth District—W. F. POSTON, of Crockett.
Tenth District—T. F. CASSELS, of Shelby.

FOR GOVERNOR,
SAM. W. HAWKINS,
OF CARROLL COUNTY.

FOR CONGRESS,
L. C. HOUK,
OF KNOX COUNTY.

FOR STATE SENATOR,
E. F. MYNATT,
OF KNOX COUNTY.

FOR JOINT REPRESENTATIVE,
CHARLES H. STEVENS,
OF MORGAN COUNTY.

Tennessee, 1888. National and statewide candidates are pictured.

Republican Ticket
Sixth Congressional District.

For President,
BENJAMIN HARRISON
OF INDIANA.

For Vice-President,
LEVI P. MORTON,
OF NEW YORK.

Sixth Congressional District of Maryland.
LOUIS E. McCOMAS.

Election Tuesday, November 6th, 1888.

Maryland, 1888.

Nine

Third Parties: A Quixotic Quest

"Supremacy of the Laws."

WIRT

ANTIMASONIC REPUBLICAN TICKET

FOR

Electors of President and Vice President.

ELECTOR AT LARGE,
JOHN D. WILLIAMS, *of Suffolk.*
Suffolk District,
JACOB HALL, *of Boston.*
Norfolk,
JOHN BAILEY, *of Dorchester.*
Bristol,
JOSEPH RICKETSON, *of New Bedford.*
Essex South,
WILLIAM B. BREED, *of Lynn.*
Essex North,
THOMAS PAYSON, *of Rowley.*
Middlesex,
BENJAMIN WYMAN, *of Woburn.*
Hampden,
JOHN CHAFFEE, *of Springfield.*
Franklin,
ASA STEBBINS, *of Deerfield.*
Barnstable,
BENJAMIN HALLETT, *of Barnstable.*
Plymouth,
ZECHARIAH EDDY, *of Middleborough.*
Worcester South,
PLINY MERRICK, *of Worcester.*
Worcester North,
STEPHEN P. GARDNER, *of Bolton.*
Berkshire,
JAMES W. ROBBINS, *of Lenox.*

FOR GOVERNOR,
Hon. **SAMUEL LATHROP.**

FOR LIEUT. GOVERNOR,
Hon. **TIMOTHY FULLER.**

FOR SENATORS,
John Bailey,
George Hawes,
Christopher Webb.

Massachusetts, 1832. William Wirt, former Attorney General of the U.S. under Andrew Jackson, carried Vermont in this election. His party won two governorships and fifty-three House seats, but quickly faded from view.

"We'd all like to vote for the best man, but he's never a candidate."

–Frank McKinney "Kin" Hubbard

"Everything is changing. People are taking their comedians seriously and the politicians as a joke."

–Will Rogers

The American electoral landscape has changed immeasurably since 1789. We quickly progressed from a single party to a two-party system, and while the two parties occasionally changed their names they never changed their stripes. Despite perodic changes they almost always solidly represented the political center. Dissatisfaction with this status quo has spasmodically given rise to viable third parties. The first was the Anti-Masonic Party which nominated William Wirt for the 1832 presidential election. Even though several of our early presidents were Freemasons, many citizens viewed Masons – not to mention the plethora of other secret societies – as suspect and nefarious. The sensational 1826 New York murder of William Morgan, who had threatened to publish and thus divulge secret Masonic rituals, precipitated enough outrage to create this new political party. Wirt had a poor showing at the polls. The conspiracy-minded Anti-Masons quickly disappeared back into the landscape, so much so that Andrew Jackson – a Mason – was elected in 1832. But the Anti-Masons have the distinction of having held America's first national nominating convention. Fringe movements have not infrequently spawned great ideas later appropriated by the political establishment.

LIBERTY TICKET.

For President
JAMES G BIRNEY of Michigan

For Vice President
THOMAS MORRIS of Ohio

For Senatorial Electors
Samuel Lewis of Hamilton county
James H Paine of Lake county

1st District	John Matson
2d "	Joseph Howell
3d "	James Morrow
4th "	John T Stewart
5th "	Alex'r Templeton
6th "	Joshua Maynard
7th "	William Keys
8th "	Robert Stewart
9th "	Hugh C Stewart
10th "	Lewi W Knowlton
11th "	Allen McNeil
12th "	William Blackstone
13th "	David Putnam Jr
14th "	Peter B Sarchet
15th "	William Watters
16th "	Luther Boyd
17th "	Jacob Heaton
18th "	Robert Taggart
19th "	Augustus Fuller
20th "	Lucretius Bissell
21st "	Tench C Stiles

Ohio, 1840. The first anti-slavery party to run in a presidential election.

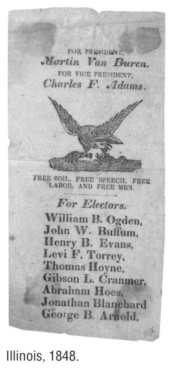

FOR PRESIDENT,
Martin Van Buren.
FOR VICE PRESIDENT,
Charles F. Adams.

FREE SOIL, FREE SPEECH, FREE LABOR, AND FREE MEN.

For Electors.
William B. Ogden,
John W. Buffum,
Henry B. Evans,
Levi F. Torrey,
Thomas Hoyne,
Gibson L. Cranmer,
Abraham Hoes,
Jonathan Blanchard
George B. Arnold.

Illinois, 1848.

Free Soil Democratic Ticket!!

VAN BUREN & ADAMS.

For Electors of President and Vice President.

ELECTORS AT LARGE.
SAMUEL HOAR, of Concord,
WILLIAM JACKSON, of Newton.

Dist. No. 1. JOSEPH WILLARD, of Boston,
    2. JOHN B. ALLEY, of Lynn,
    3. JOHN G. WHITTIER, of Amesbury,
    4. NATHAN BROOKS, of Concord,
    5. ALEXANDER DE WITT, of Worcester,
    6. JAMES FOWLER, of Westfield,
    7. THOMAS ROBINSON, of Adams,
    8. BENJAMIN V. FRENCH, of Braintree,
    9. PHILO LEACH, of Bridgewater,
    10. ISAAC C. TABER, of New Bedford.

Massachusetts, 1848. Once again, John Greenleaf Whitter is listed as a Presidential Elector – the poet and abolitionist was active in politics for many years .

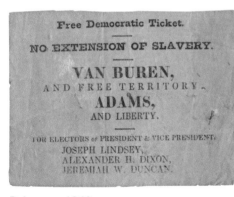

Free Democratic Ticket.

NO EXTENSION OF SLAVERY.

VAN BUREN,
AND FREE TERRITORY.

ADAMS,
AND LIBERTY.

FOR ELECTORS OF PRESIDENT & VICE PRESIDENT.
JOSEPH LINDSEY,
ALEXANDER H. DIXON,
JEREMIAH W. DUNCAN.

Delaware, 1848.

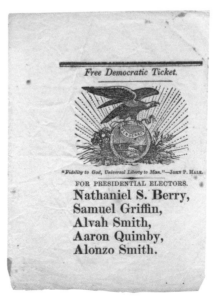

Free Democratic Ticket.

"Fidelity to God, Universal Liberty to Man."—JOHN P. HALE.

FOR PRESIDENTIAL ELECTORS.
**Nathaniel S. Berry,
Samuel Griffin,
Alvah Smith,
Aaron Quimby,
Alonzo Smith.**

New Hampshire, 1852. John P. Hale was the standard bearer of the Free Soil Party that year.

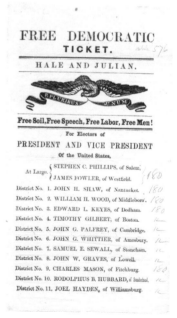

FREE DEMOCRATIC
TICKET.

HALE AND JULIAN.

E PLURIBUS UNUM

Free Soil, Free Speech, Free Labor, Free Men!

For Electors of
PRESIDENT AND VICE PRESIDENT
Of the United States,

At Large. {	STEPHEN C. PHILLIPS, of Salem,
	JAMES FOWLER, of Westfield,
District No. 1.	JOHN H. SHAW, of Nantucket,
District No. 2.	WILLIAM H. WOOD, of Middleboro',
District No. 3.	EDWARD L. KEYES, of Dedham,
District No. 4.	TIMOTHY GILBERT, of Boston,
District No. 5.	JOHN G. PALFREY, of Cambridge,
District No. 6.	JOHN G. WHITTIER, of Amesbury,
District No. 7.	SAMUEL E. SEWALL, of Stoneham,
District No. 8.	JOHN W. GRAVES, of Lowell,
District No. 9.	CHARLES MASON, of Fitchburg,
District No. 10.	RODOLPHUS B. HUBBARD, of Boston,
District No. 11.	JOEL HAYDEN, of Williamsburg,

Massachusetts, 1852. Hale got 22% of the vote in Massachusetts and 155,825 votes nationwide.

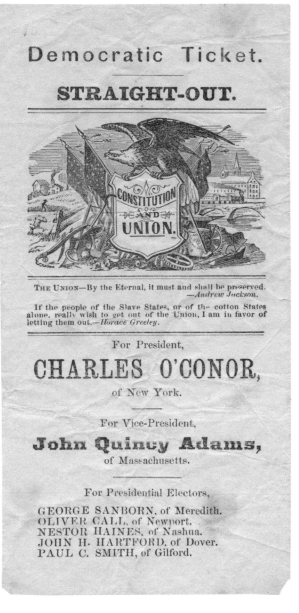

Democratic Ticket.

STRAIGHT-OUT.

CONSTITUTION AND UNION.

THE UNION—By the Eternal, it must and shall be preserved.
—*Andrew Jackson.*

If the people of the Slave States, or of the cotton States alone, really wish to get out of the Union, I am in favor of letting them out.—*Horace Greeley.*

For President,

CHARLES O'CONOR,

of New York.

For Vice-President,

John Quincy Adams,

of Massachusetts.

For Presidential Electors,

GEORGE SANBORN, of Meredith.
OLIVER CALL, of Newport.
NESTOR HAINES, of Nashua.
JOHN H. HARTFORD, of Dover.
PAUL C. SMITH, of Gilford.

New Hampshire, 1872. The Straight-out Democrats reprint a quote from Horace Greeley, made at the time of the secession crisis in order to discredit him. Greeley was also criticized for donating bail money to help free imprisoned ex-Confederate President Jefferson Davis in 1867.

Some third parties existed for but a single election, such as the Anti-Masons (1832) and the Constitutional Union Party (1860). Some managed to last for two elections, such as the Liberty Party (1840, 1844) and the Free Soil Party (1848, 1852). Some have had greater staying power, such as the Socialists. The hoariest of current third parties is the Prohibitionists who organized in 1872 and have fielded slates of candidates ever since. Often parties will merge or "morph" as the situation demands: the Republican Party, born in 1854, absorbed adherents from the Liberty, Free Soil, Whig and American (Know Nothing) Parties; the Populist or People's Party inherited members from the National Greenback Labor Party, but following one electoral defeat after another, eventually returned to the fold of the Democratic Party.

Occasionally disagreement over a candidate or a platform has caused a schism in a mainstream party and created a new one. Democrat Martin Van Buren, disappointed in not receiving his party's nomination in 1844 and unhappy with 1848 standard bearer Lewis Cass, chose to run as the Free Soil candidate in 1848. A former "loco-foco," he represented the "Barnburner" faction of the Democratic Party, as opposed to the "Hunkers" (somewhat arcane we admit, but when have New York politics ever been easy to understand?). In 1872 conservative Democrats – displeased when Horace Greeley was nominated by both the Liberal Republican *and* Democratic parties – split off and nominated Charles O'Conor as the Straight Democratic candidate. 1872 also witnessed the rise of the National Equal Rights Party which nominated Victoria Woodhull and Frederick Douglass as its standard bearers. Woodhull was the first woman to run for President and even though her chances were "slim to none," she made a statement that has resonated with time. Her policy of women's suffrage and equal rights was ulti-

National Democratic Ticket.

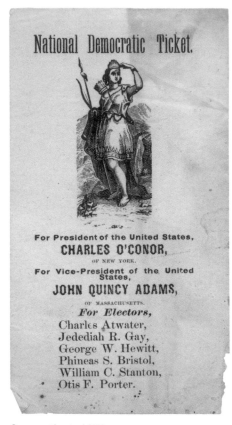

For President of the United States,
CHARLES O'CONOR,
OF NEW YORK.
For Vice-President of the United States,
JOHN QUINCY ADAMS,
OF MASSACHUSETTS.
For Electors,
Charles Atwater,
Jedediah R. Gay,
George W. Hewitt,
Phineas S. Bristol,
William C. Stanton,
Otis F. Porter.

Connecticut, 1872.

NATIONAL
PROHIBITION TICKET.

For President of the United States,
JAMES BLACK,
Of Pennsylvania.

For Vice President of the United States,
JOHN RUSSELL,
Of Michigan.

For Presidential Electors,
SAMUEL E. ADAMS, } Electors
CHARLES H. DeWOLF, } at large.
[District Electors:]
1. CHARLES W. EVANS.
2. JOSHUA WADSWORTH.
3. WILLIAM L. COOK.
4. PETER M. WEDDELL.
5. WILLIAM H. HARRIS.
6. JOHN S. MAHER.
7. ALONZO LOKEY.
8. JAMES W. HORTON.
9. LYMAN POTTER.
10. JEROME W. HENDERSON.
11. ENOCH G. COLLINS.
12. JOSEPH HELMICK.
13. J. P. DARLING.
14. ROBERT LOCKHART.
15. ISAAC PARKER.
16. DAVID H. TWEEDY.
17. RICHARD BROWN.
18. DR. MILO MOODY.
19. REV. W. F. MILLIKIN.
20. JAY ODELL.

Ohio, 1872. This was the first year in which the Prohibition Party ran candidates.

For President,
PETER COOPER.
For Vice President,
SAMUEL F. CARY.

SIDNEY MYERS,   A. J. STREETER,
JAMES W. SINGLETON, H. K. DAVIS,
ANDREW J. GROVER,   JOHN McCONNELL,
A. C. CAMERON,   THOMAS SNELL,
H. B. BURRITT,   JESSE HARPER,
S. M. SLADE,   CHARLES VORIS,
J. M. KING,   ROLLA B. HENRY,
S. M. SMITH,   JOHN HINCHCLIFFE,
JOHN M. THOMPSON,   S. I. DAVIS,
JAMES G. BAYNE,   JOHN LANDRIGAN.
H. CHRISTMAN,

For Governor,
LEWIS STEWARD.

For Lieutenant Governor,
JAMES H. PICKRELL,

For Secretary of State,
M. M. HOOTON,

For Auditor of Public Accounts,
JOHN HISE.

For State Treasurer,
HENRY T. ASPERN.

For Attorney General,
WINFIELD S. COY.

For Member of Congress,
STEPHEN A. HURLBUT

For Member of State Board of Equalization.
MOSES DEAN

For Representative in the General Assembly.
ANDREW ASHTON.
THREE VOTES.

For Clerk of the Circuit Court,
H. C. DeMUNN.

For States' Attorney,
WALES W. WOOD.

For Sheriff,
SIMEON L. COVEY.

For Coroner,
GEORGE WILLIAMSON.

Illinois, 1876. Peter Cooper, an 86 year-old millionaire, ran as the standard bearer of the Greenback Party. He remains the oldest candidate ever put forward by a significant political party.

AMERICAN PARTY TICKET.
FOR PRESIDENT,
JAMES B. WALKER of Illinois.
FOR VICE PRESIDENT,
DONALD KIRKPATRICK, of New York.
FOR ELECTORS:
At Large, { Samuel W. Abbott,
          { Moses Morse,
1st District, O. Brooks,
2nd   "   Isaac Stearns,
3rd   "   John N. Brown,
4th   "   Jas M. Currier,
5th   "   Joseph Sweetzer,
6th   "   J. G. Smith,
7th   "   Daniel F. Pratt,
8th   "   J. Leadbetter,
9th   "   Henry M. Tower,
10th   "   Nelson Smith,
11th   "   N. S. Dickenson.

Massachusetts, 1876.

INDEPENDENT GREENBACK TICKET!

FOR PRESIDENT,
PETER COOPER.
FOR VICE-PRESIDENT,
SAMUEL F. CARY.

FOR ELECTORS AT LARGE,
Alanson T. Bliss.
Thomas B. Buchanan.

FOR DISTRICT ELECTORS,
1st Dist.—John Wyttenbach.
2d Dist.—Elihu E. Rose.
3d Dist.—Ara E. S. Long.
4th Dist.—Lundsy Acres.
5th Dist.—William J. Howe.
6th Dist.—Samuel Orr.
7th Dist.—James Milleson.
8th Dist.—James W. Alexander.
9th Dist.—Archibald Johnson.
10th Dist.—George Major.
11th Dist.—Samuel P. Martindale.
12th Dist.—James J. Stewart,
13th Dist.—Norris S. Bennett.

Indiana, 1876.

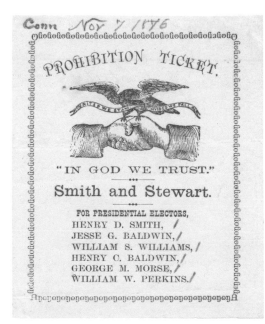

VOTE-AS-YOU-PRAY TICKETS.

GEORGE ELDEN,
Prohibition Candidate
FOR
MEMBER OF ASSEMBLY
THIRD DISTRICT, ONEIDA CO.

A wonderful, and horrible thing is committed in the land. (Jeremiah)

"Let us rise and vote it out
That will put the thing to route".

DWIGHT WILLIAMS.

ASSEMBLY.
THIRD DISTRICT.
For Member of Assembly,
GEORGE ELDEN.

Electors.
For Electors of President and Vice President.
MYRON H. CLARK,
William J. Spence,
Charles C. Leigh,
Henry Hagner,
John W. Hill,
Stephen Merritt,
William H. Barnes,
George R. Tremper,
T. S. Lambert,
S. Robert Newton,
John B. Gibbs,
Thomas Edwards,
Henry Hubble,
Mitchell Downing,
Moses McMonagle,
James O. Merritt,
Horace M. Paine.

JOHN F. HUME,
Robert Band,
Seneca R. Stoddard,
Ira Bell,
James H. Bronson,
George A. Wilson,
Peter Countryman,
George C. Law,
Rensselaer Matteson,
Wallace Kelley,
Jesse M. Frost,
Isaac Hartsen,
Robert J. Ketchum,
John Hermans,
William Hedley,
Linus W. Krahl,
Charles W. Pike.
Brookins J. Servis.

STATE.
For Governor,
WILLIAM J. GROO.
For Lieutenant Governor,
ALBERT F. BROWN.
For Canal Commissioner,
SHOTWELL POWELL
For Inspector of State Prise
ELIAS T. TALBOT
For County Clerk,
JOHN W. PRIDE.
For Sheriff,
DANIEL SMITH.
For Superintendent of Poo
ELLIS ELLIS.
For Coroners,
A. NEWTON TYL
ORIMEL GILLET
For Justice of Sessions,
IRA EDWARDS.

New York, 1876. A variety of tickets issued by the Prohibition Party headed by former Union General Green Clay Smith and Gideon Stewart. The issuers advised the recipients to "Vote As You Pray."

Conn *Nov 7 1876*

PROHIBITION TICKET.

"IN GOD WE TRUST."

Smith and Stewart.

FOR PRESIDENTIAL ELECTORS,
HENRY D. SMITH,
JESSE G. BALDWIN,
WILLIAM S. WILLIAMS,
HENRY C. BALDWIN,
GEORGE M. MORSE,
WILLIAM W. PERKINS.

Connecticut, 1876.

mately vindicated. With ex-slave Frederick Douglass, the great abolitionist orator, as her running-mate, a statement for black rights was made as well. The women's banner was elevated again in 1884 and 1888 when the party nominated suffragette Belva Lockwood.

While third parties have never captured the White House they have definitely affected the outcome of some elections. In 1848 Van Buren took enough votes from Lewis Cass to give New York's electoral vote to Zachary Taylor, costing Cass the election. When the Democrats split into two factions in 1860 – the Northern Democrats nominating Stephen Douglas and the Southern Democrats putting forth John Breckinridge – that, together with John Bell's candidacy on the Constitutional Union Party ticket, so fractured the vote that Abraham Lincoln was elected. Recently Ralph Nader's Green Party effort in 2000 likely cost Al Gore the election.

Third parties have been around for 180 years. While not to everybody's taste, they do speak for a portion of the electorate and they occasionally promulgate some important policy or innovation. If it is indeed true that in America "anyone can become President," third party candidates are obviously firm believers in that adage. ❧

INDEPENDENT GREENBACK TICKET

Electoral Ticket.

For Electors of President and Vice President of the
United States,

At Large—MOSES W. FIELD.
At Large—CHARLES C. COMSTOCK.
First District—RICHARD F. TREVELLICK.
Second District—JOHN McDONOUGH.
Third District—JOHN PEAVEY.
Fourth District—WILBER H. CLUTE.
Fifth District—WILLIAM A. BERKEY.
Sixth District—LYSANDER WOODWARD.
Seventh District—HENRY WHITING.
Eighth District—THOMAS MUNN.
Ninth District—GEORGE W. HOPKINS.

State Ticket.

For Governor,
LEVI SPARKS.
For Lieutenant Governor,
JULIUS HOUSEMAN.
For Secretary of State,
ALBERT STEGEMAN.
For State Treasurer,
JOHN G. PARKHURST.
For Auditor General,
FREDERICK M. HOLLOWAY.
For Commissioner of the State Land Office,
JOHN H. RICHARDSON.
For Attorney General,
ALBERT J. CHAPMAN.
For Superintendent of Public Instruction,
HORACE S. TARBELL.
For Member of the State Board of Education,
ETHAN RAY CLARKE.

Michigan, 1876.

NATIONAL

WEAVER and CHAMBERS.

Greenback-Labor

TICKET.

For Electors for President and Vice President,
ADOLPH DOUAI,
SAMUEL A. DOBBINS,
BENJAMIN F. McCOLLISTER,
ALFRED SATTERTHWAITE,
BENJAMIN URNER,
SAMUEL BARBER,
AUGUST SEMMINDINGER,
AGUR JUDSON,
THOMAS JACOBS.

For Governor,
THOMAS D. HOXSEY.
For Member of House of Representatives,
ERASTUS E. POTTER.
For Surrogate,
JOHN LISTER.
For Member of Assembly, 3d District,
JAMES B. HARRISON.

New Jersey, 1880. James Weaver ran again as the People's Party candidate in 1892 and got over a million popular votes as well as 22 electoral votes. He didn't fare as well in 1880.

NATIONAL GREENBACK-LABOR TICKET.

FOR PRESIDENT,
JAMES B. WEAVER,
Of Iowa.
FOR VICE-PRESIDENT,
BENJAMIN J. CHAMBERS,
Of Texas.

FOR PRESIDENTIAL ELECTORS,

At Large, { EUGENE J. FLAHERTY, of Boston.
{ HERBERT B. ROWLEY, of Shelburne Falls.
District 1,—ALEXANDER HARVEY, of Middleboro.
District 2,—HENRY GARDNER, of Braintree.
District 3,—PETER O'NEIL LARKIN, of Boston.
District 4,—BENJAMIN S. GOODWIN, of Chelsea.
District 5,—JOHN M. DEVINE, of Boston.
District 6,—LUTHER DAY, of Haverhill.
District 7,—HIRAM K. EASTMAN, of Lawrence.
District 8,—THEODORE N. SHERMAN, of Milford.
District 9,—JOHN HOWES, of Worcester.
District 10,—WILLIAM C. JOHNSON, of Fitchburg.
District 11,—THEODORE HESS, of Westfield.

For Governor,
HORACE BINNEY SARGENT,
Of Salem.
For Lieutenant Governor,
GEORGE DUTTON,
Of Springfield.
For Secretary of State,
JONATHAN ARNOLD, of North Abington.
For Treasurer and Receiver General,
WILBUR F. WHITNEY, of Ashburnham.
For Auditor,
CHARLES F. WARNER, of Northampton.
For Attorney General,
ISRAEL W. ANDREWS, of Danvers.
For Representative to Congress, Tenth District,
LEVI STOCKBRIDGE, of Amherst.
For Councillor, Seventh District,
JASON WATERS, of Sutton.
For Commissioners of Insolvency,

For Sheriff,
E. M. ELDRIDGE, of Worcester.
For District Attorney,
H. L. HERSEY, of Charlton.
For County Commissioners,
THORNDIKE LEONARD, of Grafton, 3 s.
DAVID M. FINCH, of Worcester, 2 y.
For Special Commissioners,
HENRY J. SHATTUCK, of Barre.
BENJAMIN B. NOURSE, of Westboro.
For Senator, 4th Worcester District,
LEANDER B. MORSE, of Athol.
For Representative, 9th Worcester District,

Massachusetts, 1880.

WEAVER AND CHAMBERS

GREENBACK NATIONAL TICKET.
For President,
GEN. J. B. WEAVER,
Of Iowa.
For Vice-President,
COL. B. J. CHAMBERS,
Of Texas.

FOR PRESIDENTIAL ELECTORS,
At large, { S. N. WOOD, of Chase.
{ J. J. McFEELEY, of Labett
First Dist—B. O. DRISCOLL, of Mitchelle.
2d Dist—HENRY BRONSON, of Linn.
3rd Dist—J. G. BAYNE, of Harper.

GREENBACK STATE TICKET.
For Governor,
H P VROOMAN, of Greenwood.
For Lieutenant Governor,
H L PHILLIPS, of Miami.
For Secretary of State,
A B CORNELL.
For State Treasurer,
S A MARSHALL, of Leavenworth.
For Auditor of State,
D J COLE, of Reno.
For State Superintendent of Public Instruction,
CHARLES SMITH, of Jefferson.
For Associate Justice of Supreme Court,
D B HADLEY, of Douglas.

For Representative in Congress,
Second Congressional District,
L F GREEN.

COUNTY TICKET.
For Senator, 25d district,
J L SHINN.
For Representative, 54th District,
J BUTTS.
For Sheriff, to Fill Vacancy,
J P HOLMES.
For County Attorney,
W S SOULE.
For District Clerk,
D HITE.
For Probate Judge,
W K HORTON.
For Superintendent of Public Instruction,
A E LEWIS.

Constitutional Amendments.
Constitutional Amendment in regard to a Constitutional Convention.
"FOR—AGAINST—Constitutional Convention.
"FOR—AGAINST—The proposition to amend Section One of Article Eleven of the Constitution of Kansas, "striking out the clause exempting two hundred dollars from taxation."
Constitutional Amendment in regard to the Manufacture and Sale of Intoxicating Liquors
"FOR—AGAINST—The proposition to amend the Constitution."
Proposition for the issuing bonds to obtain a loan.
"FOR—AGAINST—The loan"

NOTE—Voters are particularly requested to observe the forms of voting on the Constitutional Amendments, and erase the proposition they desire to vote against.

Kansas, 1880.

Transmittal envelope for Greenback-Labor (Weaver and Chambers) ballots intended for distribution to party opponents who nevertheless somewhat favored Greenback principles.

New York, October, 1880.

Dear Sir:

In the enclosed Envelope will be found a number of the Electoral and State tickets of the "National Greenback-Labor Party. Please seal and direct it to some political opponent who favors greenback principles, as by so doing much good may be derived at the coming election.

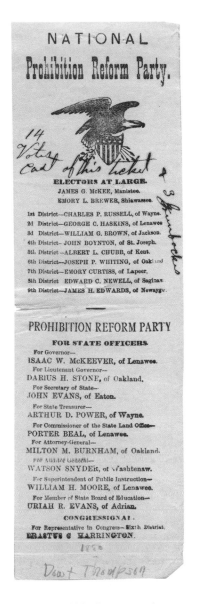

Maryland, 1880.

NATIONAL
Greenback Labor Ticket.

For President, GEN. J. B. WEAVER, of Iowa.
For Vice-President, B. J. CHAMBERS, of Texas.

PRESIDENTIAL ELECTORS.
AT LARGE.
Andrew Royal, of St. Joseph, Mo.
O. H. Baker, of Springfield, Mo.
DISTRICT.
1st—W. G. Church.   2nd—Charles Peterly.
3-Alexander Robbins. 4th—S. R. Burford.
5th—George J. Cowen. 6th—D. N. Thompson.
7th—S. A. Warden.   8th—Silas F. Allen.
9th—J. L. Johnson.   10th—A. S. Cloud.
11th—J. R. Miller.   12th—Thos. L. Anderson.
13th—W. S. Gatewood.

STATE TICKET.
For Governor, LUMAN A. BROWN.
For Lieut., Governor, HOMER F. FELLOWS.
For Secretary of State, O. D. JONES.
For Auditor of State, DR. A. C. MARKIS.
For Treasurer of State, JOHN M. SNEED.
For Attorney-General, A. N. McGINDLEY.
For Judge Supreme Court, PETER E. BLAND.
For Register of Lands, JAMES A. MATTINEE.
For Railroad Comm'r, JESSE P. ALEXANDER.

For Congressman, 12th District,
JOHN M. LONDON, of Macon county.

For Judge 27th Judicial Circuit,
Henry F. Millan
County Ticket
For Representative, GEORGE SHAW.
For Sheriff, JAMES K. P. MORELOCK.
For Treasurer, WILLIAM N. HOPE.
For Collector, DAVID C. LORD.
For Pro's. Attorney, WILLIAM P. LINDER.
For Assessor, FRANK BUCKLEY.
For Surveyor, JOHN MERCER.
For County Judge, 2d District,
JOHN H. RAINIER.
For Public Administrator, NELSON COLE.
For Coroner, A. T. STILL.
For Justice of the Peace————Township.

For Constable————Township.

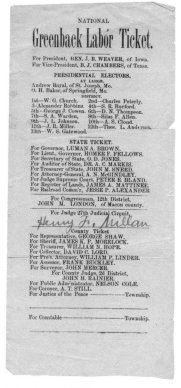

GREENBACK
Labor Ticket.

FOR PRESIDENT:
JAMES B. WEAVER,
OF IOWA.

FOR VICE-PRESIDENT:
B. J. CHAMBERS,
OF TEXAS.

Presidential Electors.
ELECTORS AT LARGE.
S. M. SCHINDELL,
URIEL GRAVES.

DISTRICT ELECTORS.
1st Dist., Howard Meeks.
2nd Dist., J. Henning Jones.
3rd Dist., Charles Luke.
4th Dist., Octavian L. Mathiot.
5th Dist., James Foreman.
6th Dist., Joseph Logsdon.

FOR CONGRESS:
6th Dist., NATHANIEL SENER.

For—Against—The Sale of Spiritons or Fermented Liquors.

Maryland, 1880. A lady is shown operating the latest in household appliances, a wringer washtub, perhaps indicating progress for the working class.

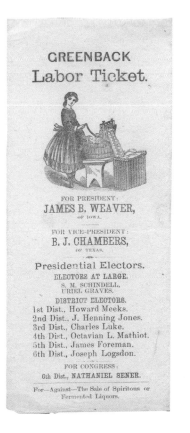

NATIONAL
Prohibition Reform Party.

14 Votes Cast of this ticket

ELECTORS AT LARGE.
JAMES G. McKEE, Manistee.
EMORY L. BREWER, Shiawassee.

1st District—CHARLES P. RUSSELL, of Wayne.
2d District—GEORGE C. HASKINS, of Lenawee.
3d District—WILLIAM G. BROWN, of Jackson.
4th District—JOHN BOYNTON, of St. Joseph.
5th District—ALBERT L. CHUBB, of Kent.
6th District—JOSEPH P. WHITING, of Oakland
7th District—EMORY CURTISS, of Lapeer.
8th District—EDWARD C. NEWELL, of Saginaw.
9th District—JAMES H. EDWARDS, of Newaygo.

PROHIBITION REFORM PARTY
FOR STATE OFFICERS.
For Governor—
ISAAC W. McKEEVER, of Lenawee.
For Lieutenant Governor—
DARIUS H. STONE, of Oakland.
For Secretary of State—
JOHN EVANS, of Eaton.
For State Treasurer—
ARTHUR D. POWER, of Wayne.
For Commissioner of the State Land Office—
PORTER BEAL, of Lenawee.
For Attorney-General—
MILTON M. BURNHAM, of Oakland.
For Auditor General—
WATSON SNYDEr, of Washtenaw.
For Superintendent of Public Instruction—
WILLIAM H. MOORE, of Lenawee.
For Member of State Board of Education—
URIAH R. EVANS, of Adrian.
CONGRESSIONAL.
For Representative in Congress—Sixth District,
ERASTUS G. HARRINGTON.

1880

Doct Thompson

Kansas, 1880. An annotation reveals that Dow got 14 votes and Weaver only 3. Hardly worth the effort!

American Ticket.
OR ANTI-MASONIC PARTY.

1880
PHELPS and POMEROY.

For Electors at Large,
MOSES MORSE, of Reading.
HENRY T. CHEEVER, of Worcester.

By Districts,
1—JAMES BALDWIN, of Provincetown.
2—ISAAC FLAGG, of Dighton.
3—SAMUEL D. GREENE, of Chelsea.
4—JOHN TANNER, of Boston.
5—J. P. ABBOTT, of Medford.
6—DANIEL FOWLER, of Lynfield.
7—JOSHUA FREEMAN, of Lancaster.
8—EDWARD PIERCE, of Wayland.
9—DARWIN BROOKS, of Shrewsbury.
10—GEORGE W. JENKS, of Shelburn Falls.
11—DAVID PRINCE, of Cheshire.

For Representatives to Congress,
1st District, WILLIAM W. CRAPO, of New Bedford.
2d District, JOHN V. SMITH, of North Bridgewater.
Eastern District of Rhode Island,
ALBERT M. PAULL, of Providence.

For Governor,
HENRY T. CHEEVER, of Worcester.

For Lieutenant Governor,
HORACE WOOD, of Boston.

For Secretary of the Commonwealth,
GEORGE H. LINCOLN, of Andover.

For Treasurer and Receiver General,
JOHN T. HATHAWAY, of Walpole.

For Auditor,
MARK SHELDON, of Sharon.

For Attorney General,
GEORGE S. RODMAN, of Boston.

For Councillors,
First District, JAMES C. CROSSLEY, of Pembroke.
Second District, GEORGE T. BRIGGS, of Boston.

For Senator (Third Bristol District),
GEORGE P. RICHMOND, of New Bedford.

Massachusetts, 1880. Little is known about this ticket, but it seems to be a last-gasp revival of the Anti-Masonic and Know Nothing Parties. They received 700 votes.

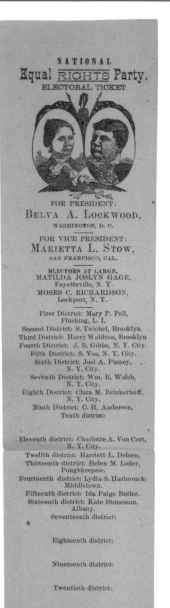

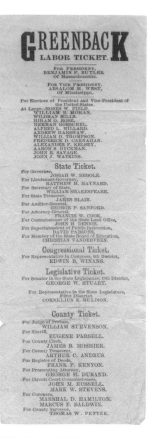

Michigan, 1884.

Massachusetts, 1884.

Kansas, 1884. Butler and West presented themselves as champions of the "National Anti-Monopoly" Party. It's hard to fight the guys with the money, then or now.

New York, 1884. Lockwood and Stow Women's Suffrage Ballot. Belva Lockwood was the second woman to run for president (after Victoria Woodhull). She ran on the "National Equal Rights Party" ticket and actually received votes – primarily from sympathetic male voters. Given the quixotic nature of the campaign and limited finances, very little campaign ephemera was issued to support her candidacy.

(Courtesy the Shlimovitz Collection of Historical Americana.)

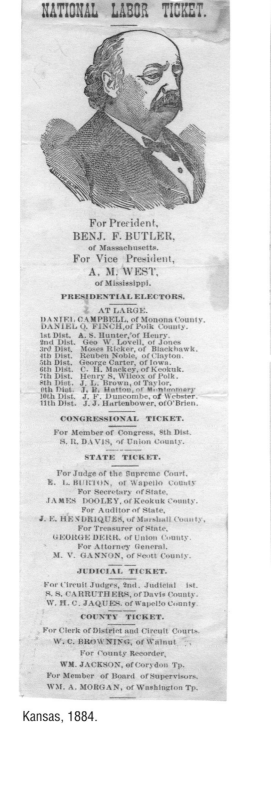

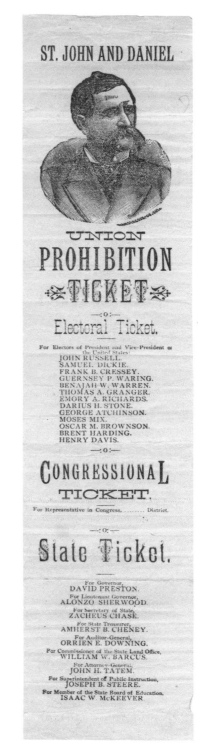

NATIONAL LABOR TICKET.

For President,
BENJ. F. BUTLER,
of Massachusetts.
For Vice President,
A. M. WEST,
of Mississippi.

PRESIDENTIAL ELECTORS,

AT LARGE.
DANIEL CAMPBELL, of Monona County.
DANIEL Q. FINCH, of Polk County.
1st Dist. A. S. Hunter, of Henry.
2nd Dist. Geo W. Lovell, of Jones
3rd Dist. Moses Ricker, of Blackhawk.
4th Dist. Reuben Noble, of Clayton.
5th Dist. George Carter, of Iowa.
6th Dist. C. H. Mackey, of Keokuk.
7th Dist. Henry S. Wilcox of Polk.
8th Dist. J. L. Brown, of Taylor.
9th Dist. J. R. Hutton, of Montgomery
10th Dist. J. F. Duncombe, of Webster.
11th Dist. J. J. Hartenbower, of O'Brien.

CONGRESSIONAL TICKET.

For Member of Congress, 8th Dist.
S. R. DAVIS, of Union County.

STATE TICKET.

For Judge of the Supreme Court,
E. L. BURTON, of Wapello County
For Secretary of State,
JAMES DOOLEY, of Keokuk County.
For Auditor of State,
J. E. HENDRIQUES, of Marshall County,
For Treasurer of State,
GEORGE DERR, of Union County.
For Attorney General,
M. V. GANNON, of Scott County.

JUDICIAL TICKET.

For Circuit Judges, 2nd, Judicial 1st.
S. S. CARRUTHERS, of Davis County.
W. H. C. JAQUES. of Wapello County.

COUNTY TICKET.

For Clerk of District and Circuit Courts,
W. C. BROWNING, of Walnut
For County Recorder,
WM. JACKSON, of Corydon Tp.
For Member of Board of Supervisors,
WM. A. MORGAN, of Washington Tp.

Kansas, 1884.

PEOPLE'S PARTY
★ TICKET. ★

For Presidential Electors,
At { JOHN I. BAKER, - - - - of Beverly
Large { ALBION C. DRINKWATER, of Braintree
By Congressional Districts.
1st Dist. THOMAS B. CHASE, - - of Harwich
2d Dist. WILLIAM L. DOUGLASS, of Brockton
3d Dist. JAMES SUMNER, - - - - of Milton
4th Dist. DENNIS O'REILLY, - - - - of Boston
5th Dist. GILMAN F. JONES, - - of Woburn
6th Dist. HENRY HASTINGS, Jr., - of Medford
7th Dist. HARRY H. HALE, - - of Bradford
8th Dist. JAMES H. CARMICHAEL, - of Lowell
9th Dist. PATRICK J. CONWAY, - of Marlboro'
10th Dist. JOHN FLINT, - - - - - of Webster
11th Dist. WILLIAM O. CROCKER, - of Montague
12th Dist. WILLIAM M. E. MELLEN, of Chicopee

FOR GOVERNOR,
MATTHEW J. McCAFFERTY,
OF WORCESTER.

FOR LIEUTENANT-GOVERNOR,
ALBERT R. RICE,
OF SPRINGFIELD.

For Secretary of the Commonwealth,
JOHN P. SWEENEY, - - - of Lawrence
For Treasurer and Receiver-General,
NATHANIEL S. CUSHING, of Middleboro'
For Auditor,
ISRAEL W. ANDREWS, - - - of Danvers
For Attorney-General,
THOMAS W. CLARKE, - - - of Boston

For Congress, Second District,
EDGAR E. DEAN, ... of Brockton
For Councillor, Second District,
EDWARD HAMILTON, ... of Boston
For County Commissioner,
JAMES MACKINTOSH, . . . of Needham
For Senator, First Norfolk District,
FREDERICK LA FOREST, . of Weymouth
For Representatives to the General Court, Seventh Norfolk District,
WILLIAM W. HURLEY, . . of Randolph

WILLIAM NEALE, ... of Stoughton

Massachusetts, 1884.

ST. JOHN AND DANIEL

UNION
PROHIBITION
★ TICKET ★
—:o:—
Electoral Ticket.

For Electors of President and Vice-President of
the United States:
JOHN RUSSELL.
SAMUEL DICKIE.
FRANK B. CRESSEY.
GUERNSEY P. WARING.
BENAJAH W. WARREN.
THOMAS A. GRANGER.
EMORY A. RICHARDS.
DARIUS H. STONE.
GEORGE ATCHINSON.
MOSES MIX.
OSCAR M. BROWNSON.
BRENT HARDING.
HENRY DAVIS.
—:o:—

CONGRESSIONAL
TICKET.

For Representative in Congress, ... District.

—:o:—

State Ticket.

For Governor,
DAVID PRESTON.
For Lieutenant Governor,
ALONZO SHERWOOD.
For Secretary of State,
ZACHEUS CHASE.
For State Treasurer,
AMHERST B. CHENEY.
For Auditor-General,
ORRIEN E. DOWNING.
For Commissioner of the State Land Office,
WILLIAM W. BARCUS.
For Attorney-General,
JOHN H. TATEM.
For Superintendent of Public Instruction,
JOSEPH B. STEERE.
For Member of the State Board of Education,
ISAAC W. McKEEVER.

Michigan, 1884.

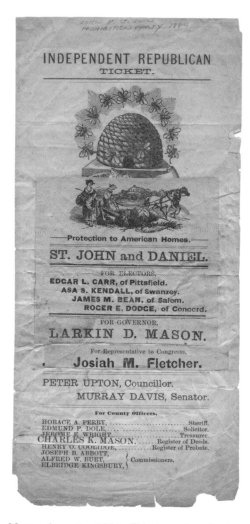

Massachusetts, 1884. This is truly a "split ticket" with local Republican nominees and a paste-down of national Prohibition candidates.

Maryland, 1884.

Massachusetts, 1884.

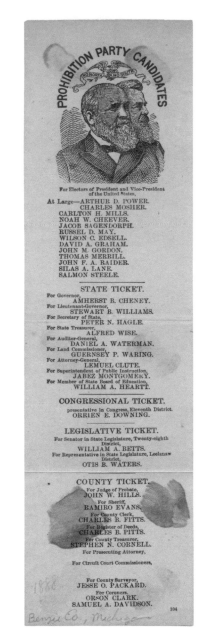

Michigan, 1888.

Kansas Union Labor Ticket.
1888.

For President,
ALSON J. STREETER.

For Vice-President,
C. E. CUNINGHAM.

For Presidential Electors,
At Large { JOHN DAVIS.
{ CYRUS CORNING.

First District, T. D. FRASER.

Second District, D. O. MARKLEY.

Third District, J. L. SHINN.

Fourth District, P. B. MAXSON.

Fifth District, L. G. FRYBARGER.

Sixth District, ALBERT FULLER.

Seventh District, CHARLES RUMSEY.

For Congressman,
First District, ALONZO J. GROVER.

STATE TICKET.

For Governor,
P. P. ELDER.

For Lieutenant Governor,
S. B. TODD.

For Secretary of State,
M. J. ALBRIGHT.

For Auditor of State,
J. H. LATHROP.

For State Treasurer,
SAMUEL NUTT.

For Attorney General,
W. F. RIGHTMIRE.

For Superintendent of Public Instruction,
H. F. HIXSON.

For Associate Justice Supreme Court,
H. A. WHITE.

For State Senator First District,
F. J. CLOSE.

COUNTY TICKET,
For Representative Forty-fourth District,
C. A. SAYLOR.

For Probate Judge,
....

For County Attorney,
....

For Clerk of the District Court,
S. WEAVER.

For Superintendent of Public Instruction,
D. L. WELLER.

For Coroner,
....

For Commissioner ....District.

TOWNSHIP TICKET,
For Trustee,
....

For Township Treasurer,
....

For Township Clerk,
....

For Justice of the Peace,
....

For Constable,
....

For Road Overseer,
District No..............

CONSTITUTIONAL AMENDMENTS.
"FOR the amendment to Section one, Article eight, of the Constitution."
"AGAINST the amendment to Section one, Article eight of the Constitution."
"FOR the proposition to amend Section seventeen of the Bill of Rights of the Constitution of the State of Kansas, concerning the purchase, enjoyment and descent of property."
"AGAINST the proposition to amend Section seventeen of the Bill of Rights of the Constitution of the State of Kansas, concerning the purchase, enjoyment and descent of property."

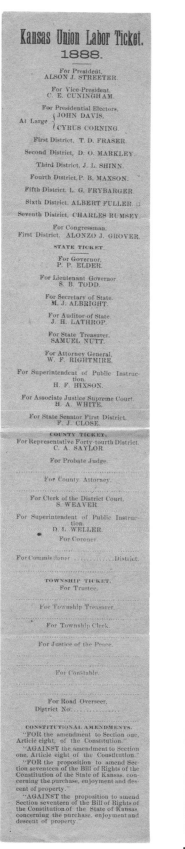

Kansas, 1888.

PROHIBITION TICKET.
FISK and BROOKS.

For Presidential Electors,
At Large,
THOMAS WIGGIN, of Portsmouth
JOHN H. GOODALE, of Nashua

By Congressional Districts,
1st District,
LARKIN D. MASON, of Tamworth
2nd District,
CHARLES H. THORNDIKE, of Concord

For Governor,
EDGAR L. CARR, of Pittsfield

For Councilor,
FRANK K. CHASE, of Dover.

For Representative to Congress,
DANIEL C. KNOWLES, - - of Tilton

For Senator,
JOHN A. FALL, of Somersworth.

For County Officers,
SHERIFF,
WILLIAM M. COURSER.

SOLICITOR,

TREASURER, of Somersworth
WILLIAM H. TASKER.

REGISTER OF DEEDS,
COURTLAND H. TURNER.

REGISTER OF PROBATE,
CHARLES L. MORRISON.

COUNTY COMMISSIONERS,
JOHN BARTLETT,
ALFRED W. JONES,
HIRAM FELKER.

New Hampshire, 1888.

UNION
LABOR TICKET.

For President,
ALSON J. STREETER,
of Illinois.

For Vice President,
CHARLES E. CUNNINGHAM,
of Arkansas.

For Electors,
GEORGE CARPENTER,
of Swanzey.

ELIAS M. BLODGETT,
of Wentworth.

JOHN F. WOODBURY,
of Manchester.

NATHANIEL WIGGIN,
of Portsmouth.

For Member of Congress,
JARED I. WILLIAMS,
of Lancaster.

New Hampshire, 1888.

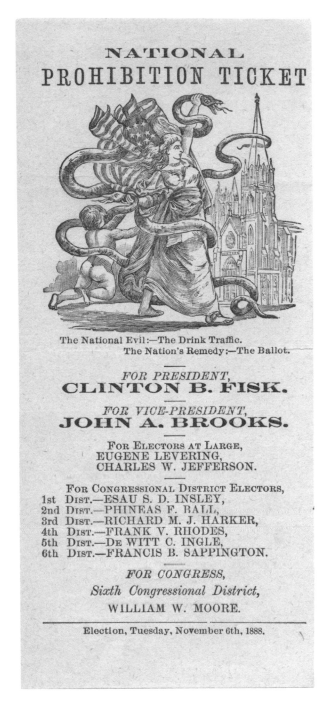

NATIONAL
PROHIBITION TICKET

The National Evil:—The Drink Traffic.
The Nation's Remedy:—The Ballot.

FOR PRESIDENT,
CLINTON B. FISK.

FOR VICE-PRESIDENT,
JOHN A. BROOKS.

FOR ELECTORS AT LARGE,
EUGENE LEVERING,
CHARLES W. JEFFERSON.

FOR CONGRESSIONAL DISTRICT ELECTORS,
1st DIST.—ESAU S. D. INSLEY,
2nd DIST.—PHINEAS F. BALL,
3rd DIST.—RICHARD M. J. HARKER,
4th DIST.—FRANK V. RHODES,
5th DIST.—DE WITT C. INGLE,
6th DIST.—FRANCIS B. SAPPINGTON.

FOR CONGRESS,
Sixth Congressional District,
WILLIAM W. MOORE.

Election, Tuesday, November 6th, 1888.

Maryland, 1888.

Ten

Appealing to Prejudice

READ BEFORE YOU VOTE!

This circular is intended merely as a matter of necessary information, that each citizen may cast a Free ballot by an intelligent choice; that he may be, possibly, better enabled to know for whom and for what purpose he is voting. The Protestant American desires to maintain the supremacy of the General Government which guarantees equal rights for each with every other citizen, in all matters of mutual interest, and believes with WASHINGTON that: "Every man, who conducts himself as a good citizen, is accountable to GOD ALONE FOR HIS RELIGIOUS FAITH, and should be protected in worshiping God according to the dictates of his own conscience."

It is sincerely hoped that the Catholic candidates are not imbued with the intention, or seeking office for the purpose, which their leading representatives promulgate in the following terse and unmistakable declarations:

We are Catholics first and citizens next.—*Bishop Gibbons.*

Education outside of the control of the Catholic Church, is a damnable heresy.—*Pope Pius IX.*

Education must be controlled by Catholic authorities, even to war and bloodshed.—*Catholic World.*

I frankly confess that the Catholics stand before the country the enemies of the public schools.—*Father Phelan.*

It will be a glorious day in this country when, under the laws, the school system is shivered in pieces.—*Catholic Telegraph.*

Protestantism has not, nor never can have any rights where Catholicity has triumphed.—*Catholic Review.*

Religious liberty is merely endured until the opposite can be carried into effect, without peril to the Catholic Church.—*Bishop O'Connor.*

We must take part in the elections, move in a solid mass in every State against the party pledged to sustain the integrity of the public schools.—*McClosky.*

The Pope doubts not that the Catholics of America will labor that they may once more re-acquire that independence and liberty which, by divine institution, appertains to him as sovereign head of all the church.—*Sotolli.*

The time is not far away when the Roman Catholic Church of the Republic of the United States, at the order of the Pope, will refuse to pay their school tax, and will send bullets to the breasts of government agents rather than pay it. It will come quickly as the click of a trigger, and will be obeyed, of course, as coming from God Almighty himself.—*Migl. Coppel.*

We call on all Catholics to take an active part in ALL MUNICIPAL affairs and ELECTIONS, and to make themselves FELT as active elements in daily POLITICAL life; do ALL in their power to cause the Constitutions of States and Legislation to be modeled in the precepts of the true CHURCH. All Catholic writers and Journalists should never lose for an INSTANT from view the above prescriptions. All CATHOLICS should indissoluble their submission to AUTHORITY and UNITE.—*Encyclical, Pope Leo XIII.*

DEMOCRATIC TICKET.	INDEPENDENT TICKET.	REPUBLICAN TICKET.
COUNTY TICKET.	**COUNTY TICKET.**	**COUNTY TICKET.**
SENATOR. WILLIAM GOEBEL.	SENATOR.	SENATOR. H. P. STEPHENS.
REPRESENTATIVES. First District. S. H. KENNEDY.	REPRESENTATIVES. First District.	REPRESENTATIVES. First District. CLARENCE WILMOT.
Second District. G. F. AHLERS.	Second District.	Second District.
Third District. JOEL BAKER.	Third District. JOS. W. POMFREY.	Third District.
COUNTY ATTORNEY. H. J. GAUSEPOHL. C	COUNTY ATTORNEY.	COUNTY ATTORNEY. C. E. CLARK.
COUNTY COMMISSIONER. PETER McVEAN.	COUNTY COMMISSIONER.	COUNTY COMMISSIONER.
COUNTY SCHOOL SUPT. NEANDER STEPHENS.	COUNTY SCHOOL SUPT.	COUNTY SCHOOL SUPT.
CITY TICKET.	**CITY TICKET.**	**CITY TICKET.**
MAYOR. JOSEPH RHINOCK.	MAYOR.	MAYOR. J. T. THOMAS.
CITY JUDGE. R. A. ATHEY.	CITY JUDGE.	CITY JUDGE. C. M. STRIGER.
PROSECUTING ATTORNEY. WM. D. BRENT.	PROSECUTING ATTORNEY.	PROSECUTING ATTORNEY.
CITY TREASURER. JOHN O'MEARA. C	CITY TREASURER.	CITY TREASURER. J. T. HATFIELD.
CITY SOLICITOR. WM. BYRNE. C	CITY SOLICITOR.	CITY SOLICITOR. W. McD. SHAW.
CITY ENGINEER. THOS. KENNEDY.	CITY ENGINEER. D. E. CONNOR.	CITY ENGINEER. WM. T. MENEFEE.
CITY CLERK. THEO. VON HOBUH. C	CITY CLERK. H. H. THRELKELD.	CITY CLERK. D. M. FIELDER.
CITY ASSESSOR. JNO. WHITNEY. C	CITY ASSESSOR.	CITY ASSESSOR. GEO. STEVENTON.
CITY COLLECTOR. DAN'L. KINGSLEY. C	CITY COLLECTOR.	CITY COLLECTOR. CHAS. STEINBORN, jr.
CITY JAILER. J. G. KRUZE. C	CITY JAILER. JOHN McKNIGHT.	CITY JAILER. A. TAYLOR HERBERT
MARKET MASTER. JNO. WOODALL.	MARKET MASTER.	MARKET MASTER. FRANK H. MEYERS. C
SEALER AND GUAGER. HENRY MEYERS.	SEALER AND GUAGER.	SEALER AND GUAGER. JOHN NIEHAUS.
WHARF MASTER. JOHN BODDE. C	WHARF MASTER.	WHARF MASTER. JAMES HERBERT.
CITY WEIGHER. BEN. DRESSMAN. C	CITY WEIGHER.	CITY WEIGHER. W. D. CHERRINGTON.
ALDERMEN. JNO. C. DROEGE. C E. J. MOORE. C JOS. JONAS. C H. HOLTRUP. C	ALDERMEN.	ALDERMEN. WM. RIEDLIN. GEO. M. CLARK. ED. R. WALKER. A. J. CRAIG.
COUNCIL. 1. W. S. NOWLAND. C 2. JOS. L. RUH. C 3. A. NIENABER. C 4. B. HOLTMAN. C 5. J. B. LINNEMAN. C 6. JNO. H. TEIPEL. C 7. HENRY MEYER. C 8. JNO. H. WESSELN. C 9. M. Messingschlager. C 10. FRANK LOHRE. C	COUNCIL. 1. 2. 3. 4. 5. 6. 7. 8. JOS. KNOLL. 9. GEO. W. HARDIN. 10. HENRY HEMPEL.	COUNCIL. 1. R. F. ERNST. 2. GEORGE T. BEACH. 3. EDWARD WILSON. 4. K. F. BENNDORF. 5. FRED. REHFUSS. 6. THOMAS R. GOCKEL. 7. DAVID B. SERENA. 8. THOS. C. RANSHAW. 9. C. W. HOUSE. 10. CHARLES HAIS. C
SCHOOL BOARD. 1. THOS. SULLIVAN. C THOS. REED. C 2. CHAS. NOCK. C J. W. BOOTH. 3. JAS. MULCAHY. C H. STUNTEBECK. C 4. MAX HERBST. L. L. BRISTOW. 5. C. POHLMAN. C J. B. GLENDEMYER. C 6. THOS. G. WOODS. DAVID FINNEGAN. C 7. J. A. AVERDICK. C JAS. GAHAN. C 8. JAS. McCOURT. C A. THOMAN. C 9. F. WILLENBRINK. C THOS. ASHBROOK. C 10. B. B. HUELEFELD. C B. SAALFELD. C	SCHOOL BOARD. 1. 2. 3. J. THOS. BERRY. 4. 5. 6. 7. 8. 9. 10.	SCHOOL BOARD. 1. E. B. SAYERS. CHAS. J. DAVIS. 2. DR. JNO. R. ALLEN. J. E. MITCHELL. 3. J. M. McCLUNG. H. C. THOMAS. 4. JNO. C. WEAVER. MAURICE WILLIAMS. 5. ROBERT WELLING. J. H. MINDERMAN. 6. CHAS. AHLERS. J. T. GEDGE. 7. JNO. F. SELMEIER. GEORGE HOUSTON. 8. JOHN EVANS. H. STACEY. 9. RUDOLPH WALKER. F. H. PIEL. 10. ALEX. EVANS. MICHAEL GOEBEL.

☞ All names marked thus—**C**—are Roman Catholic.

CAUTION—Every voter will remember that two members for School Board in each ward and all Councilmen are to be voted for by the city AT LARGE. Put your **X** in the [ ] opposite the candidates you wish to vote for.

Kentucky, circa 1890's. Handbill targeting Catholic candidates for office, each Catholic has a letter "C" next to his name.

"A ballot is like a bullet. You don't throw your ballots until you see a target, and if that target is not within your reach, keep your ballot in your pocket."

—Malcolm X

Unfortunately voters are not always rational and logical. Often their convictions are grounded in fear and prejudice. Sometimes economic factors, such as competition for jobs, underlie offensive terms. At other times, pure xenophobia, in the wake of war or the influx of immigrants, has promulgated ugly rhetoric.

The 1840's saw the rise of the Native American Party. The name does not refer to the true Native Americans (American Indians) but to white people born in the United States alarmed by the many Germans and Irish entering the country. They also thought Roman Catholicism a sinister conspiracy to dominate Protestant America. The Party was particularly active in Philadelphia and Baltimore. They burned churches and rioted in the City of Brotherly Love to express their grievances. The American or Know Nothing Party reached its zenith in 1856, electing many lesser government officials counted President Millard Fillmore among its supporters.

African Americans were targeted for the most persistent and egregious attacks. In addition to being denied voting rights (in 1860 only five states allowed free blacks to vote), they were abused through a variety of stratagems; "Black laws" passed in Illinois, for example, prohibited new settlement there by any free blacks. Republicans generally favored granting civil rights while Democrats did not. In 1864 Democrat George B. McClellan considered negotiating a peace with the South that would have included continuance

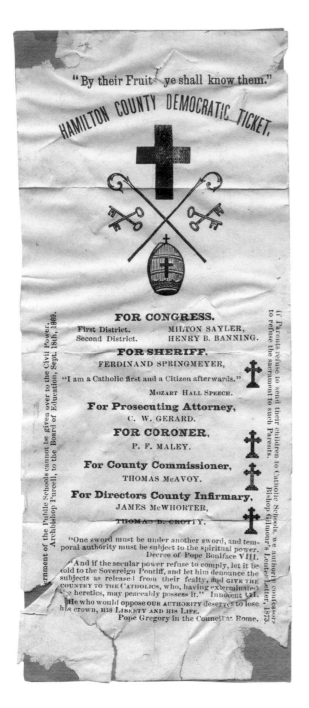

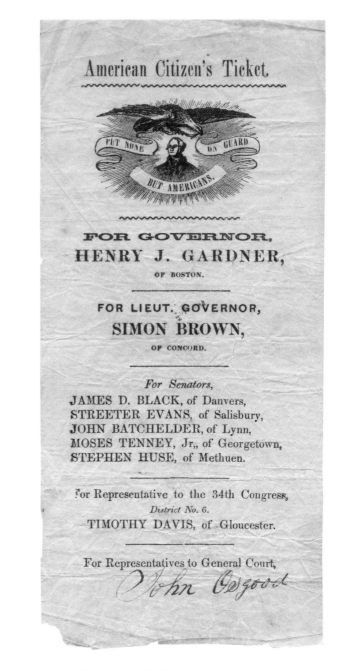

Ohio, 1873. Catholic candidates for office are targeted on this ballot, evidently issued to alert voters as to which candidates were Catholic (those with crosses by their names). They were accused of putting allegiance to Rome ahead of allegiance to America and secular values. The mantle of anti-Catholicism was eventually assumed by the Ku Klux Klan.

Massachusetts, 1857. Henry J. Gardner lost in his bid for re-election as Governor. The American or Know Nothing Party was anti-Catholic and anti-immigrant. It proposed a naturalization period of 21 years before citizenship would be granted.

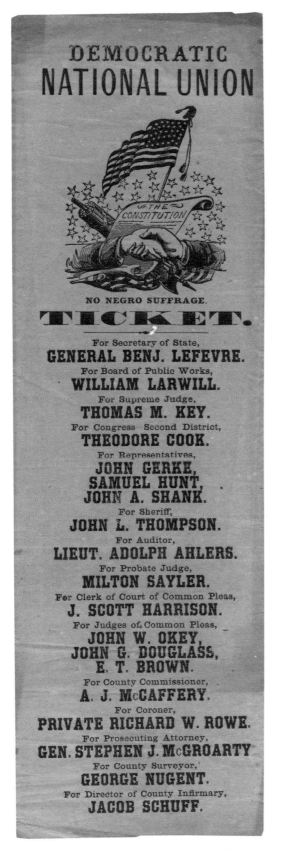

Ohio, 1866. Statewide ballot opposing Negro suffrage.

of slavery and the return to slavery of those freed by the Emancipation Proclamation. In the immediate post-war years many Democrats actively opposed Negro suffrage; in 1868 Democratic presidential candidate Horatio Seymour appealed to voters with the slogan "This is a White Man's Government – Let White Men Rule." Such politicians acceded the end to slavery but adamantly opposed granting blacks any rights normally enjoyed by the white population… including the vote.

Following the Irish and Germans, it was the turn of Chinese immigrants to be vilified. With the discovery of gold in California in 1848, the Chinese began to settle on the West Coast, working in mining camps the big cities such as San Francisco. Although they were critical to the building of the transcontinental railroad, sentiment against them coalesced and resulted in the Congressional Chinese Exclusion Act of 1882. This barred anyone of Chinese ancestry from becoming an American citizen or voter. The horrid goal of the new Workingmen's Party in California was to effect mass deportation of all Chinese; ballots for statewide elections typically show a cartoon "coolie" in pigtails being kicked out of the country, accompanied by the slogan "The Chinese Must Go!" These and similar sentiments can be seen on ballots issued by various organizations throughout the 19th century and even later.

Sometimes an appeal to prejudice was sufficient to win elections and pass restrictive laws. Overcoming such setbacks – tearing out the pages of hatred – has been a frustrating but ultimately strengthening experience in the evolution of our democracy. ❧

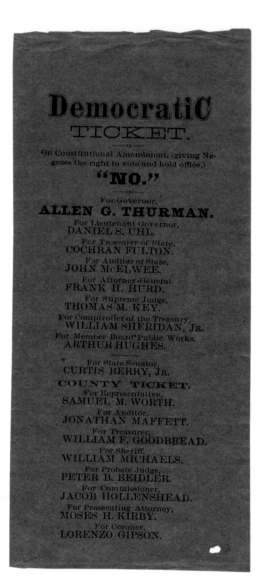

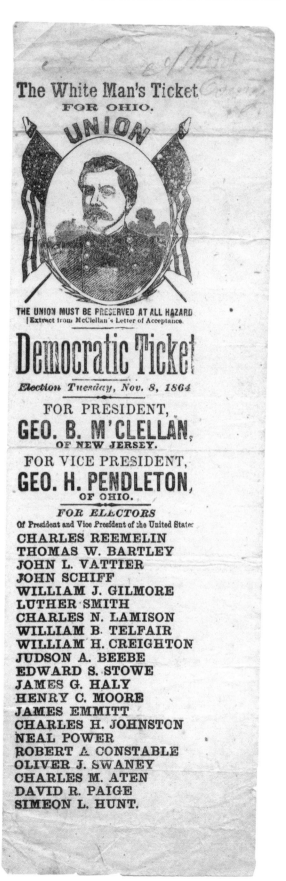

Democrat Allen G. Thurman ran for Governor of Ohio in 1866 urging a "No" vote on the question of whether the state constitution should be amended to give Negroes the right to vote and hold office. Although the 14th and 15th Amendments to the U. S. Constitution granted them these rights, many obstacles were still placed in their way.

Ohio, 1864. Many Civil War soldiers fought for maintenance of the Union, not abolition of slavery, and felt betrayed when Lincoln issued the Emancipation Proclamation. Lincoln's opponent, George McClellan, is presented here as the head of the "White Man's Ticket," at a time when the Democratic Party was very reactionary and racist.

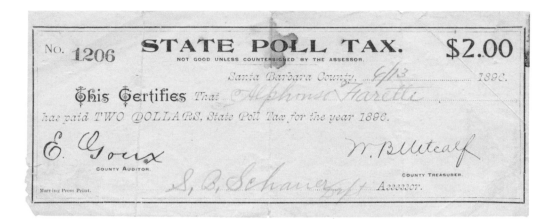

California, 1896. Receipt for $2 poll tax issued in Santa Barbara, California. The poll tax was a thinly-veiled attempt to prevent African Americans and the "lower classes" from voting.

DEAR SIR:

You are sent herewith three Democratic Electoral tickets. *Vote* one yourself; give the others to your friends.

Vote this ticket, because it is a vote against BEN. HARRISON, the Indianapolis lawyer, who says "A dollar a day is enough for any man, but that or any amount is too much for a striker."

To the strikers, he says: "I would force you back to work at the point of the bayonet, or shoot you down like dogs."

He believes in Springfield rifles and Pinkerton's detectives to suppress American workmen.

VOTE AGAINST HIM!

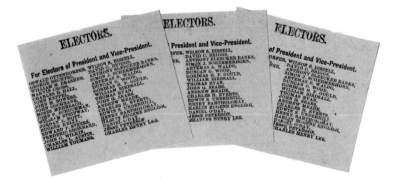

New York, 1888. The last quarter of the 19th century witnessed growing conflict between labor and capital. Workers began to organize unions, conduct strikes and demand better working conditions and wages, while the moneyed interests fought them at every turn. This had the makings for class warfare with each side vilifying the other. The establishment viewed labor as rabble, guided in their actions by communists, anarchists and foreign-born agitators. This circular reflects those stereotypes and fears.

Eleven

Vote Early and Often
or
Stuffing the Ballot Box

> "When I was a boy I was told that anybody could become President; I'm beginning to believe it."
>
> *–Clarence Darrow*

> "In America, anyone can become president. That's the problem."
>
> *–George Carlin*

> "Those who vote decide nothing; those who count the votes decide everything."
>
> *–Joseph Stalin*

REPUBLICANS BEWARE!

It is known from undoubted authority that our Democratic opponents have printed 10,000 split tickets of various kinds and well calculated to deceive, and which they will endeavor to force upon Republican voters in lieu of the regular nominations· Look well to your tickets or else many will be inveigled into casting votes, unawares, for Democrats, when nothing of the kind is intended. Look out for roorbach, colored split tickets and the ones headed the **"Independent Republican Ticket."** The regular Republican nominees are as follows :

Republican State Ticket.

For Governor,
REDFIELD PROCTOR, Rutland.
For Lieutenant Governor,
E. P. COLTON, Irasburgh.
For Treasurer,
JOHN A. PAGE, Montpelier.

Republican County Ticket.

For Senators,
LOVELAND MUNSON, Manchester.
WM. D. ARNOLD, Pownal.
For Assistant Judges,
EDWARD RICE, Bennington.
IRA COCHRAN, Dorset.
For State's Attorney,
J. K. BATCHELDER, Arlington.
For Sheriff,
MYRON BARTON, Shaftsbury.
For High Bailiff,
W. S. BENTLEY, Sandgate.
For Judges of Probate,
E. L. SIBLEY, Bennington,
District of Bennington
RANNEY HOWARD, Manchester,
District of Manchester.

Read your Tickets Carefully.

Vermont, 1878. Handbill warning voters of fraudulent "roorbach,* colored split tickets" designed to fool Republican voters "into casting votes, unaware, for Democrats." The official Republican State Ticket is reproduced for comparison purposes. The final line says it all: "Read your Tickets Carefully."

*A "roorbach" is a falsehood used to discredit a political candidate. The term was coined during the campaign of 1844 when a pamphlet, written under the pseudonym "Baron von Roorbach," published lies about James K. Polk.

W e hear of voting fraud all over the world: unbelievable majorities for a "strongman" in a supposed African democracy; stolen elections in the Middle East; irregularities in counting the vote in former Soviet republics. Unfortunately the United States has not been immune from such malfeasance.

Examples of note include the infamous "Ballot Box #13" (the contents of which gave Lyndon Johnson the margin of victory in his 1946 bid for the U. S. Senate) and *post facto* allegations of fraud in tabulating Illinois votes during the Kennedy-Nixon contest of 1960. While modern deviations are, hopefully, the exception, 19th century politics is full of stories of vote fraud, especially in cities controlled by powerful bosses and organizations such as Tammany Hall.

A favorite ploy, as shown by the material culture left in its wake, was the use of fraudulent ballots. When there were no *official* ballots – provided and sanctioned by state officials – tickets were obtained from a variety of sources. As need arose they were ordered from local printers, published in partisan newspapers, created by party

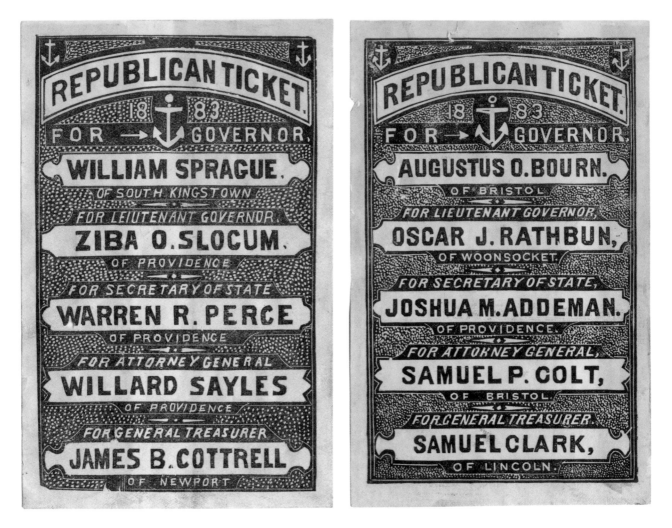

Rhode Island, 1883. The real "Republican Ticket" named William Sprague for Governor, while the counterfeit ballot lists Augustus O. Bourn and other candidates who were actually Democrats. Pretty sneaky, but here's the proof!

FALL RIVER, *Nov. 3d, 1840.*

SIR—You have been appointed one of the *WHIG VIGILANCE COMMITTEE* in the coming Election. The Committee will meet at the Firemen's Hall on *THURSDAY EVENING NEXT,* at quarter before 8 o'clock.

Per order,   SAM'L. L. THAXTER, Sec'ry.

Massachusetts, 1840. Printed notice advising the recipient he has been "appointed one of the Whig Vigilance Committee in the coming Election." Apparently the Democrats of Fall River were not to be trusted.

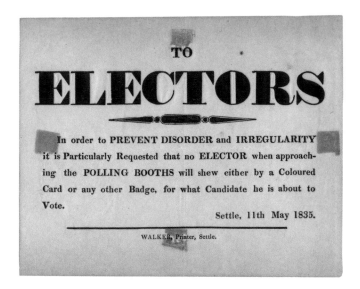

Small 1835 broadside cautioning voters ("electors") to not indicate their choice of candidate either "by a Coloured Card or any other Badge" when approaching a polling place in order to prevent "disorder and irregularity."

functionaries and sometimes even hand-written by the voter himself. If a ballot that was actually cast had correct names upon it, it was accepted and counted; if not, it was voided and not counted. The most devious ploy had political tricksters distribute ballots containing a list of electors which did not match the title on the ballot. For example, a "Democratic Ticket" might actually list Republican electors. Such a ticket deposited in the ballot box would be counted as a Republican vote. This subterfuge was so subtle that many a voter was duped into voting for the opposition. Voters were often warned to carefully examine their tickets prior to depositing them, failing which their vote was lost to the "good cause."

In an effort to minimize dirty tricks, challengers and poll watchers monitored polling stations for suspicious activity just as they do today. Intricate color patterns and woodcut illustrations

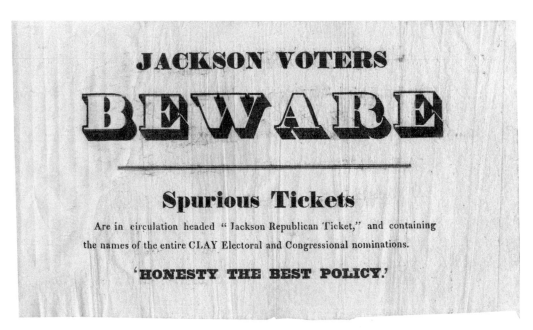

Andrew Jackson supporters are reminded that "Honesty is the Best Policy" and warned to watch for fake ballots. This 1832 broadside reflects how Jackson was bested by Henry Clay in the "Corrupt Bargain" election of 1824. The two clashed horns again in 1832 and evidently the Jackson camp was ready for a repeat performance by insidious Clay operatives. The idea of the "old switcheroo" may have originated in this contest.

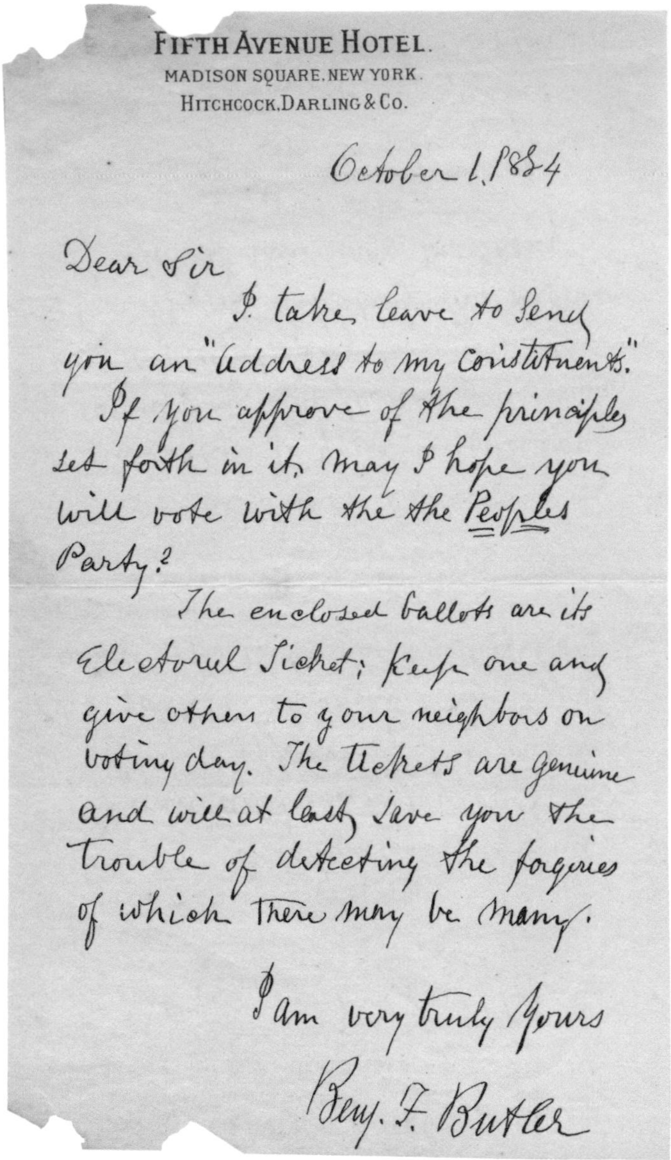

FIFTH AVENUE HOTEL.
MADISON SQUARE, NEW YORK.
HITCHCOCK, DARLING & CO.

October 1, 1884

Dear Sir

I take leave to send you an "Address to my Constituents." If you approve of the principles set forth in it, may I hope you will vote with the the Peoples Party?

The enclosed ballots are its Electoral Ticket; keep one and give others to your neighbors on voting day. The Tickets are genuine and will at last save you the trouble of detecting the forgeries of which there may be many.

I am very truly Yours

Benj. F. Butler

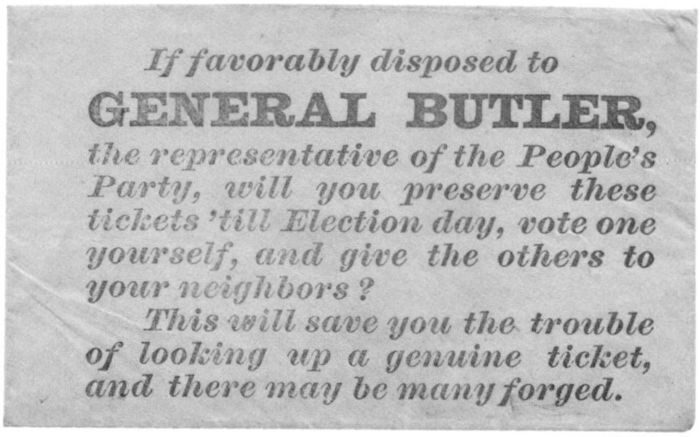

If favorably disposed to

GENERAL BUTLER,

the representative of the People's Party, will you preserve these tickets 'till Election day, vote one yourself, and give the others to your neighbors?

This will save you the trouble of looking up a genuine ticket, and there may be many forged.

This envelope contained official ballots for the People's Party candidate, Benjamin Butler, for the presidential election of 1884. It urges voters to use them rather than risk casting a forged one. The letter, sent by Butler, forwards a speech and a supply of legitimate ballots which will "save you the trouble of detecting the forgeries which there may be many."

1880 THE TISSUE BALLOTS, *S. C.*

That is a natural curiosity which leads people to inquire how a State with 25,000 Republican majority could be carried by a Democratic majority of 70,000; how a Congressman could be elected by a *majority* greater than the legal vote in the district. This was done in Mississippi and Louisiana by the plan known as the shotgun policy. It remained for South Carolina to adopt the tissue ballot policy. It did not ignore the shotgun policy altogether. It had its reign of terror as an aid to the tissue ballot.

The readers of the GAZETTE have heard of the tissue ballot. In order that they may see and be able to preserve for future reference this little instrument of fraud, we have printed a fac simile of the ticket, including the paper used, and a specimen will be found inclosed in this issue of the paper, as a *supplement*. It is a very small specimen of printing, and the person opening the paper must look out for it, or he will be likely to miss it.

The fraud was perpetrated in the following manner: From ten to thirty-five of these tickets were inclosed in a regular ballot and dropped into the box. At intervals during the day one of the judges stirred up the box, as a cook would stir a pot of mush. In this way the little jokers were shaken out. Meantime fraudulent names were written on the pollbooks, in order that the number of names might correspond with the number of tickets. The work of voting the tissue tickets, however, was overdone, as might be expected, where enthusiastic red shirts were charged with depositing them. When, therefore, there was a surplus in the box, a blindfolded person was employed to withdraw the extra number. How fair that seemed! But the blindfolded person took care to not withdraw a tissue ticket. Thus the work was done, and this was the way, in part, South Carolina was made solidly Democratic. The other part was in intimidating voters.

Preserve the tissue tickets. They will prove a curiosity one of these days.

were printed on the back of many ballots to discourage counterfeiting. This precaution may have been effective but it also alerted polling station moles to a voter's preference. Standing in line while holding a clearly recognizable ballot might attract a "plug-ugly" or other party thug, whose job was to intimidate a voter into changing his vote – or not vote at all. It is unclear how widespread the practice was but it undoubtedly had a decisive effect in some elections, mostly on the local and statewide level. In sum, the best advice remains found with a slogan on some 1860 Lincoln ballots: "Eternal vigilance is the price of liberty." ❧

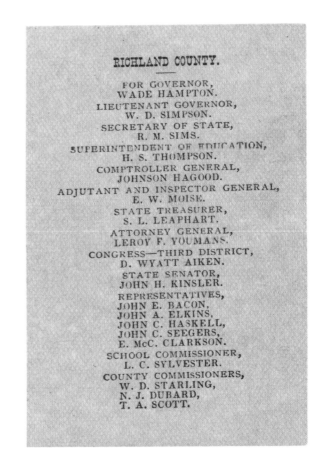

RICHLAND COUNTY.

FOR GOVERNOR,
WADE HAMPTON.
LIEUTENANT GOVERNOR,
W. D. SIMPSON.
SECRETARY OF STATE,
R. M. SIMS.
SUPERINTENDENT OF EDUCATION,
H. S. THOMPSON.
COMPTROLLER GENERAL,
JOHNSON HAGOOD.
ADJUTANT AND INSPECTOR GENERAL,
E. W. MOISE.
STATE TREASURER,
S. L. LEAPHART.
ATTORNEY GENERAL,
LEROY F. YOUMANS.
CONGRESS—THIRD DISTRICT,
D. WYATT AIKEN.
STATE SENATOR,
JOHN H. KINSLER.
REPRESENTATIVES,
JOHN E. BACON,
JOHN A. ELKINS,
JOHN C. HASKELL,
JOHN C. SEEGERS,
E. McC. CLARKSON.
SCHOOL COMMISSIONER,
L. C. SYLVESTER.
COUNTY COMMISSIONERS,
W. D. STARLING,
N. J. DUBARD,
T. A. SCOTT.

South Carolina, 1880. Former Confederate General Wade Hampton was elected Governor in 1880, possibly with the help of one of these tissue ballots. Very small and very thin, an operative would fold a bunch of them inside a regular ballot and deposit the whole into a ballot box. Once the polls closed, an "inside man" would retrieve the ballots. Adding names to the poll book and/or destroying opposition ballots ensured that these tissue ballots were counted and that the number of ballots in the box matched the number of names on the list of voters.

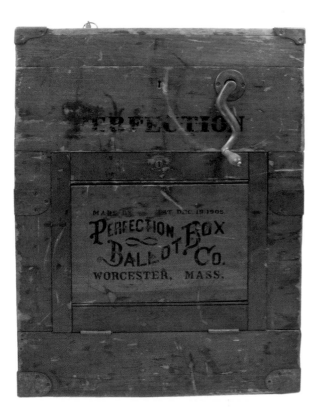

Ballot boxes from the Brian D. Caplan Collection.

Strongboxes of Democracy

"The ballot box is the surest arbiter of disputes among freemen."

—James Buchanan

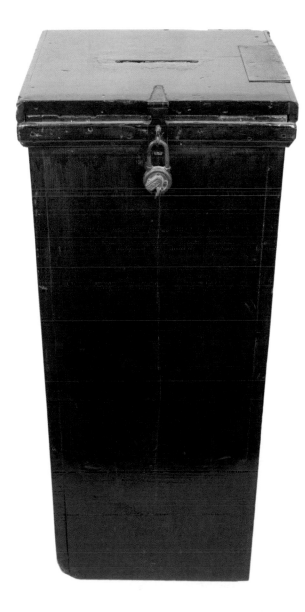

The ballot box, a symbol of democracy, has served as a vehicle for the people to elect political candidates since the inception of the United States. Whether used in local, state, or presidential elections, in schools, firehouses, libraries or one of a host of other polling places, the ballot box safeguarded the sanctity of every vote. Prior to the advent of free-standing polling booths, long before "hanging chads" and electronic methods of casting and tabulating votes, the ballot box stood alone. Sturdy and secure, whether made of wood, metal or glass, in whatever shape or size, ballot boxes withstood the test of time. Incredibly many polling precincts in the Southwest, including Texas, continued to use metal-barrel ballot boxes, manufactured in the late 1860's, right through the general election of 1984.

There is little written history about the manufacture and distribution of ballot boxes throughout the United States. Many were made locally as the need arose, without government regulation or standardization. Ballot boxes evolved quite slowly from 1789, when George Washington was inaugurated for his first term in office, through the 1960's, by which time the presidential voting process was becoming more fully automated.

Ballot boxes made of oak, mahogany, maple and pine were in use from our earliest days. Following the Industrial Revolution in the United States (which lasted from the 1820's thru the late 1860's), metal-barrel ballot boxes were introduced, first during the election of 1868 between U.S. Grant and Horatio Seymour. They have been used in various configurations ever since. Glass receptacles in the shape of goldfish bowls have been used for ballots at least as far back as the Civil War. More sophisticated, square, glass

ballot boxes with chicken wire mesh date to the early 1920's.

Since ballots usually designated a specific candidate and party, ballot boxes were sometimes adorned with a party label. A voter would drop his ticket in the ballot box labeled for the political party and candidate of his choice. This practice continued until the 1930's. Many wood and glass ballot boxes from the 1880's through the Great Depression incorporated a mechanism that tabulated incoming votes as they were fed through the opening in the box. With the post-1888 advent of single ballots listing all candidates from every party, use of separate ballot boxes for particular parties and candidates fell out of favor. At the completion of an election which used ballot boxes, all boxes were taken to a centralized location for tallying.

As humble as any particular ballot box may be – whatever its form, or material, or age – its common purpose with its fellows is to maintain and preserve the vote, ensuring that every vote counts, and see that every person who votes can do so freely and with confidence.

—*Brian D. Caplan*

EXPANDING AND RESTRICTING THE FRANCHISE: A TIMELINE

1848: The Treaty of Guadalupe-Hidalgo ends the Mexican War. Mexicans in newly-acquired territories are granted citizenship but not given the right to vote.

1866: The Civil Rights Act declared "all persons born in the United States...excluding Indians not taxed" were citizens and were to be given "full and equal benefit of all laws."

1868: The 14th amendment gave citizenship to all people born or naturalized in the United States, regardless of race, prohibited states from abridging the "privileges and immunities" of citizens and afforded all citizens "equal protection of the laws." African Americans, Native Americans, women and Asian Americans were still almost entirely excluded from voting.

1869: Wyoming Territory grants women the right to vote; when admitted to the Union it was the first state to grant voting rights to women.

1870: The 15th Amendment finally extends the right to vote to African Americans. The right cannot be denied "on account of race, color, or previous condition of servitude."

1882: The Chinese Exclusion Act bars people of Chinese ancestry from becoming citizens.

1887: The Dawes Act gives citizenship to Native Americans willing to sever their tribal affiliation.

1890: The Indian Naturalization Act grants citizenship to Native Americans upon completion of the same naturalization process used for immigrants.

1890: Southern states begin to enact poll tax laws and literacy tests as a requirement for voting.

1895: Utah women regain the right to vote after having it taken away from them in 1887.

1896: Idaho grants women the right to vote.

1898: In *United States* v. *Wong Kim Ark* the Supreme Court decides that children of Chinese parents, if born in the United States, are citizens.

1901: Native Americans living in Indian Territory in Oklahoma are granted citizenship.

1910: Washington State grants women the right to vote.

1911: California grants women the right to vote.

1912: Oregon, Arizona and Kansas also grant woman suffrage.

1913:   Illinois grants women the right to vote in municipal and presidential elections.

1915:   The United States Supreme Court rules "grandfather clauses" unconstitutional. The laws had exempted those with the right to vote *prior* to the Civil War from paying poll taxes and taking literacy tests – further disenfranchising blacks and impoverished minorities.

1917:   North Dakota, South Dakota, Indiana, Nebraska, Michigan, New York and Oklahoma grant woman suffrage.

1920:   The 19th Amendment grants women the right to vote.

1920:   The United States Supreme Court rules that Native Americans who live on reservations and pay no taxes are ineligible to vote.

1922:   In *Takao* v. *United States*, the Supreme Court upholds a 1790 law that effectively bars Asian Americans from becoming citizens and voting.

1923:   In *Bhagat Singh Thind* v. *United States*, the Supreme Court reverses its earlier decision and rules that Asian Americans are eligible for citizenship.

1924:   The Indian Citizenship Act grants citizenship to Native Americans.

1943:   The Chinese Exclusion Act is repealed after sixty years.

1944:   White-only primaries are ruled unconstitutional.

1947:   Courts rule that Native Americans have the right to vote in every state.

1952:   The McCarran-Walter Act repeals racial restrictions of the 1790 Naturalization Law, allowing first generation Japanese-Americans to become citizens.

1961:   The 23rd Amendment grants the right to vote to residents of Washington, D.C.

1964:   The 24th Amendment bans poll taxes in national elections.

1965:   The Voting Rights Act bans literacy tests and similar racially-based practices.

1971:   The 26th Amendment lowers the voting age to 18 nationwide.

1990:   The Americans with Disabilities Act mandates free access to the polls for handicapped citizens.

CHAPTER ILLUSTRATIONS

1. "Congressional Pugilists." (Artist unknown, published in Philadelphia, 1798.) Political cartoon depicts the first physical brawl on the floor of the House of Representatives. Vermont's Congressman Matthew Lyon, a radical Democratic Republican, had earlier spit in the face of Roger Griswold, a Federalist from Connecticut, over an alleged insult. In the following session, Griswold came at Lyon with a hickory cane while Lyon picked up a pair of fire tongs to strike back. Other congressmen would separate the combatants and neither representative was expelled.

2. "The County Election" by George Caleb Bingham, 1852; 38" x 52" oil on canvas. (Courtesy of the Saint Louis Art Museum [Gift of Bank of America 44:2001].)

3. *A Bake-Pan for the Dough Faces. By One of Them. Try It.* (Leonard Marsh, Burlington, VT. 1854.) An anti-slavery booklet.

4. "Grand Procession of Wide-Awakes at New York on the Evening of October 3, 1860." (*Harper's Weekly*, New York, October 13, 1860.)

5. "Inauguration of President Jefferson Davis of the Southern Confederacy, at Montgomery, Alabama, February 18, 1861." (*Harper's Weekly*, New York, March 9, 1861.) The event took place at the original capital of the Confederacy in Montgomery, later moved to Richmond. Jefferson Davis stands in front of the building taking the oath of office.

6. "The True Issue or 'Thats Whats the Matter.'" (Currier & Ives, New York, 1864.) A political cartoon.

7. "Soldiers Voting For President." (*Frank Leslie's Illustrated Newspaper*, New York, December 3, 1864.)

8. "In The Robber's Den. Jay Gould Surprises Even the Hardened Monopolists." (*Judge*, New York, March 25, 1882.)

9. "Grand, National American Banner." (Currier & Ives, New York, 1856.) Campaign print presenting the standard bearers of the Know Nothing ticket, Fillmore and Donelson.

10. "The Ignorant Vote – Honors Are Easy." (*Harper's Weekly*, New York, December 9, 1876.)

11. "The City of Dust – The Fruits of the Democratic Victory… Shadows of Forthcoming Events." (Detail from a Thomas Nast political cartoon for *Harper's Weekly*, New York, August 13, 1870.)